Ironclads and Big Guns of the Confederacy

Studies in Maritime History
William N. Still, Jr., Series Editor

Ironclads and Big Guns of the Confederacy

The Journal and Letters
of John M. Brooke

Edited by

George M. Brooke, Jr.

UNIVERSITY OF SOUTH CAROLINA PRESS

© 2002 University of South Carolina

Published in Columbia, South Carolina, by the
University of South Carolina Press

Manufactured in the United States of America

06 05 04 03 02   5 4 3 2 1

Library of Congress Cataloging-in-Publication Data

Brooke, John M. (John Mercer), 1826–1906.
  Ironclads and big guns of the Confederacy : the journal and letters of
John M. Brooke / edited by George M. Brooke, Jr.
    p. cm. — (Studies in maritime history)
  Includes bibliographical references and index.
  ISBN 1-57003-418-4 (alk. paper)
  1. Brooke, John M. (John Mercer), 1826–1906—Diaries. 2. Brooke, John
M. (John Mercer), 1826–1906—Correspondence. 3. Confederate States of
America. Navy—Officers—Diaries. 4. Confederate States of America.
Navy—Officers—Correspondence. 5. United States—History—Civil War,
1861–1865—Naval operations, Confederate. 6. United
States—History—Civil War, 1861–1865—Personal narratives, Confederate.
7. Virginia (Ironclad) 8. Confederate States of America.
Navy—Ordnance and ordnance stores. 9. Inventors—Confederate States of
America—Biography. I. Brooke, George M. II. Title. III. Series.
E467.1.B768 2001
973.7'57—dc21

                                                              2001005642

To Professors William Gleason Bean of
Washington and Lee University and Fletcher M. Green of
the University of North Carolina, eminent historians,
who shaped my course for the future.

Contents

Illustrations

Foreword

The purpose of this book is to define the contributions of John Mercer Brooke (1826-1906) to the Confederate navy. After twenty years of service as a line officer in the United States Navy, Brooke at the age of thirty-four resigned his commission at the outbreak of the Civil War and offered his services to, first, Virginia and, then, the Confederacy. Most of his work during the conflict was in the field of naval ordnance, where despite a lack of formal or specialized training he made significant contributions.

In recording Brooke's services I have used the journals he kept and his copious correspondence. The journals are uneven, but when possible Brooke noted events and his actions daily. In such cases he usually wrote carefully and legibly. At other times when rushed he would skip a number of days and try to catch up later. When in the field conducting gun experiments Brooke often jotted rough notes and accompanied them with pencil drawings of gun bursts made at the time, which I have reproduced. In the course of the war he received many letters commenting on ordnance matters. Brooke's many letters to his wife present a personal picture of his hectic life we would not have otherwise.

Generally I have followed the journals and letters exactly as written, but sometimes it has been necessary to correct spelling and punctuation so that an entry makes sense. Except in the case of the Merrimac, where variant spellings have been retained for academic reasons, misspellings of place names and personal names, as well as misrepresentation of a person's initials, are followed by correct spellings in brackets. Upon first mention in each chapter, full names, where known, have been supplied in brackets.

Many historians over the years have shown a continuing interest in my grandfather's variegated naval career. In my biography of him published in 1980 I sought to cover all aspects of his life. But the continuing interest in the Civil War and Brooke's unique contributions make a publication of his journals and correspondence, which are in my possession, seem advisable.

As in the past I am indebted to the George C. Marshall Research Library at Virginia Military Institute, which has given me storage space for the Brooke Papers and an ideal atmosphere in which to work.

Two typists over a considerable period of time have shown great skill and the utmost patience in helping me translate rough journals and drawings into a comprehensible text. They are Sherri Wheeler and Janet Cummings.

To my wife and son, a budding historian, I express gratitude for their continuing support.

Preface

I nterest in the American Civil War continues apace, but it is concentrated on the land battles and famous generals. Interest in the naval aspects of the war continues to lag. After all, the Union navy clamped a blockade on the Confederacy at the beginning of the war, so most of the naval fighting was on inland waters: rivers and harbors. There were duels between ships and shore batteries, but lacking were the dramatic fleet actions of World War II or the hard-fought battles between single ships on the high seas reported in the War of 1812.

On the surface it would appear that the Union won the battle at sea almost without fighting. To begin with, only one-fifth of the officers in the United States Navy in 1861 entered Confederate service, and few enlisted personnel went south. In population and industrial resources the South was dwarfed by its antagonist. Being basically agricultural, the Confederacy had few factories, machine shops, shipyards, foundries, or skilled workers. Norfolk was the only important shipyard, and it soon fell to the Federals. The Tredegar Iron Works in Richmond, initially, was the only facility capable of producing heavy ordnance and armor plate. The South was compelled to import and improvise. Yet, despite many handicaps the South developed ship-building facilities, machine shops, powder mills, and an iron industry dependent on the iron furnaces of the Shenandoah Valley. Much of the effort was behind the scenes, but it is important to remember that the South did not fail because of a lack of naval armament.

Interest in the Confederate navy has focused on the exploits of public cruisers such as Raphael Semmes's *Alabama* and the *Shenandoah*, the skills of the blockade runners, and the epic duel between the *Merrimac* and the *Monitor*, the first battle between ironclads. But behind all of this was an effective Office of Ordnance and Hydrography that pushed production of material and evaluated inventions.

Considerable credit for these accomplishments should be attributed to John Mercer Brooke, a veteran of twenty years' service in the United States

Navy. When President Abraham Lincoln called for troops to invade Virginia, Brooke, as did a number of other officers, resigned his commission and offered his services to Virginia, where he was commissioned in the Virginia navy and assigned to Gen. Robert E. Lee as naval aide. When Virginia joined the Confederate states and the latter's capital was moved from Montgomery to Richmond, Brooke was given a commission in the Confederate navy and assigned to the Office of Ordnance and Hydrography under Comdr. George Minor. There he designed the plan for the conversion of the *Merrimac* into the ironclad *Virginia* and the Brooke Guns, notably the 7-inch and 6.4 rifles. He developed fuses and range tables and soon was put in charge of all experimental work in the Confederate navy. In April 1863 he succeeded Minor as chief of the Office of Ordnance and Hydrography.

It is remarkable that John Brooke could adapt to his scientific duties so well. His formal education was limited to the nine-month course given at the Naval Academy in its early days. A series of routine cruises was followed by a tour on the Coast Survey under Samuel Phillips Lee, where he learned much of surveying, and at the Naval Observatory under Matthew Fontaine Maury, where he studied hydrography and astronomy. While at the observatory he invented a deep-sea sounding lead for measuring the depth of the sea at more than two thousand fathoms. Later Brooke won recognition for his work in astronomy and hydrography on the North Pacific Expedition under John Rodgers. Yet none of this scientific work pertained to ordnance, his area of work during the Civil War.

At the beginning of his Confederate service Brooke established a close relationship with Secretary of the Navy Stephen Russell Mallory, a veteran legislator from Florida, who had been involved in naval affairs while serving in Congress in the 1850s. Brooke foresaw the difficulties the South faced through a lack of facilities and materials, and he suggested steps that might be taken. Although these problems did not coincide with Brooke's previous training, Mallory listened and added steadily to Brooke's responsibilities. Prior to the war Brooke had had a vast and varied career as a "blue water sailor," but he soon became involved in a multitude of specialized duties that revealed his latent scientific talents. Despite a wealth of difficulties Brooke fulfilled his tasks with pertinacity. The South did not fail because of a deficiency in naval ordnance.

Abbreviations

BP Brooke Papers (collection of the author)
LC Library of Congress
NA National Archives
NR *Navy Register*
RG Record Group

Ironclads and Big Guns of the Confederacy

Introduction

Brooke's Actions on the Eve of War

J ohn Brooke's surveys in the western Pacific and on the coast of Japan were interrupted when his ship, the *Fenimore Cooper*, was beached on the Japanese coast in a storm; he and his crew were stranded for six months. After his cruise in the Pacific, Brooke returned to the United States in the warship *Kanrin Maru*, which he helped navigate across the Pacific at the same time staff of the Japanese Embassy crossed in the *Powhatan* under Capt. Josiah Tattnall. Both vessels landed in San Francisco, and from there the embassy staff and Brooke proceeded to Washington, D.C., separately.[1] When Brooke reached the East Coast, Charles Wolcott Brooks notified him: "The *pony express* brought us the news of your safe arrival in New York in season to communicate it to the Japanese previous to the sailing of the 'candinmurrah' (*Kanrin Maru*) [for Japan] on the 8th inst. The Japanese were much pleased at your safe arrival. The steamer was put in fine order by Commodore [Robert B.] Cunningham [commandant at Mare Island] and was the prettiest vessel in port when completed. . . . Ten Japanese Seamen were left here in my charge, and are now in the hospital but getting better rapidly. Causes, Dysentery and fevers. I have a sort of apointment [*sic*] as commercial Agent to represent the Japanese people, take charge of the sailors and finally send them home. Funds were left with me to pay their passage back. I am promised the Consulship if the Emperor is willing."[2]

In New York City, Brooke notified Secretary of the Navy Isaac Toucey of his arrival on 27 April 1860. Proceeding quickly to Washington, D.C., to resume work on the report and charts of the North Pacific Expedition, Brooke learned that his wife Lizzie, who was living with relatives in Lexington, Virginia, was very sick.[3] Despite the many pressing duties he had with John Rodgers relating to the North Pacific Expedition, Brooke requested leave to travel to Lexington. Secretary Toucey responded promptly, granting three months' leave effective 3 May.[4] This prevented Brooke from being appointed to a select commission of naval officers that took care of the

1

Japanese Embassy in the United States.[5] In a letter to an old friend, the oceanographer Lt. Matthew Fontaine Maury, Brooke indicated that the timing of his return was poor. "I regret exceedingly," he wrote, "that in consequence of the illness of Mrs. Brooke I was compelled to leave Washington without seeing you. I have specimens of bottom from the Pacific and some water from the depths of 3,300 faths. We had quite an eventful cruise. . . . I shall be in Washington as soon as possible, the day I cannot now fix. Please remember me to your family."[6]

While in Lexington, Brooke continued to plan his work in Washington. He informed the secretary of the navy that he had brought "to the Atlantic States the records, etc. of the survey of the route between California and China, and of portions of the nearly unknown coasts of Japan, with the data necessary to correct the positions of numerous reefs, islands, capes, etc., erroneously placed upon the latest and best charts." Brooke stressed that "a timely publication of the results of the Cooper's survey" could avert such wrecks as that of an American clipper ship on French Frigate Shoals, which he had surveyed. He also noted, "Several wrecks have recently occurred on the Coast of Japan, near the port of Simoda, in consequence of the want of correct charts." With no inkling of impending disaster in the United States, Brooke, who had been out of the country for two years, wrote, "It will be necessary in preparing the results of these surveys and rendering them available to navigators to incur the expenses incidental to the hire of drafting rooms, the employment of draftsmen, etc. An appropriation of $5,000 would be sufficient for this purpose and ensure the speedy accomplishment of the work."[7] It was barely more than seven months to the secession of South Carolina from the Union, but it is clear that such thoughts as civil war, ironclad ships, and naval ordnance were far from John Brooke's mind. More to be expected was the letter from the chief of ordnance and hydrography directing him to "please make a return to this Bureau, showing the disposition made of the Nautical Instruments and other articles which were supplied you by direction of this Bureau to be used in the survey between California and China."[8]

John Brooke's sojourn in Japan in 1859–60 had made him an expert of sorts in Far Eastern affairs. He wrote to Lizzie, who remained in Lexington, "I have not only my own business to attend to but am called upon to give information etc. to Senators and others in reference to Eastern Russia the Amour [sic] and Japan, so my time is much occupied." On a personal note, Brooke said: "I read your pa's letter this morning, it was of the 18th. Tell him I will follow his advice implicitly. . . . I love you more than ever. Kiss Anna for me say Papa sends his love but *Uncle Sam* keeps him a few days from her."[9] At this time Brooke returned to Lexington because of Lizzie's recurring sickness.

While at home Brooke had time to write an extremely long letter to Sen. William Gwin of California. The senator, whose state had the most to gain by developing trade with eastern Asia, had strongly supported Brooke's survey in the *Fenimore Cooper* for the purpose of determining the best steamship route between San Francisco and China. The beaching of the *Cooper* in Japan had prevented completion of the project. Rodgers and Brooke felt that it was essential to finish the survey and publish the charts. Such work would require an appropriation by Congress, so once again the two officers turned to Senator Gwin.[10] In his letter to Gwin, Brooke elaborated on his views of the Far Eastern situation.

At this time when Russia in the North and England in the South are striving to get a foothold in Japan and the United States can prevent only by indirect means the accomplishment of their purpose—the absorption of that country—and consequent control of the Western Pacific, it is of the utmost importance that such situations commercial and other as will enable the United States to exert a decided and effective influence in that quarter of the globe should be cultivated. The Japanese already see that their existence as an independent nation depends upon two things, intercourse with the United States and improvement. The sending of the Candinmarruh [*Kanrin Maru*] to California was in accordance with this view and is a significant fact.

During my intercourse with the Japanese in their own country and onboard the Candinmarruh I found that unlike other oriental people they were perfectly aware of their inability to maintain the Empire in its integrity without availing themselves of the improvements inventions and discoveries of other nations. . . .

They anticipate war with foreign nations but not with the United States. They are familiar (sufficiently so to put them on their guard) with the history of the British occupation in the East, and they are impatient to avail themselves of every kind of information which may tend to put Japan on a footing with other nations. It is providential that Japan has been closed until the present day when we have California on the Pacific and steamers at command. Now is the time to secure to the United States what may be called the "right of way to China," as well, as the commerce of Japan. Having opened the country we are indeed responsible for its preservation as well as entitled to the first reward of a success obtained in the peaceful and legitimate extension of our Western influence. The Russians are now disputing the boundary on the North. . . . With the English at Nagasaki commanding the Straits of Corea and the Russians at Hakodadi commanding the Straits of Tsugar the interests of the United States in that quarter are materially diminished. . . . But if England with the consent of Russia occupies Nagasaki then I presume Hakodadi may fall to the former without dispute, the French having no further interest in the matter than to retard the encroachments of both.[11]

This long quotation is only a small part of the letter's contents. Brooke goes on to describe in detail the aspirations of the European powers, the political organization of Japan, and the economic strengths and weaknesses of Japan and Okinawa, a fief of the feudal lord of Satsuma in southern Japan.

Brooke's letter to Senator Gwin shows that he had a profound interest in U.S. diplomatic and economic destiny in eastern Asia. Perhaps he had a greater knowledge of Japan than any of his contemporaries in the naval service. Had the Civil War not come, Brooke might have played a significant role as the United States became the dominant foreign influence in Meiji Japan. Although a naval officer, his emphasis had been on peace and friendship, diplomacy, and scientific development. Unfortunately, the Civil War ended such dreams for the United States and John Brooke. After Appomattox the United States was consumed by hate and domestic problems, so the Meiji leaders of Japan turned to Great Britain, France, and the new German Empire for help in modernizing their army and navy, establishing an educational system, and drafting a constitution. For Brooke, too, it was a sad turn of events. Throughout his career and in the letter quoted above he had shown a pride in the United States. In his early years he had demonstrated a competence in surveying, oceanography, and astronomy as well as some talent as an inventor. To this he had added, as a result of his cruising in the Pacific, some knowledge of diplomacy and geopolitics. But Virginia's secession changed all that. It was a time of war, not peace, and the opportunities in Brooke's fields of accomplishment were slight. So Brooke turned to naval ordnance and shipbuilding, areas of vital importance to the Confederacy in which he had shown little interest and had no specific training.

In 1860 after his return to Washington, Brooke had considerable correspondence with Secretary of the Navy Toucey and must have gotten to know him quite well. It seems to have been a smooth relationship, as Toucey granted his requests without quibble. For example, when Brooke reported that from San Francisco he had brought home Edward Kern, his draftsman, and two other members of the *Fenimore Cooper*'s crew, John Rodgers warned him that Charles W. Welsh, chief clerk of the Navy Department, had said bringing home the men was "irregular" and that Brooke "ought to have waited for instructions from the Department."[12] But the secretary informed Brooke "that the Department approves your course under the circumstances."[13]

In the 1850s Brooke had invented the Brooke Deep Sea Sounding Lead, which made it possible to sound the sea over two thousand fathoms deep and by bringing up a sample from the ocean floor to prove the bottom had been reached. This discovery greatly stimulated the laying of a cable across the Atlantic. Cruising in foreign waters and associating closely with the Japanese did not diminish Brooke's interest in scientific matters. Two months after his return to the United States, Brooke wrote to Cyrus Field, the philanthropist who promoted the laying of the Atlantic cable, "Having been absent from the U.S. for some two years I am desirous of learning something in relation to the Atlantic telegraph project."[14] There is nothing in the Brooke Papers to indicate that Field ever replied.

While Brooke was concerned with Lizzie's poor health, publishing of the Pacific charts, the establishment of strong relations with Japan, and the laying of the Atlantic cable, he was directed by the secretary of the navy to testify at a court martial to be held at the navy yard in Boston, Massachusetts.[15] The case involved Lt. Charles E. Thorburn, who had served under Brooke as the only other officer on the *Fenimore Cooper*. The two officers had parted company in Japan, Brooke returning to America in the Japanese warship *Kanrin Maru* and Thorburn returning with the Japanese Embassy staff on the U.S. warship *Powhatan*. The American vessel had proceeded from Japan to San Francisco and thence to Panama. "The charge against Thorburn was deserting from his station," and the specification was "that Thorburn on or about May 15, 1860 left without permission the *U.S.S. Powhatan* on which he was then stationed. He was accused of leaving the ship, which was then at Panama, with the intent to desert." The court found Thorburn guilty of being absent without leave and sentenced him to be dismissed from the service. Although Brooke had complained in his journals of Thorburn's inefficiencies, that officer requested that Brooke be present at the trial as a character witness. Though present at the trial, Brooke was not called to the stand.[16] President James Buchanan and Secretary Toucey approved the sentence but remitted the sentence to permit Thorburn to resign. Perhaps Brooke intervened in Thorburn's behalf.

While in Boston at the time of the trial Brooke wrote to Lizzie, who had moved to Washington. When he wrote, his plans were indefinite, but he was eager to return to her and Anna. He noted, however, "that a rail-road runs to Plymouth which is in sight from Duxbury and I have half a notion of going there one day to see my relatives. It takes two hours to go to Plymouth and less than an hour to Duxbury. Yet I cannot make up my mind to go if I can start for home sooner by not going. . . . If you were only here we could pay a visit together to my Yankee relatives. . . . The Great Eastern attracts much attention [and] if your health permits I will stop a day in New York to see her and talk to William. But I wish to see you and Anna so much that I can hardly make up my mind to delay at all."[17] Correspondence indicates that Brooke did visit Duxbury at that time. Lizzie apparently had had tuberculosis for a long time, and her ill health was a constant worry to Brooke.

On 28 June, Brooke submitted to Secretary Toucey a detailed "Estimate of expenses for the ensuing fiscal year to prepare a report of the Route between California and China."[18] The total amount of $4,640 was quickly approved by the secretary, who told Brooke to regard himself "on special duty under this Department" for preparation of the survey charts.[19] The secretary showed his confidence in Brooke at that time when he proposed ordering him "to Chiriqui [on the Caribbean coast of Panama] under Capt. [Frederick] Engle to survey that port and the one on the West Coast of Golfita [in Costa Rica on the Pacific side of the isthmus]," although the next day Brooke noted that Secretary Toucey "withdrew the proposition in consequence of my wife's ill health."[20] Certainly Toucey was acquainted with Brooke's vast experience as a surveyor in foreign waters.

While many Americans in 1860 were absorbed in the question of slavery and African Americans, Brooke attempted to shed light "upon the obscure relation of races." This came about because when he was in San Francisco following the voyage of the *Kanrin Maru*, he and some of the Japanese from the ship visited Capt. J. B. Frisbie's plantation in Vallejo where they met Martinez, supposedly an Indian boy who had been taken into the Frisbie family. A number of the guests remarked on how much Martinez resembled the Japanese. Brooke's friend Manjiro Nakahama, who was highly intelligent, noticed that several words used by Martinez's tribe were identical to Japanese. When Brooke reached Washington he found that there was considerable interest in the subject, so he asked Frisbie to get more words from Martinez's tribe to compare with Japanese. Two months later, at Secretary Toucey's request, Brooke described the incident in detail. He then elaborated on his view that over a long period of time shipwrecked Japanese had been carried east by the currents and washed ashore in America. Even though this subject was "occupying the attention of many scholars," the inferno of war would divert Brooke from any further study of the subject.[21]

On the *Fenimore Cooper*, Brooke had had to assume the duties of purser, and by late July he had settled the accounts of his expedition with a balance due him of $191.44. But he was soon ordered by the Bureau of Ordnance and Hydrography to compensate for two Colt pistols he had given away in line of duty on the *Cooper:* one to the American consul in Yokohama during disturbances and the other to the governor of Tanegasima "for refreshments and aid in obtaining observations etc. on shore." Brooke was told that the Bureau of Ordnance and Hydrography had decided it had "no power to sanction the expenditure of arms as presents to persons abroad."[22]

On 21 July, having settled the accounts of the *Cooper* and being worried about Lizzie's health, Brooke took a month's leave with her and Anna, then four years old. They apparently visited relatives in eastern Virginia between the James and the York Rivers. Despite the joy of being together, there was a cloud of foreboding. While in Hampton, Lizzie, who must have had a premonition of early death, wrote her husband and daughter letters that were not to be opened until after her death. This would occur four years later, and in the meantime her failing health hung as a cloud over John Brooke.

The first reference in the Brooke Papers to the political situation in 1860 was a letter from Brooke's old shipmate John Van McCollum six weeks before the election. McCollum, born in Illinois and a native of Wisconsin, had entered the navy five days before Brooke. They had served together as passed midshipmen on the North Pacific Expedition and with the Mediterranean Squadron. In 1859 McCollum had resigned from the service and entered the mill business in Erie, Pennsylvania. He wrote:

> I am sorry your wife is not strong. . . . I must say viva the Democratic Party. . . . Although somewhat scared I do not think "honest Old Abe" will be elected. . . . In this section the Union and Douglass parties will vote together, and so it will be in the border Southern States. In the rest of the Southern States I am inclined to think Bell will beat Breckenridge.
>
> Douglass is to speak here on the 21st. He appears to be the only person capable of getting up a furor. I have seen several Abolition turnouts in favor of Lincoln. At none of them was there the show of enthusiasm. . . .
>
> I am still milling. Paying very little attention to politics and my object in mentioning the noisy subject at all is just to let you know who I am supporting viz Douglass for Prest and Foster for Gov. Breckenridge was my choice before the announciation [sic] at Baltimore. But I am sorry to say I must now regard him as the most politically dead man in the whole United States. I don't think he can carry more than five Southern States. His true policy would be to withdraw from the field in favor of Bell.[23]

Like his friend McCollum, Brooke had little time for politics. Responding to orders of the secretary of the navy, Brooke in October filed "a brief statement of the progress that had been made, during the current year in the work under my charge, its present condition, and the portions of it yet to be completed":

> Since the 7th July, when the preparation of the report was commenced, the meridian differences between San Francisco, Honolulu, Guam, Hong Kong, Loo Choo and Kanagawa, primary stations in the survey of the route between California and China, have been determined

after a careful examination and comparison <u>interse</u> or rates etc. of the chronometers of the "F. Cooper," and with those of the Vincennes.

It is gratifying to find that the results are excellent.

The observations determining intermediate points, reefs, shoals and coastlines are now in process of reduction.

The deep sea soundings are under discussion; the specimens, obtained from depths ranging from 12,000 to 19,800 feet, are being examined by eminent microscientists with results of great interest.

There remains to be completed, the plotting of the work, and the report upon the results, embracing determinations of positions (final) of reefs, shoals and islands, with surveys of positions of the Coasts of Japan, causes of storms, routes to be prepared etc.[24]

It is obvious that on the eve of the Civil War, Brooke was busy and still had much to do.

John Brooke could not get Lizzie's poor health out of his mind. In October she gave him a second letter to be opened on her death, having "left some things unsaid" in her letter written in Hampton in the spring. The October letter shows how much religion meant to Brooke's wife. "All I ask for my child," she wrote, "is that she sh'ld be religious, and if we do all we can, we must trust the aid to God—as long as she is with you let her say her prayers to you, as she does to me, commence from the very first. God bless you both and make you His own servants is the Prayer of Yr devoted and loving Wife."[25]

While absorbed in a variety of activities Brooke received evidence that his duties on the *Kanrin Maru* had been well done. Before leaving San Francisco he had alerted the minister of foreign affairs of the Kingdom of Hawaii that the Japanese corvette *Kanrin Maru* would arrive in Honolulu en route to Japan. The minister replied: "I had great pleasure in receiving . . . your letter of the 5th April, advising me of the rank and character of the Admiral, Captain and officers of the Japanese Steam Corvette. . . . The King and His ministers looked upon it as an act of great and very considerate kindness in you, to anticipate to us that useful information."[26]

Secretary of the Navy Isaac Toucey's annual report to Congress dated 1 December 1860 was of much interest to Brooke. The secretary reported the arrival of the Japanese Embassy staff in the *Powhatan* and described in detail Brooke's work on the *Fenimore Cooper* and the *Kanrin Maru*, basing his statements on Brooke's report to him. No doubt this was gratifying. But for the future, what the secretary said about the state of the navy was of intense interest to an officer who would soon be fighting the U.S. Navy. Toucey had "appointed a board of officers . . . to examine the sailing ships of the Navy in order to determine the expediency of converting them into efficient war steamers." The board found "that it is not expedient to introduce steam power into the brigs, sloops, and frigates, but that it is expedient to introduce it into these ships-of-the-line, except the Delaware, now too defective to permit it, and by razing them to convert them into first class steam frigates." The secretary stated that there were seven steam frigates, including the *Merrimac*, a screw frigate of thirty-two hundred tons that was stationed at Norfolk. These forty gun ships, carrying mixed batteries of eight- and nine-inch guns, had cost an average of $725,000. The *Merrimac* had been built at Charlestown, Massachusetts, in 1855, but the secretary reported that its engines "should be renewed." Toucey was a conscientious secretary of the navy and earnestly recommended "the policy of a gradual, substantial, and permanent increase of the Navy, accompanied by the universal introduction into it of the motive power of steam." Looking ahead, Toucey, a former member of the House of Representatives and senator from Connecticut, warned: "The provision in the act of Congress of June 23, 1860, which prohibits the purchase of patented articles for the use of the Army and Navy will be found injurious to the latter service. Since the introduction of steam to propel ships of war, a great variety of patented articles have, in the construction and repair of a steamship, become of daily use, and in many cases of indispensable necessity." Toucey then listed a score or more of significant inventions. But it is interesting to note that he did not mention applying armor or building ironclads, even though the British and French had such vessels.[27]

In December, John Brooke wrote to his brother William, who worked in the New York Customs House. The two brothers apparently were in need of money and discussed the possibility of selling land Brooke owned in Wisconsin and Kansas. William wrote, "The Wisconsin lands must be worth several hundred dollars and our title is perfectly clear and unembarrassed except by a slight tax." The brothers also apparently were exchanging views on the political situation. William, who was five years John's junior, wrote: "I cannot see any way out of our present political troubles except secession. The Republican party will not concede what the South demands and ought to have and the South cannot yield without giving up at once and forever her just share of power and influence in this union and consenting to the inevitable ultimate abolition of slavery, not directly in so many words, but indirectly and surely." With this letter came a disappointing report. Brooke seems to have submitted a manuscript, supposedly on his recent surveying cruise, to William for possible publication in New York. William wrote that the agent said the manuscript "is excellent as far as he has gone but there is very little now doing in the book line and he does not think it politic to press the work on for publication at present."[28]

Following the secession of South Carolina from the Union on 20 December 1860, a number of events occurred in rapid succession between 26

December and 10 January 1861: the evacuation of Fort Moultrie and occupation of Fort Sumter in Charleston Harbor by forces under Maj. Robert Anderson; the seizure of Castle Pinckney and Fort Moultrie by South Carolina authorities; the seizure of Fort Pulaski on the Savannah River by state forces; the seizure of Mount Vernon Arsenal in Alabama by Alabama volunteers; the taking of Fort Morgan in Mobile Bay, Alabama, by Alabama militia; the departure on 5 January of the *Star of the West* from New York for the relief of Fort Sumter; an attack on the *Star of the West* by South Carolina troops on Morris Island as the vessel tried to enter Charleston Harbor; and the seizure of Fort Jackon and Fort St. Philip on the Mississippi River by Louisiana troops on 10 January.[29] By that time Mississippi had followed South Carolina out of the Union, and on that very day Florida would do likewise. Up to this point there is nothing in the Brooke Papers to show how Brooke felt. But on 11 January he wrote to his cousin Col. Charles Garnett in Hanover County: "Since our conversation on the subject of a system of defense for the coast of the United States against foreign aggression, affairs have taken such a course that it would not be proper for me whilst holding a commission under the General government to pursue the subject further."[30]

On 12 January state commissioners in Florida accepted the surrender of the navy yard at Pensacola from the United States Navy, and twelve days later Georgia seized the U.S. arsenal in Augusta.[31] Events were moving so fast that by 25 January, Brooke felt compelled to record his impressions in his diary:

> It is seldom that I feel like recording incidents of the day. The Union is broken, and no one can tell what will be the result of the present difficulties. They may be settled. There may be two Confederacies or more. Abraham Lincoln, the choice of the Abolitionists, is president elect. Virginia is trying to mediate [and] has sent commissioners to confer with others to be appointed by border states.
>
> My work in the office, preparation of report goes on. I have sent to [Christian] Ehrenberg some notes on deep sea soundings etc. through Baron [F. von] Gerolt.[32]

Evidence shows that John Brooke's time was filled on the eve of the Civil War with compiling charts and making reports based on his Pacific cruise, meditating on future relations with Japan, and worrying about Lizzie's health. But his inventive mind was not idle. He wrote: "Occasionally an idea occurs to me with reference to some invention or improvement. If after consideration it seems plausible others, by association and confidence inspired, present themselves. Some may be valuable and as within a short period several such inventions have suggested themselves to me I will record them with others of older date." In brief, he mentioned "1st, A war rocket, winged and so arranged as to rebound from a ship's side in striking and to dart beneath her and explode" and "No. 2. Boats to carry troops over water under the fire of artillery."

Brooke also had three other inventions or improvements in mind: an improved anchor, a transit stand column, and a post-hole cutter.[33]

While cogitating over new inventions Brooke was still endeavoring to obtain some compensation from Congress for the Brooke Deep Sea Detaching Apparatus he had invented while serving at the Naval Observatory in 1852. To aid his cause Brooke wrote to Matthew Fontaine Maury, superintendent of the Naval Observatory, and Alexander Dallas Bache, superintendent of the U.S. Coast Survey, to secure their evaluations of the device. Maury wrote: "The works of this Office, as well as that of my own on the 'Physical Geography of the Sea,' abound with its praises. All we now know about what is at the bottom of the *deep* sea, we owe to that instrument."[34] Bache, with whom Brooke did not have the intimate relationship he had with Maury, wrote: "I take pleasure in referring to the fact that no invention for the purpose for which this is intended has gained a wider celebrity than yours. It has been adopted and employed in every country where scientific explorations of the greater depths of the sea have been attempted, either for the purpose of sub-marine lithographs, or for purely scientific objects, and is referred to in nearly all the reports on deep sea explorations, of late years, in a manner highly flattering to the genius and skill of American hydrographers."[35] The eminent Joseph Henry, head of the Smithsonian Institution, added his praise: "[I] have learned that the important improvements of the means of detaching the weight from the line when the former touches the bottom, is due to Lieut. Brooke of the U.S. Navy. Whatever improvements may be made in this apparatus hereafter, the invention of Lt. Brooke will always be considered as a valuable addition to the means of accurately determining the depths of the ocean."[36]

Thus it can be seen that a week before the formation of the Confederate government in Montgomery, Alabama, Brooke enjoyed an international reputation in the fields of hydrography and scientific invention. Brooke's active mind was constantly seeking answers, and he turned his talents to questions whose needs for answers were greatest.

At this time Brooke gave some thought to the design of ships. He wrote:

> Some years ago prior to my departure in the "Cooper" I thought that the speed of the English screw steamers . . . was due to the fact that the squareness of their bows retaining the water instead of partially dividing and keeping it up permitted the formation of what might be termed a water bow which increasing in sharpness with the speed of the vessel altered the usual laws of resistance to increase [the] speed of vessels.

A mass of water, the inertia once overcome, would assume the form of least resistance, perhaps. It is said that water runs equally well over surfaces of different character provided the irregularities are within certain limits. . . . If this is so then a water bow should move as easily through water as a wooden bow under all circumstances and far more easily at high speed."

Brooke concluded that this principle is also applicable to projectiles for rifled cannon elongated shell or shot.[37]

As the kettle began to boil in the United States in mid-February, John Brooke wrote his friend Robert C. Wyllie, the minister of foreign affairs in the Kingdom of Hawaii: "The unsettled condition of the country has in fact led me to defer writing in the hope of having at least some pleasant information to convey in relation to the disposition of the agitating questions which are now convulsing the country. But whilst I have great faith in the good sense of my countrymen I can not but apprehend disastrous consequences from the violent and aggressive disposition of party heads in and out of power."[38] This was certainly a neutral statement. On the same day Brooke reported to the secretary of the navy that it would cost three thousand dollars "to complete the preparation of report on Survey of the Route between California and China, and portions of the Coast of Japan, including Construction of Charts."[39]

By now Brooke's close friend in Erie, Pennsylvania, John Van McCollum, seems to have made up his mind on the secession crisis and must have had some influence on his old shipmate of two cruises.

And so you are a Union man Sub-modo. Well I am for the Union too, but I do not see how we are ever to get together. . . . Mr. Lincoln passed through here on Saturday, and made a small speech, but it was just sufficient to discover his want of knowledge of the real state of the country, inasmuch as he distinctly stated that the present difficulties were simply artificial, that the South was working along without injury to anybody and that all would be in good shape soon. . . . Mr. L. is an honest man and of fair ability in his specialty, I knew him when I was a boy, but just now we are in need of a prodigious executive. My own opinion is, that Jeff Davis will ere long somewhat astonish the Northern mind. Persons laboring under the idea that we are a great nation, one and indivisible have much more faith than I possess. I shudder to think of the uncertainty, anarchy and misery so closely upon us. We who in our pride mocked the King of Naples must now slink cowering away and hide our faces for very shame.

My notions concerning the cause of this frightful fact are such that I should have my habitat in the South since I hold negro slavery to be not only morally right, but politically expedient.[40]

Less than a week before Lincoln's inauguration Brooke received a letter from Sen. John R. Thomson of New Jersey, chairman of the naval committee of the Senate, with reference to his sounding lead:

> It was the purpose of the Naval Committee, and of the Senate, in making an appropriation of Five Thousand Dollars for the use of your instrument for deep sea soundings, to pay you for the use which the vessels of the United States had made of it, without compensation.
>
> Not only this, but by the use they made of it you were prevented from taking out a Patent for it.

Thomson had fought hard in the Senate as a committee of the whole to secure passage of the Brooke amendment to the "appropriation for the naval service for the year ending 30th of June, 1862." He informed his colleagues that by Brooke's invention "the bottom of the ocean has been completely mapped out."[41]

The question now was what to do with the money. Brother William, still in New York, congratulated Brooke and added that on receipt of the money, "do not invest in a house in Washington until you are sure the Border States will not secede. I think they will before many months have elapsed."[42]

A cousin in Norfolk also offered advice. "I think as a temporary investment a deposit in the Savings Bank would be safe; and as a permanent investment United States, or Virginia State Stock be judicious—but the difficulty is in deciding upon the moment *when* to make the investment. If Virginia secedes, as I hope she will, her stock might temporarily decline, but ultimately would, I think, advance."[43]

By this time the country was drifting rapidly toward war. The Confederate general Braxton Bragg on 18 March forbade the "passage of supplies to Fort Pickens [Fla.] and U.S. Squadron at Pensacola"; and two days later a major at Mobile, Alabama, seized the sloop *Isabella* "with supplies for U.S. squadrons at Pensacola, Fla."[44] On 9 April, Capt. Gustavus V. Fox left New York in the steamer *Baltic* "in charge of the second relief expedition to Fort Sumter." Four days later Fort Sumter capitulated to the Confederates despite the attempted relief by the warships *Pawnee, Harriet Lane,* and *Baltic.*[45] This climactic event brought on the Civil War when Lincoln labeled the firing on Sumter as an insurrection and called for seventy-five thousand volunteers to suppress it. Four days later on 19 April he called for a blockade of the seven states of the lower South that formed the Confederacy.

These events led Virginia to secede on 17 April, and Brooke's resignation from the United States Navy followed quickly. Why, one might ask, did John Brooke resign after twenty years of service? There are many good reasons why he might not have done so. He was settled in Washington with his wife and daughter and deeply involved in scientific matters in which he had established a reputation. Moreover, he had promoted good relations with Japan, and if that course were to be followed he would have a role to play. He had just, after years of effort, been compensated by Congress for his invention of the Brooke Deep Sea Sounding Lead, in which action a Northern senator had played a significant part. He still owned a little land in the Old Northwest. In his cruising in the Pacific and his residence in Japan he had carried the American flag with pride. Brooke's father had had a distinguished career in the U.S. Army, dying after forty years' service, and John Brooke had spent his early years on army posts. In the navy Brooke had spent most of his time at sea, and when ashore he had spent most of his duty hours in Washington. His mother was from Massachusetts, and relations with her family had been good. He had spent a brief but happy visit with them shortly before the outbreak of hostilities. There were officers who stayed with the Union and who became admirals, such as John Rodgers and Samuel Philipps Lee, whom he admired greatly. Lee had been born in Virginia. Also, Brooke's relationship with Secretary of the Navy Isaac Toucey during Brooke's last tour in Washington had been good. Moreover, he was not political and had expressed no strong feeling when the crisis came to a boil. His wife's health was not good, and if he remained in the U.S. Navy his future would seem to have been assured.

The question is: Why did he set aside these arguments and go south, as the expression was, and face an uncertain future? Lincoln's call for seventy-five thousand troops to invade the South and Virginia's secession prompted Brooke's first response. In addition Gov. John Letcher seems to have urged him to defend Virginia. Brooke had long demonstrated his loyalty to the United States, but like many of his contemporaries in those days of states' rights he felt a stronger tie to his native state. To many the war had come about because of conflict between those who wanted a strong union and those who put their native states first. Virginia had existed long before the United States. Also Brooke had close relatives in Congress, including Robert M. T. Hunter and Muscoe Russell Garnett, who supported the Southern cause. But perhaps the strongest reason was that Lizzie was Southern to the core. Her father, William Garnett, a former collector of customs in Norfolk, supported Virginia, as did her brother Richard Brooke Garnett, a West Point graduate, who resigned his commission in the U.S. Army to fight for the Confederacy. Such time as John Brooke had lived in the South consisted of his short leaves in Norfolk and Lexington, but he owned no property in the South and no slaves.

1

Brooke's Resignation from the United States Navy and Appointment to Confederate Service

■ **20 April 1861**

Lt. John M. Brooke, Washington, D.C., to Secretary of the Navy Gideon Welles, photostatic reproduction (from RG 45, Naval Records Collection of the Office of Naval Records and Library, Letters from Officers Tendering Their Resignations but Dismissed Instead, November 1860–December 1861, Ltr. #29), NA

I hereby resign my Commission as a Lieutenant in the Navy of the United States.[1]

■ **30 April 1861**

Baron F. von Gerolt, Washington, D.C., to Brooke

I have received your kind letter of the 27th April which gave me great comfort with regard to my friends who left Washington and I hope we shall meet here again under more favorable circumstances for the peace of the country.

In the meantime I sent you a portrait of Professor Ehrinberg [Christian Ehrenberg] which he sent me for you with his warm thanks for all the valuable things you sent him and of which he made a report to the Academy of Science in Berlin. . . . He seems to think that there is life and light at the Depths of the Sea. . . .

He writes me also that the Prussian Govt. intended to present you with a decoration of honor for your scientific contributions and inventions.[2]

■ **4 May 1861**

John Rodgers, Washington, D.C., to Brooke, Virginia navy

I received your letter yesterday. No political diference [sic] between us shall ever interrupt the kind feeling, the affection which I entertain for you and however politics may go, I hope you will not suffer them to put a division between our private sentiments. I shall ever be rejoiced and proud to hold you as my friend. I will take care as far as I can to advance your interests in the office here and I have your orders about your letters. I will take as good care as I can of all your private papers—I should like to keep those private journals of which you speak until I shall be able in quieter time to write out our common history of the Expedition to which you so largely contributed—but of course they are yours, subject to your orders. I was so kindly treated in Virginia, that all Virginians have my thanks.

Remember me kindly to Mrs. Brooke and your little girl—I shall be happy to attend to any thing for you here.

I told your employees in the office that I should dismiss them at the end of this month thus giving them a month to look around—the money of yours remaining unexpended will be about $1,000 dollars, the main part of which may be required for engraving. . . .

P.S. I conclude of course that you are in the Virginia Navy, but as I do not know it I simply put Esq. to your name.[3]

■ **6 May 1861**
   Brooke, Richmond, to Secretary of the Navy Stephen R. Mallory (rough draft), BP

As the strict blockade which the U.S. Government proposes will render the importation of arms very difficult, and the process of manufacture is too slow to provide [?] a sufficient number even if we had the best machinery, it has occurred to me that if the French Emperor is favorable to the Confederate States, an iron plated ship might be purchased in France loaded with arms and brought into port in spite of the wooden blockade.

To bring such a vessel in that could be taken by boarding, it would be advisable to have a strong crew, the difficulty would be getting them to France.

I do not know what condition the Fulton is in—she had the reputation of being the swiftest steamer in the Navy, she might be refitted and she might get to sea, once outside I think she could get over, with a crew for the vessel to be purchased.[4]

■ **14 May 1861**
   Secretary of the Navy Gideon Welles, Washington, D.C., to Brooke, late lieutenant, United States Navy, Lexington, Virginia, Appointments, Orders, and Resignations, RG 24, NA

Your letter of the 20th ultimo tendering your resignation as a Lieutenant in the U.S. Navy has been received.

By direction of the President your name has been stricken from the rolls of the Navy from that date.[5]

■ **28 [May 1861]**

Memo book, drawings, sketches, figures, names

Left Richmond on the 28th, reached Zuni about 9 a.m. Wrote to Smithfield . . . station force of 1 Regiment at junction of road from Burrel's [Burwell's Bay] and Smithfield. Destroy Broadwater bridge. Have telegraph at Zuni Subsistence from Norfolk. Wire the Baltimore [?] for Zuni.

Modifications of instructions in regard to detaching companies transportation. Order for fuze. Paid by State of Virginia June 6th inclu. 221–62.

■ **28 May 1861**

Brooke, Zuni, Virginia, to Lizzie Brooke, c/o Henry L. Brooke, Richmond, BP

I arrived here all right, but as I expected the company from Powhatan did not meet me at Petersburg, they will probably come on tomorrow. I am only a few miles from Smithfield and have written a note to Cousin Mary Ann, also to several people in the neighborhood to send early notice of any attempt on the part of the enemy to come this way. I have started up quite an enthusiasm. Everything is quiet, a real sleepy place. I feel like taking a nap now, seeing as I did not get a winks sleep last night. I keep wondering whether you will start on Wednesday. I know you would probably be better off in Lexington particularly in regard to sleeping. Kiss Anna for me and tell her I am writing in a little country store very near cousin Mary Ann. I wish I had time to go to Smithfield.

I suppose I shall be here until tomorrow as the down train goes only once a day.

■ **4 June 1861**

Brooke, Richmond, to Lizzie, Lexington, BP

I hope you have had cooler weather today than we have here. It is a hot oppressive drizzly day. . . . Mallory arrived last night. I had some conversation with him but it was quite late and he was very tired. I spoke to Gen. [Robert E.] Lee about going into the Confederate Navy. But I have not done so yet. There is no news. A portion of the Louisiana Artillery 8 guns 300 men arrived last night, a first rate set of men and well equipped. I hardly know what to do. I dislike the idea of leaving Genl Lee and yet I wish to do something in the ordnance line.

There is no truth in that report about the <u>last</u> fight at Fairfax C.H. The Genl is going off for a day or so. The weather is terrible hot and close.

[Anton] Schönborn is here, says old Knorr and Waldecker talk very largely about what they would have done if they had known I was going to take up arms against the Govt. All nonsense. They knew perfectly well, and their report would have had no influence. . . .

I will write every day. . . .

Keep your spirits up and don't fret about me. Don't get to imagining. I read in the book last night.

■ **5 June 1861**
  Brooke, Richmond, to Lizzie, Lexington, BP

All quiet here. Govr. [Henry A.] Wise has started or is about to start for Grafton, he will have ample force and full powers to wind up the traitors of that section.[6]

I have been very uneasy about you and the weather. It has rained here for two days and I presume you have had a miserable time. I do hope you did not take cold. I have not had any further conversation with Mallory.

The house is lonesome since you and Anna left. I enjoy very good health. The Northern papers are full of lies about the engagements at Aquia Creek and Fairfax C.H. Give my love to all. I reckon you had better send on my uniforms and white pants. They are in my large trunk. . . . We are getting on very well. I wish I could remain with Genl Lee. He is a true man in every sense of the word.

■ **7 June 1861**
  Brooke, Richmond, to Lizzie, Lexington, BP

It is said that Robt. [Garnett?] is going to Beverly with troops a sufficient number to repel these Ohio people. I would not be surprised if we were to have quite an invasion from that quarter.[7] Troops are coming in pretty rapidly from the South. [Jefferson] Davis is knocking the Council in a lively way. Mallory wants me to make some calculations in regard to floating batteries which I shall do today. It is impossible for me to tell whether I shall be more likely to remain in Richmond or be stationed at Norfolk. . . . I will try to find out soon. In the meantime I don't know what course to pursue in regard to our house which ought to be purchased somewhere soon. The news from England is very cheering.

I suppose that Lexington is safe as the country is very wild between that place and Beverly. In a few days we shall know whether anything very serious will result from the invasion of the North West.[8]

It was a great piece of neglect to permit the state to remain unarmed after the appropriation was made by the legislature. I doubt whether we have heard the last of that.

Davis dont seem to admire the Council—I dont—I spoke to Robert about William Williamson he will try to find a place for him.[9]

■ **9 June 1861**

Brooke, Richmond, to Lizzie, BP

I have just returned from Cousin Theodores, we spent a very pleasant day there. . . . The farm pleased me very much. I think Theodore must be an excellent manager. We hear nothing new. The Yankees appear to be much exercised by the foreign news. It pleases me to think of the discomfiture of that prince of asses and Rascals Seward. I think Robert G[arnett] has started for the N.W. My health is very good indeed. But I feel a longing desire to see you and Anna. . . . Keep your spirits up and dont give room for imagination. I shall very probably be able by and by to go to Lexington, so you must not fret. We are getting on very well here. I am very glad to think I am not going off to Africa or China. There is a fair prospect in my humble opinion for the future. I can not feel dissatisfied when I think of the many advantages and blessings we enjoy. Your health is improving etc. to say nothing of a home feeling which rises when I think that we have at last a homogeneous country. I never wish to have anything to do with the late U.S. or rather the Northern people.

■ **15 June 1861**

Brooke, Richmond, to Lizzie, Lexington, BP

Yesterday I went to the War Dept. and saw Col. [Albert T.] Bledsoe. He told me that Davis has determined not to appoint any Lieutenants from civil life, that he had refused to appoint [Pierre G. T.] Beauregard's son on that ground. No steps have been taken to form a Corps of Engineers. I mentioned Herbert Bryant's case to Bledsoe and he thinks a cadet's appointment may be obtained for him whenever any shall be appointed. From all I can learn Jeff. is very decided in these matters and there is still some confusion. I think Thomas would do better to keep his permanent position at the Institute than to enter Confederate service. But if he wishes to enter he ought to apply directly to headquarters.[10] I will see Col. [Andrew] Talcott today he may know something about the Engineer Corps. I hear of nothing for William yet. Tell Willie Williamson he need be in no hurry to go to the war. There will be ample opportunity before it closes. . . .

What I said about being in Lexington was this. I probably will be able to be with you. I don't want you to believe that I can not come for I may do so. . . . You used to bother yourself about what we should do in Washington this summer all of which never came to pass. . . . I will try to be with you. Dont fatigue yourself writing to me or anyone else.

■ **19 June 1861**

   Brooke, Richmond, to Lizzie, Lexington, BP

Have been hard at work all day drawing plans etc. We have now all told about 80,000 armed troops in Virginia and the number is being rapidly increased. Old Abe will be surprised before he is done. . . . Our prospects improve every day. . . . Don't write very long letters if it hurts you to do so.[11]

■ **20 June 1861**

   Samuel Barron, captain in charge, Office of Orders and Detail, Navy (by command of the secretary of the navy), to Brooke, Richmond, BP

Report to the Hon. Secretary of the Navy in person for duty on Wednesday morning next, the 24th instant, at 8 o'clock.

■ **20 June 1861**

   Samuel Barron, captain in charge, Office of Orders and Detail, Navy Department, Confederate States Army, to Brooke, BP

Report to Capt. D. W. [Duncan N.] Ingraham for Ordnance duty.
   Reported June 24/61
   D. N. Ingraham
   Chief of the Bureau.

■ **21 June 1861**

   Brooke, Richmond, to Lizzie, Lexington, BP

Col. [Francis Henney ?] Smith goes up tomorrow and will take the spools of thread and two books. I wanted something for you to read, was afraid to buy a novel as <u>you have read them all</u>, so I got a copy of Michelet for you. There are some good things in it which will bear reading twice and then there is a good deal of truth in the book. I would like to read it myself being just at this time peculiarly susceptible of impression. . . . I send Anna the adventures of Dandy Jack, the pictures are good, you will have to simplify the text for her. I am writing this in the Dept. No news except the defeat of 250 Federalists by 4 companies Va. and Ten troops the enemy ran as usual leaving 2 cannon and colors. There is much arrant cowardice amongst them. . . .

   Politically speaking it will be best for the South to have war for some time to break up all the old connecting ties. I despise the North as a nation and never wish to have relations with them. Troops continue to arrive, some 2 and 3,000 daily. All in first rate condition.

   Tell Anna Papa sends her a book but feels very sorry when he hears she dont obey her mother. . . . I enclose Robert T's letter for your consideration. My own opinion is that the sooner I can purchase property the better. . . .

   Hope and trust that I shall be able to be with you when you want me. You must let me know as soon as you begin to think the probability is in favor of a speedy—what do you call it. Tell me when you expect the little stranger. I suppose it will keep me awake for the next six months if I chance to be with you. . . .

If you have a good opportunity send me the drawings of my patent book etc. they are I believe in the large trunk on top.

Let me know what <u>you</u> think of the houses Bob mentions.

2

Conversion of the *Merrimac* to the *Virginia* and Experiments in Ordnance

■ **23 June 1861**
Brooke journal, BP

Yesterday [William P.] Williamson and [John L.] Porter, Engineer and naval constructor, arrived from Norfolk. The latter brought a model of a floating battery which he submitted to Mr. [Stephen R.] Mallory.[1] We then discussed the matter and by unanimous consent a plan proposed by me was adopted and Mr. Porter immediately set to work on the draft. The following sketch will give an idea of it. I was afraid that Mr. P. would, having an idea of his own, make objections to my plan, but he did not, regarding it as an improvement. Major Williamson and I then went to the Tredegar Works to make inquiries for boilers, etc.[2] [We] found several locomotive boilers, also a new steam hammer which has never been used, cost $6,000—[originally] purchased to forge shafts etc. of steam frigates; the boiler had however been sold. I procured a room in the Navy Dept. for our secret work and then I drew my plans for the iron plated gunboat.[3] The model will be made and then perhaps she will require some modifications. At present the plans stand as follows:

Figure 1 showed shields and ends of the ship sharp and submerged. Figure 2 sections of shield and hull. Figure 3 sheer plan showing ends submerged 2 feet with false upper work to divide the water—to be of boiler or tank iron.

Constructor Porter's plan omitted the submerged ends, the extremities of the shield being on the bow and stern. My objection to the plan was that no speed could be obtained and the least head swell would enter the ports.[4]

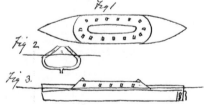

I regret very much that I did not commence keeping a journal when I first reached Richmond from Washington, as I performed some quiet service —of which I should like to leave a trace.[5] I was appointed a Lieutenant in the Va. Navy on the 23rd. of April, having resigned on the 20th. Upon my arrival here I reported to General Lee who appointed me actg. A.D.C.[6] My first employment was writing letters, copying etc. stirring [?] up percussion cap machine makers etc. At one time great fears were entertained as we were without a sufficient number of caps for one good fight, nor were we better off for flints. The state had a few rifles, about 1,000 revolvers, 2,500 sabers and 46,000 old flintlock muskets of inferior make, 37 new brass six pdrs. without carriages, 12 parrot Rifle Cannon, mounted.[7] Every effort was made to procure communication and we managed to hurry up enough to say we had some. But for a month we were in a very critical situation and yet editors who knew everything wished Alexandria stormed, Washington taken etc.[8]

The General sent me with Colonel [Andrew] Talcott, Engineer to select a site on the James for battery and to examine the works already erected. We recommended Wilson's at Kennon on the James as a good position for the guns now at Powhatan. Mr. Wilson was dreadfully distressed at the idea of losing some plum trees in his yard.[9]

Soon after, the General was apprehensive that the enemy would land at Burrils bay [Burwell's Bay] and cut off communication with Norfolk, the R.R. was exposed.[10] He therefore sent me down suddenly to take measurements to secure it at Zuni [Bridge ?] over the Blackwater. I met Capt. Scott, Cockade rifles, who joined me the day after my arrival. Stationed some [men] at New Bridge and some at Broadwater bridge with order to destroy the latter upon receipt of information of the landing of an enemy. I wrote to Smithfield requesting early information, also to Isle of Wight C. H. directing such information to be sent to Zuni and Suffolk. Also wrote to the Powhatan Co[mpany] of Cavalry expected at [Burwell's] Bay making some suggestions etc. Then went on to Norfolk. Saw General [Benjamin] Huger and arranged with him to send men if necessary from Suffolk to Zuni.[11] From Zuni I wrote to Cousin Mary Ann Garnett, but had not time to visit her.[12]

If I had kept a journal could have mentioned many little incidents that would now be interesting.

Several days ago I remarked to Genl. Lee that the enemy, finding their fire upon the Aquia Creek batteries ineffective, would resort to heavy Rifle Cannon and that it would be well to secure those batteries with railroad iron. He directed me to draft a letter to Gen [Theophilus H.] Holmes, Comdg there, which I did.[13]

The enemy has now a Rifle Cannon on the Rip Raps from which they throw shells far beyond Sewell [?], probably at Norfolk. A brig lays off beyond range and indicates by signal the elevation etc. No damage has been done so far. We should get up one of those <u>enormous</u> mortars. I shall propose it.[14]

Some five or six weeks ago I took steps to get a powder mill started, but it fell through in consequence of dilatory proceeding on the part of the Council.[15]

I am now in the Confederate Service under the Secretary of the Navy.[16] Am getting up signal fires [?] and incendiary composition for shells, parrott shells.[17] There is no news of consequence today. We anticipate a battle soon. Beauregard is at Manassas Junction, has some 14,000 men.[18] Genl Holmes is at Fredericksburg with some 7 or 8,000.

[Joseph E.] Johnston near Winchester with 7 or 8,000. Col. [Thomas J.] Jackson to the West at Hanging Rock with about 3,000, [Henry A.] Wise and [Robert Selden] Garnett with 4 or 5,000 towards Beverly. [John] Magruder near Yorktown with five or six thousand. Gen Huger at Norfolk 10,000. Then other scattered forces, in all about 68,000 men. The numbers alone amount to only 43,000 men so there must be more than I have estimated for each commander.[19]

There are however some four or five thousand here [Richmond]. But it is said that [Winfield] Scott's Army numbers over 100,000. We have no fears for the result. If we once get hold of a large Northern Army the slaughter will be terrific.

In every engagement so far we have driven the enemy before us at odds, that is where our troops have been engaged.

They are behind the times. Their cannonading of our river batteries are perfectly futile. I hope to have the pleasure of capturing one of their frigates with an iron plated boat. I believe we can do [so], the superiority of their sea forces over their land forces notwithstanding. I saw today my old friend Com. [Josiah] Tattnall of Geo. [Georgia]; he is here looking up some gun boat constructors.[20] I am attached to the [Naval] Ordnance Dept.[21]

■ **24 June 1861**
Brooke, Richmond, to Lizzie, Lexington, BP

After breakfast I shall go to work at the office or visit some steam engine establishment with Major [William] Williamson. I wish I could tell you what we are doing as you might take interest in it. You must not be uneasy about the war. The South is considered by Military men here to be in a very defensible position. . . . Well I will dress now and go down to the hotel for breakfast and a paper. . . . Afternoon. It is very warm in my room darling. But I have come up to add a few lines to my letter for if you experience as much pleasure in receiving my communications as I do in receiving yours it is well worth the time and the temporary discomfort of writing in an oven. Major Williamson, the constructor and myself have been at the Dept. all day and this evening will make a report in relation to the subject upon which we are engaged. . . . The Genls here hope to <u>get the enemy into the field</u>. Our preparations have so alarmed the Federalists that they are unwilling to advance unless they can do so very <u>safely</u>. Enough has been done in the little skirmishes to show which side has the fighting element. I shall feel much relieved when <u>we</u> have the new baby. My thoughts turn constantly to you and I watch the signs of the times very closely indeed for I do hope to be with you my darling. Today I shall take the 20 yds. linen to Adams Express office and send it to Mrs. John M. Brooke, Lexington etc. care of Mr. Hawkins Staunton. You will soon have it [the linen was for sheets]. . . . You might in case you desired send a note to telegraph office in Staunton if you should happen to have signs of a strong sail, in the offing. I could then perhaps leave next day and arrive in the evening at Lexington. But I see no reason to apprehend an advent before the 4th or 5th. [Dr.] Yelverton [Garnett] thinks if absolutely necessary you could use ether but then it certainly is not good for you. Checking action and perhaps affecting you injuriously. You must keep your spirits up my dear wife. You are in far better health than you were, when I got home, there is indeed no comparison, and you are on the way to perfect recovery.

■ 28 June 1861
Brooke journal, BP

Since 23 June very little change in the posture of affairs. My plan for a floating battery will be applied to the Merrimac now at Norfolk.[22] Major Williamson and Mr. Porter returned to Norfolk to go on with the work at once. Today I saw Mr. [Albert T.] Bledsoe at the War Dept. in relation to a cadetship for Herbert Bryant and a commission for William Williamson.[23] Suggested to the Secretary of the Navy the building of 8 light row boats for river service, so light as to admit of easy transportation.

I have also been to the Foundry Sampson and Pae to have a projectile of my invention cast. It is intended for smooth bore cannon. I am in hopes of getting it to rotate in the guns. While at the foundry saw one of Dahlgren's rifle shells unexploded.[24] Bore 3.75 in[ches] weight in all 15½ lbs., lead 5 lbs. It has been fired from a gun of 12 grooves and has four guides, 1 inch in breadth and extending along the cyclindrical portion. We took off the lead.

I see nothing very remarkable about this shot, nothing original. Too much lead, its center of gravity near the base.

Saw Genl. Lee at his office, and also at his house this evening.

■ 28 June 1861
Brooke, Richmond, to Lizzie, Lexington, BP

I shall try to get off on Monday as it is possible that just about the 4th you may be confined. . . . Am extremely thankful that there is so good a prospect of my getting off. For at one time I had great doubts yet tried to hope on. I am bent upon being with you my darling to do what I can to soften your troubles. . . . I am now making a shell to be fired from ordinary cannon which will I hope go as far and as straight as the best rifle cannon projectiles. . . .

I was at the War Dept. today and did what I could for Willie Williamson and Herbert Bryant.

There is a tremendous pressure. After you get well over your confinement I shall be able probably to go to Norfolk. I shall I think have a great deal to do there in the ordnance line.

[There are no journal entries or letters for the period 29 June–22 July 1861.]

■ **22 July 1861**
  Brooke, Richmond, to Lizzie, Lexington, BP

I arrived yesterday after a very fatiguing day in the cars as the weather was oppressively warm. At Gordonsville we first heard of the engagement at Bull's Run. Genl. [Jefferson?] Davis passed up whilst I was there. . . . I saw Yelverton and told him all you told me. He thinks with Dr. E [Andrew Estill] that your pains are due to the pressure etc. . . . I do trust my darling that you are easier than you were when I left. I think of you all the time. If you were well the victory over the Northern hordes so gallantly achieved would make me very happy. [He then writes a page giving details of the great victory at Manassas.] Mr. Mallory was at Theodore's when I arrived, he returned this morning. Seemed glad to see me was much elated by the victory. . . . Troops are coming in every day, the Florida Regiment has arrived. . . . The means of transportation are not very good. . . . Old [Winfield] Scott must feel worried indeed and all that traitor crew in Washington. . . . I feel very sad when I think of you suffering so much. [The baby was named Lucy.]

■ **23 July 1861**
  Brooke journal, BP

On the 1st ins. I went up to Lexington to be with Lizzie during a critical period.[25] Lucy was born. I was detained by Lizzie's illness until the 20th. Left Lexington that evening and Staunton the next morning. At Gordonsville heard that a battle was being fought at Bull Run. Presdt. Davis passed up towards Manassas. He telegraphed from Gordonsville to know if the action was general; the reply was that it could not yet be determined. I arrived on the 21st at Richmond.

Have been employed arranging Signal books etc. This evening heard Jeff Davis address the people in front of the Spotswood hotel. They paid Genl.

Johnson [Johnston] and Beauregard very high compliments. Our people are much elated by the victory of the 21st but not too much so.[26]

Called on Genl. Lee. He wishes me to hurry up my shell for smooth bore guns.[27] One is cast now. I took Herbert Bryant to the War Dept. to see Colonel Bledsoe who will try to get his cadet's appointment for him.

■ **25 July 1861**
Brooke journal, BP

By letter from Lexington I heard that Lizzie is better. Yesterday got sketches of signals made and sent off to New Orleans, read proof sheet of an abstract of signals from the old U.S. Signal book. Have not seen Mr. [William James] Hubard since my return. Suspect he has not done anything in regard to the Signal lights he was to prepare.[28]

Capt. Maury has been trying some experiments with torpedoes. Had an argument with him upon that subject. He appeared quite indignant at the idea that I proposed to cause floating bodies connected by a string to spread athwart current by using stopwater and applying inclined surfaces.[29]

■ **30 July 1861**
Brooke journal, BP

Nothing new. Yesterday and today engaged with the Secretary, Capts [Duncan N.] Ingraham and [George] Hollins and Constructor Pearce [Joseph Pierce] in devising plans to meet the enemy's gun boats on the Mississippi. Concluded to use tugs and armed vessels in tow or lashed alongside. I propose plated batteries to be towed also. Will get up a plan. Hollins goes to New Orleans. The enemy is quiet. Some of the Yankee soldiers brought greased cords in their knapsacks to hang rebels with. There were captured at Manassas two wagon loads of iron. Genl. Lee has gone to the North West. My shell progresses slowly at the Foundry. Visited the Tredegar Works today; they are rifling heavy cannon there. I think that a large portion of our field guns should be smooth bores for grape and canister [*sic*], otherwise the batteries can not protect themselves.[30]

■ **2 August 1861**
Brooke, Richmond, to Lizzie, Lexington, BP

The more I ponder over your letter of the 30th the less reason can I see for the cruel charges you make. You have made me very miserable for if anything can wound ones feelings it is to have their keenest sufferings ignored their efforts to control feeling for the objects sake charged upon them as evidence of heartlessness etc.

My love is strong and has controlled me, and for you thus deliberately to charge me with want of affection and to say that I wean you from love of life,

I who would lay down my life for you, whose only consolation is to be loved by you is too hard. It is cruel and I think calculated to wean me from the love of life. You don't know what you are doing when you write such letters to me.

■ 8 August 1861
Capt. Lawrence Rousseau, Office of Orders and Detail, to Brooke, BP

You will please attend at the Surgen [*sic*] General's office, Navy Department, to morrow morning at 10 o'clock, as one of a board of officers . . . to consider the subject of a uniform for the personnel of the Navy.

■ 12 August 1861
Secretary of the Navy Stephen R. Mallory, Richmond, to Brooke, BP

you will without delay proceed to test the iron plates now being prepared at the Tredegar Works, in the best manner to determine what their powers of resistance to shot and shell will be when placed on the Merrimac according to the plans adopted.

Herewith you have access to the Master Carpenter at Richmond and upon the Tredegar Works for the framework and the plates. You will report results as early as practicable.

■ 14 August 1861
Brooke, Richmond, to Lizzie, Lexington, BP

Tomorrow I shall probably get a letter from you. God grant that Lucy is better. I have been very uneasy about her. . . . I am very busy [and] shall probably try my experiments at Jamestown island. Would much prefer to try them here but there is no suitable place and moreover there would be publicity. At Jamestown Island we can be comparatively quiet. I can not tell you how long it will take, or when I shall be ready to go but soon I think. . . . Afternoon. . . . I am going this afternoon to see a new style of gun fired, a little brass piece of small calibre. I am worried at not getting a place for William. Of course he waits for me to provide for him, jogs along just so waiting to be told what to do instead of moving round or stirring things up on his own account. A total want of energy or enterprise. I suppose he will become a second Alfred Herbert. Well let us hope for the best. I have enough to fret about without taking all the drawbacks into consideration. . . . I look for the raising of the blockade pretty soon by England and France, and also the recognition of our independence, they have shown sufficient courtesy to the Yankees by waiting so long. They must now be satisfied that there never can be reunion. Thank Heaven we are separated from those scoundrels. Bitterly are they paying for their base attempt to subjugate a free people. . . . Everything here is unsettled as far as I am concerned. I suppose however that I shall be about Richmond for some time. I want to get a place—a local habitation—

before my means become too small to get a good one, there is a constant ebb which will I suppose continue and probably increase. I see no reason to believe that I shall be stationed at Norfolk any more than at any other place, and Richmond may not be the capital. In fact I am pretty sure it will not be. . . . We have been separated 25 days, it seems longer to me, much longer, particularly as many things have occurred to annoy me. The failure of that box to reach you worries me a good deal, as it contained everything you needed. . . . The Express Co. is extortionate anyhow and I think there ought to be some special legislation in regard to their charges.

■ **15 August 1861**
Capt. Lawrence Rousseau Navy Dept., Richmond, to Brooke, Richmond, BP

You have been appointed one of a Naval Board by the Hon. Sec. of the Navy, to examine and report upon, the Naval floating battery and fort invented by Maj. Gamble of Florida, and you will please attend at this office to morrow morning, at 10 o'clock, for the purpose specified.

■ **16 August 1861**
Brooke to the editor of the *Mobile Register* [not sent], BP

There is reason to apprehend that certain sympathisers with the Lincoln abolition Government have adopted and put in successful operation a system of communication with the enemy of so ingenious a character as not only to perfectly attain the object but to make southern patriots do the work for them and that most willingly, totally unsuspicious of the fact that they are serving Lincoln, adding immensely to the loss of southern life and even spirelling [imperiling] the cause in which we are engaged.

The suspicion is confirmed by the appearance in your issue of the 11th ins of a paragraph in relation to the "Merrimac." It was hoped that this vessel the only one suitable in the Confederate Navy might be converted into a formidable iron plated ship capable of performing the service so fully detailed in the paragraph alluded to, and it is probable that notwithstanding the inadequate means at the disposal of the Confederate Government to construct an iron plated battery, she might have been so far advanced as to enable us to put her forth before the enemy could make ready to meet her at the threshold. Feeling great interest in this matter I carefully scrutinised the papers in hopes that no allusion calculated to attract the notice of the enemy or the northern press would appear but I was disappointed, first came a notice that the Merrimac was to be plated that amounted to little for it would probably be to serve as a harbor defence. But the Mobile Register informs the world that her powerful engines great speed impentrable sides etc. will enable us to break up the blockade destroy half Lincoln's Navy bombard cities etc. The result will be that before the Merrimac is ready we shall probably have two iron plated batteries either a match for the Merrimac blockading the Elizabeth river.

■ **17 August 1861**
Brooke journal, BP

After some days of intensely hot weather we have had a cool spell with rain. Tonight reliable dispatches were recd. from the West, of a victory over [Nathaniel] Lyons forces by [Ben] McCullochs forces, 3,000 of the enemy reported killed and wounded, 11 guns taken much equipage etc. The mail between Richmond and Lexington is very irregular, but I recd. a letter from Lizzie today. Lucy is not well.[31]

Since my return from Lexington I have been variously employed. Shall try some experiments on the capacity of plate rolled iron to resist shot at various angles, a section similar to that proposed for the Merrimac. Day before yesterday I went into the country with a Mr. Jas Lynch of Petersburg to try some experiments with a gun of his invention, a cylindrical chamber and flat sided rectangular bore intended to spread shot horizontally and limit vertical deviations. We fired four times, the indications were very favorable and I hope some further experiments will be made.[32] We spent the night at Mr. Drury's, a fine place about 3 miles from the city.[33] Made the acquaintance of Mr. D. who invited me to call and see him again, also of his daughter and son in law Mr. Rhodes, very kind and agreeable people. Two or three days ago, Mr. Mallory directed me to examine or consider a plan proposed by Mr. Wm G. Cheeney for the destruction of blockading ships. The plan I believe practical and effective, reported accordingly. The Secretary gave him an order to commence operations etc. Several forms of floating battery have been presented, but their good points have already been adopted. The Mobile Register contains information in relation to the Merrimac of much value to the enemy. Editors are doing infinite harm in that way. I shall begin to think that not even the South can tolerate a free press. A temporary uniform has been adopted for the Navy. I was to my regret one of the board. We have made something that certainly will not be objectionable on the ground of display. We were limited to gray or sky blue. My shell is finished, only two, and I am in hopes of having the bullet mould in a few days. Shall try both soon. A musket has been fitted up for me at the Armory. Brother William is here in hopes of finding some employment. It is said that Genl. Johnston is moving a column towards the fords of the Potomac. Our forces are increasing slowly but surely.[34]

■ **17 August 1861**
  Brooke, Richmond, to Lizzie, Lexington, BP

I recd. today yours of the 15th ins. . . . I am sorry to hear of the continued trouble with Lucy. . . . I do hope Dr. Estill may succeed in finding a nurse for her. . . . I feel very very anxious about you both. . . . I do not hear of any one going up by the road, peaches are very dear the best 15 cents each. . . . I am not sick as you feared. If I were to be sick I would of course inform you, but that would only make you uneasy. I don't intend to stay long at Jamestown Island if I go there, only long enough to try a few experiments. You must be very careful of your health too. . . . William has the room next to me, both small rooms and generally the weather too warm to admit of both sleeping in one. . . . Well as I feel excessively dull I will lie down and try to forget my troubles in sleep. . . . Night, now darling before going to bed I will write you a line or so and then write in your prayer book. I am trying as I intimated in a preceding letter to improve a little for I need it. But I have failed so often that my confidence requires much aiding. All I want you to do is to hope that your long cherished wishes are not altogether unattainable. I write this in confidence to you and want no approval from anyone but yourself, not that I do not love approbation, but that I do not care to be observed or to have my conduct commented upon by anyone but yourself.[35] . . . Now of other things. A bearer of dispatches has arrived from Missouri. The federal army was thoroughly routed 3000 their loss. Our troops captured 11 eleven cannon and a large amount of stores etc. The south has been more successful than we could have anticipated Lincoln's hordes are learning to their cost the iniquity of their ways. I suspect the Germans of Missouri will wish they had remained in faderland. Those bullet headed ingrates will be severely punished. I suspect that the rumor of recognition by England and France is premature. . . . A Brussels paper "Le Nord" says that the recognition has been decided upon by England and France, and they only await a favorable opportunity to promulgate it. The battle of Manassas affords such a one. Recognition will be a terrible blow to the Northern hounds in power, Lincoln, Seward and other demons. You ask the price of tea, that I sent Matilda cost $1.25 I sent her good tea.

■ **18 August 1861**
  Brooke, Richmond, to Lizzie, Lexington, BP

There is not much fever in this city. But there is a great deal among the troops in the country. . . . I wish I had a home for you so that when you do come you could be very comfortable. I must go to church today and try to maintain such resolution as I have. Sometimes when I think what joy it would be to you for me to be a good Christian I wish I could put my arms round you and tell you how hard I shall try to be better than I have been.

There is no true happiness without religion, that I know perfectly well. Love me darling and pray for help for me. You know that it is hard for me to persevere, that I have tried before and always failed, for that reason even now I hardly dare promise anything. But will try. Well darling, I went to church, took your prayer book with me. Heard a very good sermon. Mr. Pendleton was there but did not preach.[36]

■ **22 August 1861**
   Brooke, Richmond, to Lizzie, Lexington, BP

I am glad to hear of your success in getting a wet nurse for Lucy. . . . I hope you won't write anything more about my faults and my likes and dislikes. You are mistaken in regard to my feelings towards people. There are certain manners etc. that I can't admire and when people have disagreeable ways it is impossible for me to feign fondness for their society. Young people who assume dominion and interrupt grown people in the midst of a sentence, and speak impertinently are not agreeable companions however much one may appreciate their good qualities. As to your father no one esteems him more highly than I do. But when he is continually contrasted with me and held up [as a model] one becomes tired, insensibly the husband becomes a simple adjunct—his family absorbed, and his the role of a child. Therefore it is better not to imagine dislikes for people, but rather to discover wherein the cause of apparent estrangement lies. Here in Richmond I am some 34 years of age. In Lexington I become a youth not yet arrived at the age of discretion with a scale of guardians from the oldest to the youngest, with an almost total absence of the sense of individuality which all grown people should enjoy. . . . I presume that if circumstances were the same now that they were in Norfolk you would not accuse me of not liking your father. I like him well, but I don't like to be continually told that in whatever I am wanting he overflows, all of which is doubtless true. . . . Now I have every earthly reason to love Uncle William and I do love him. But whenever you differ from me you associate him with your opinion and opposition. You fly from me to your father, so that my feelings towards him are not those which naturally exist or would exist. I seldom hear you speak of him except in connection with my faults. . . . I love you just as dearly as I did in the old time. . . . Let us stop arguing and mutual recrimination.[37]

■ **24 August 1861**
   Laws for the army and navy of the Confederate States

The Congress of the Confederate States of America do enact. That there be appropriated, out of any money in the treasury, not otherwise appropriated, for the year ending February eighteenth, eighteen hundred and sixty-two. . . . For repairing and fitting the steamer Merrimac as an ironclad ship, the sum of one hundred and seventy-two thousand five hundred and twenty-three dollars.[38]

■ **28 August 1861**
Miscellaneous notebook, BP

Yesterday about 1 p.m. left Richmond for Jamestown Isd. in the Northampton, Capt. Hicks, with the target representing a section of the Merrimac side to be fired at with shot. It is 12 feet square and 27 in thick including 3-in iron plates 8 in each by 1, and its face is inclined to the horizon at 36°. The target was in pieces to be put together at the Isd. Lt. [Robert D.] Minor, wife and three children took passage for Shirley. We stopped alongside the wharf near Patrick Henry at City Pt. I went on board saw Capt. [John Randolph] Tucker & made arrangements with him. Capt Hicks could not wait as we had the target forward on his bow and we thought it strained the vessel. Mr. Pierce and 16 men came down with me to put up the target. We arrived at Jamestown after dark. Capt. [Catesby ap R.] Jones gave me quarters with him. Col. Nelson Tift came down with me to witness experiments. Fired one or two of the leaden musket bullets of my invention they tore apart.[39]

■ **28 August 1861**
Miscellaneous notebook, BP

At work today (Mr. Pierce) putting up target, light rain. About noon Capt. Jones read a dispatch from Yorktown informing him that an expedition was afloat from Fort Monroe and that all batteries must be in readiness for instant action.

■ **29 August 1861**
Miscellaneous notebook, BP

During the night sentinel reported firing down the river, proved to be thunder. Patrick Henry arrived and anchored about midnight. Rain during the day cessation towards evening, Recd 12, 8 inch solid shot from Patrick Henry. Variable reports from down the river as to number of vessels off New Port News. Wrote to Cousin Mary Ann [Garnett]. . . . Saw exercise at battery. Target nearly ready. May fire at it tomorrow afternoon. I propose to make a sketch of the ruins of Jamestown Church.[40] Many memorials of the early settlers and the Indians are found in the soil. Coins fragments of tobacco pipes in abundance. Graveyard is in ruins the wall falling, slabs broken etc.

■ **31 August 1861**
Brooke, Jamestown Island, to Lizzie, Lexington, BP

The target was completed this morning and I am now only waiting for a boat to take the carpenters away. It is desirable that they should not witness the

experiments as they live in Richmond and would probably report to their friends, leading to the publication of the whole affair in our indiscreet newspapers. We heard yesterday that a strong expedition consisting of the whole available force of the U.S. Navy and a number of troops had succeeded in taking a battery at Hatteras, capturing some of our people including Capt. [Samuel] Barron.[41] It is also reported that our battery had but 20 rounds of ammunition which did not serve for the occasion. I know nothing of the battery taken. It certainly occupied a very exposed situation liable to be attacked by an overpowering force at any time. As winter approaches, the enemy will find it extremely difficult to operate effectively on our eastern coast. I am very sorry for Barron's family, as they will be very uneasy about him. . . . Barron has been very energetic but I think he was less prudent than enterprising. There is but one way of successfully combating the North, that is to avail ourselves of the means we possess and build proper vessels superior to those of the enemy. This we can do as the vessels of the enemy must be built <u>for sea</u> whilst ours need only navigate the southern bays rivers etc. I shall try my best to direct our efforts that way. We are already beginning and I hope the experiment we shall try today will help us on. . . . I hope to return to Richmond tomorrow.

■ **31 August 1861**
   Miscellaneous notebook, BP

This morning Mr. Pearce [Pierce] reported target ready, about 8 a.m. Fine day. Shall defer firing until the mechanics who were employed upon it leave for Richmond. Heard last night that the expedition from Fortress Monroe had captured battery at Hatteras & 300 men including Capt. Barron. Several officers of Patrick Henry on shore today. Clear weather light breeze from W.N.W. at 11 a.m.

After the boat left yesterday we fired three shots from the 8 in Columbiad at the target, experiment witnessed by Capt. Tucker, Jones, Powell, [David P.] McCorkle, [Robert] Minor, [James] Rochelle, Dr. Garnett, Col. Tift, myself, Mr. Pearce [Pierce] and the troops of the Isd.[42] The first shot struck center plate ungreased, broke through three plates and indented wood 5 inches 2 & 3d shots grazed target. I am inclined to believe that the shot will glance from greased part of target.[43]

■ **1 September 1861**
Miscellaneous notebook, BP

Fine day attended divine service at the old church tower amid the ruins. There is in the graveyard a slab with inscription in memory of Ursula Beverley wife of Robt Beverley she died at the early age of 16.[44]

■ **2 September [1861]**

1st shot, 8in. 10lbs, powder shot struck ground 4½ feet from target [scoring] it 1 ft. deep. Struck target at seam of 11th & 12 plates counting from right. Broke through three plates splintering wood slightly inside. All three plates broken in the wake of bolt holes. Ball broke, leaving 4 small pieces in hole, the remainder glancing & humming loudly. Right bolt head of 2 bolts broken off. 3rd one driven an inch. 2nd shot 2nd September. Shot struck 10th plate, center of the plate, grazed, lower edge of fracture 5ft. 7in. 8in in depth including iron. Grazed head of bolt, broke it down very slightly, 1/12 in slip before fracture, small fragments of ball in hole. Aperture 10in. to edge of bends 17 heads of bolts on two adjoining plates started a little three dogs under target, the center plate between two <u>sheared</u> showing cut surface.

2nd shot. September 2nd. No damage within, 1 bolt head at top of plate next to left broken off. A fragment scraped along the plate leaving mark in grease. The bend above fracture slightly depressed. Whereas the first shot of first experiment raised the bend nearly the thickness of the plate, the bolted planks did not

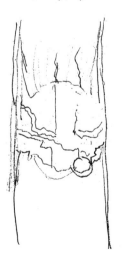

start. Some intermediate planks simply spiked or started an inch or two.

3rd shot 2nd September. Struck ground 6 ft from target. Fracture 7in long. Broke out of lower edge, 9in at base or edge, 8in at top. Bolts disappeared, two in number. Struck at seam, break very short. Penetration in wood including iron 8in. Scraped 6in. Bend about 8. Sheared at seam as before, not quite so clean, no fragments in hold.

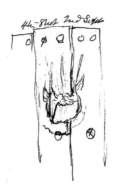

4th shot. 2nd, Sept. Shot struck near top of target, lower edge of fracture 26in from top edge, 3in above bolt. All three plates broken and sheared at seams. Shot broke. Plate in fragment at bottom forming [?] plated bottom. Plate deeply scarred by fragments of shot, adjoining bolts chipped on flange of head. Depth of pocket 8in including iron between 10th & 11th plates, greased bar rising a little, 1in. above ½in. below fracture. No fragments of shot in hole.

5th shot. 2nd Sept. Grazed left edge on bend above former shot 4ft 5in from bottom of target, ½in deep, 4in long. The shot was deflected to the left passing through the timber clear of supporting stanchion. Prior to this 5th shot, removed two middle stanchions.

6th shot. 2nd Sept. Shell, 10lbs. powder. Struck 10th plate little to right of center and breaking all three plates, but this part of the target weak in consequence of old fracture.

Shell broke in many fragments scored 3 in to break bolt above gone 2½ inches penetration 8in. Effect less than solid shot.

7th shot. 10lbs load. Struck target, 6th plate from right side, 2ft 9in from lower edge of impression, indented plate 4in. 20 inches includes slope and indentation. All plates fractured, ¾ across from left. Bolt stood.

8th shot missed. Shell 8lbs.

■ **2 September 1861**
   Miscellaneous notebook, BP

9th [shot]. 8lbs. powder, shell filled with earth. Struck target four feet six in from bottom, indented 3in deep length end plate from left. Grease on the score evidently eased the shell off.

Fired rifle gun. Struck 3rd plate 4ft from top, indent ½in perhaps less, 3½ long, about 100 yards. ½lb powder.

Moved up to 50yds., no further effect. Edge left of 5th plate indent ½in.

Best position is that which presents bow or quarter, for this reason there should be ports at those points. On the bow or quarter one plate presents itself at an angle of 36°. All the others present a less angle. Alter 9in. Dahlgren gun bore. Less indepth. 1in. increase thickness forward of trunnion Vent vertical. Increase length 6 inches. Present thickness 9in bored to 42 10In bands 2–12 inches.

| Spec. gravity | 7.27 |
| Gun cast iron | 7.32 |

■ **2 September 1861**
   Miscellaneous notebook, BP

Today concluded our experiments for the present returned in Custis Peck to Richmond.

■ **3 September 1861**
   Miscellaneous notebook, BP

Loaned R[ichard] B[rooke] Garnett $200.00.[45] Reported verbally to Mr. Mallory. He gave me orders to go to Norfolk and consult the Naval Constructor and Engineer in relation to iron plating. Called at Tredegar Works, will make arrangements as soon as possible with regard to punching plates etc.

■ **3 September 1861**
   Secretary of the Navy Stephen R. Mallory to Brooke, BP

Proceed to Norfolk without delay, and report to Flag Officer [French] Forrest, for the purpose of consulting with Chief Engineer [William] Williamson, and Constructor Porter in relation to the iron for plating the "Merrimac" etc. After completing this service you will return to this city and report to the Department.[46]

■ **4 September 1861**

Miscellaneous notebook, BP

Reported to Com. Forrest to consult with Engineer & Constructor.

■ **5 September 1861**

Miscellaneous notebook, BP

Visited Navy Yd. Consulted Mr. Porter & Williamson, determined arrangement for plating Merrimac. Began to feel a little impatient to make a move. Think I shall apply for command of the Teaser.

■ **6 September 1861**

Miscellaneous notebook, BP

There are many good instruments at the Navy Yard, many broken the Merrimac is pretty well advanced.

Ship will take 9 inch guns of 9000 lbs. or 8 in of 12000.

The 9 in from muzzle to trunnions is 76 inches. It might be advisable to lengthen the gun forward of trunnions it is now about 1 foot clear. 1200 in plates for 2 tiers, 1200 half lengths for one tier & chains one ft by 8, holes same as before.

■ **8 September 1861**

Lizzie, Lexington, to Brooke, BP

In this letter you will find enclosed a letter I have written to Jeff Davis. I cannot but think he does not understand the case in relation to Herbert Bryant, but how to get him to read it. If you think there is no impropriety in sending it Edgar Garnett knows him personally very well. I wish you w'ld ask him to deliver it to Jeff & try to wait there until he reads it for Herbert is in a very unpleasant situation to be placed in now the appointments in the Provisional Army have all expired. [The letter to Jefferson Davis is dated 7 September 1861 and was never delivered. Lizzie stated that Mr. Bryant was a West Point graduate. Later he resigned his commission and became an Episcopal minister. At one time he officiated at the church in Lexington where Lizzie knew the family. Later Mr. Bryant died while minister in Buchanan, and Mrs. Bryant moved to Washington where she set up a boardinghouse. John and Lizzie Brooke boarded with her in Washington for several years. Mrs. Bryant had two sons and a daughter. One son was confined in an insane asylum near Washington, and Mrs. Bryant, hoping for his recovery, could not leave the city at the outbreak of the war. However, she sent Herbert to fight for the South.] I hope you had a pleasant visit to Norfolk and was [sic] successful in the contemplated changes you found the Merrimac wanted, if tis not a state secret what is to be done with her.

■ **8 September 1861**
  Brooke journal, BP

Yesterday evening I returned to Richmond from Norfolk whither I had gone
to consult with Mr. Porter and Williamson as to the iron plating of the Merrimac. On the [blank] I went to Jamestown Island to make some experiments upon an iron plated target.

[From 8 September to 2 November 1861 Brooke made no entries in his
journal. But the Brooke Papers reveal some of his activities through correspondence.]

■ **13 September 1861**
  Memo book, BP

Employed Mr. [A. Frederick] Volck, $3.00 per day.

■ **17 September 1861**
  Secretary of the Navy Stephen R. Mallory to Brooke, BP

You will obtain by loan or otherwise from the President of the Da vile
[Danville?] Rail Road Co. thirty bars of Rail Road, T, iron twenty four feet
long for experimental purposes.

  You will also send six men to Jamestown Island to remove the iron from
the target, and have it transported to this city.

  The Quarter masters Department (Capt. D. H. Wood) will furnish the
order for transportation.

■ **18 September 1861**
  Lt. Col. Richard B. Garnett, Cobb's Georgia Legion, Yorktown, Virginia, to
  Brooke, BP

I want to pester you with a little business, which I fear will be somewhat
annoying but to who else shall I fly for succor? I enclose you $40.00, $20.00
of which I must beg of you to have converted into small change—as follows:
Ten into "dollar notes"—Five into "Fifty-cent" notes, and the ballance [*sic*]
into "paper quarters." Should you not be able to get as much as called for
of the last denomination, do the best you can for me. Perhaps there is some
establishment in the city, or Brokers offices, where these things can be gotten
by paying an advance, which I should be willing to do, to obtain small
money, which is so much in demand in these parts. . . .

  I enclose you twenty other dollars—to deposit in your hands for any
"odds and ends" I may require. The first expenditure of this kind I desire is,
to subscribe to the Richmond Examiner. . . . I have written to Larkin Smith,
to request Evie to have 4 flannel shirts made for me, and to present to you
the bill.

■ **20 [September] 1861**

Brooke, Richmond, to Lizzie, Lexington, BP

I rec'd yours of the 19th this evening. I am glad to hear that you are willing and ready to join me. I must look about for a place. What shall we do in regard to the baby I dont like the idea of diminishing its supply of nourishment it gets on so well now I hate to disturb the arrangement and yet this separate existence is unbearable. With regard to the travelling I thought perhaps the canal would suit the baby best and you might I suppose go the day before starting in a hack taking your own time. Still I dont like the idea of your travelling without me. It would I fear not be in my power to go to Lexington for you.

■ **21 September 1861**

Col. John T. L. Preston Diary, 1861, Collections in the Manuscripts Division, LC

Went up to Norfolk. . . . The Southern Confederacy has nearly stripped this depository of all its guns—From the Chesapeake to New Orleans all the coast defence is with Virginia guns, and so also up the Mississippi, and this too when we actually need more guns for the further armament of our own state. Here at Crany Island we cannot get any of the guns that are being rifled, because the Secretary of War, C. S. has sent down an order for <u>all</u> to go to N. Orleans and even to Galveston. Virginia is a generous old mother.[47]

■ **22 September 1861**

Brooke, Richmond, to Lizzie, Lexington, BP

There is nothing new today. A British frigate will see that the Alliance and other English vessels that have run the blockade get to sea. I am curious to hear what will result when the Alliance goes out. The British frigate is the Rinaldo, of what force I do not know. I dont believe that the Yankees can whip John Bull now the best men of the Service have left them. It is said that the new U.S. officers dine in their shirt sleeves and are a dirty set. I have a great deal to do just now but don't work on <u>Sundays</u>. I must go to church today am worried about a pew. Hereafter when we are together I will rent seats at church, that point is conceded to you without trouble. I suspect it is getting quite chilly up there in Lexington, is it not? What shall we do about Lucy. If cows milk dont agree with her can the wet nurse come temporarily? or would you prefer not bringing her. I must say I feel a little as you do in regard to seeing other people nursing our children particularly people that are dark complexioned, this matter worries me very much indeed I want to see you and yet I dont want to do anything that might be prejudicial to Lucy. On the other hand Lexington climate will not do for you. I dread your being exposed to colds etc. . . . I reckon Anna is getting pretty well accustomed to separation from her papa. I see by the papers that Gallaher[48] has been arrested in Washington charged with gambling away large sums of Government money. I hope it will not be true on his wife's account as well as his own. It is strange that a man should do so. Gambling is not as common a vice now as it used to be long ago. That is one thing I have no taste for. . . . Write about what you think about the best way of coming and what you think best with regard to Lucy, for it is nearly time for you to start. I am specially desirous of having you with me in consequence of the uncertainty of my being on shore. Yet I don't want you to start without a proper understanding as to Lucy's food and a due consideration of your own health. I am of course impatient but still I wish to do exactly right. Write what you think and then I will if circumstances permit fix a day for you to start etc.

I think the bad weather is nearly over now. I dont want you to be exposed to sudden changes such as you have in Lexington, perhaps you may go further south than Richmond this winter.

■ **24 September 1861**
Memo book, BP

Recd. $40.00 from R. B. Garnett. Sent him $17 on the 26th. Subscribed to Examiner for him $6.00 which leaves $17 in my hands.

■ **26 September 1861**
Brooke, Richmond, to Lizzie, BP

I have made inquiries about rooms and anticipate great difficulty in getting them. Edgar mentioned several person who want just such rooms as we do but who are unable to find them. I shall look round however and have no doubt but that I shall find them eventually.

■ **27 September 1861**
Brooke, Richmond, to Lizzie, Lexington, BP

I recd this morning your letter of the 25th telling me of Lucy's being very ill. I hardly know what to do I have to attend to several things which no one else can do for me. There has been much delay in preparing iron for the Merrimac, then I have to give designs for cannon that are required with all possible dispatch then experiments upon Railroad iron etc.—all to be done before the vessels can be clothed with it. All this makes it nearly impossible for me to leave. I hardly know whether I am on my head or my heels. . . . William is getting on very well indeed and I derive comfort from the reflection.

■ **1 October 1861**

Brooke, Richmond, to Lizzie, Lexington, BP

I find that hard work particularly at night is hurting my eyesight again. I do have enough to do. Cant attend to all of it. Feel exhausted every day and only weigh about 133 lbs. I weighed 147 when I came home [from Japan] never as little as I do now.

■ **2 October 1861**

Secretary of the Navy Stephen R. Mallory to Brooke, Richmond, BP

Proceed to Norfolk and report to Flag Officer Forrest, for the purpose of consulting with the Naval Constructor and Chief Engineer, in relation to the steamer Merrimac.

P.S. upon completing this duty you will return and report in person to the Department.

■ **2 October 1861**

Brooke, Richmond, to Lizzie, Lexington, BP

Tomorrow I shall go to Norfolk to see about the Merrimac returning as soon as my business is completed expect to return on Saturday. In the meantime the target will be completed and then I shall go to Jamestown Island. In this case it will be better if you can come to postpone your departure until my return from Jamestown Island.

■ **2 October 1861**

Brooke, Richmond, to Lizzie, Lexington, BP

It is now nearly eleven and I must start at 4 in the morning and shall therefore have to look out to wake in time. To save [Catesby] Jones time at Jamestown Isld will fire at the target so perhaps I may be able to go for you sooner than I anticipated, that is provided Lucy has not the whooping cough or too ill to travel. I spoke to Cousin Virginia who says all her children except the youngest have had the whooping cough and that she does not mind it. But I should feel rather badly if instrumental in making the baby sick, so I hardly know what to do. [Brooke had made arrangements for his family to take two rooms at Cousin Virginia's.]

■ **3 October 1861**

Arrived at Norfolk.

■ **4 October 1861**

Consulted Mr. Porter in relation to guns. Concluded to construct two pivot gun carriages for rifle 7in guns, forward and aft, to mount as many 10 inch guns on Marsilly carriages as can be procured, the remainder 9 inch guns.

Boat False bow.

Build up false bow but leave stern clear as at present.

Maj. Wms. Will want large quantities of iron for shafting. Let us have ten ton hammer. Cost about $20,000. Afterward to be put on St. Helena sheet iron house.

Grating will weigh 45 tons. 2 inch square, 2 ½in apart.

Four hatches 4X5

Ask Archer for boiler iron for Maj. Williamson please inquire & hurry it up using tanks.

2 forges now forge 4 bands $10 per day. Prefer $2.50 ? band. They risk the bursting bands.

Average 1 rifle gun complete per day.

■ **4 October 1861**

Lt. Col. Richard B. Garnett, Cobb's Legion, Yorktown, to Brooke, BP

I was very much pleased to learn that Willie had at last got into employment. Let me know how he likes it, and ask him to write to me.

I want you to send me immediately, a <u>keg</u> of nice lard, not <u>less</u> than 50 lbs.

■ **7 October 1861**

Lt. Col. Richard B. Garnett to Brooke, BP

Please hunt out a tailor by the name of Benson, or something so near it, as will serve as a guide—who lives on the North side of Main Street, in the neighborhood of Mitchel the Jeweler, whether above or below I do not recollect—and inquire if he has the measure of Lt. Col. Garnett (I left it with him), and if he has, order him to make me a pair of uniform panteloons of sky blue cloth, and of <u>stout</u> material. If he should not have this article I wish him to make me a <u>thick</u> pair of grey pants for winter wear. Request him to build them <u>right off</u>, for am nearly ragged and send them to me by Express. You pay the bill for me and let me know the swindle. . . .

I got a letter from Lizzie a few days since, in which she said her babies had colds.

■ **30 October 1861**

Miscellaneous notebook, BP

1st shot 12in. from lower edge of fracture to lower bolts at bottom fracture 8in. width of plate scarred [?] slightly on both sides or edges of plate. Broke head off bolt 3 in to left. 9th plate started lower bolts of next plate to right and sprung the heads of next bolts right & left for 3 plates showing elasticity of target no sign of injury internally. Shot No. 2 10lbs powder. Struck left plate 2½ inches on, bent over and fractured three plates at bolt, ball evidently split.

3rd shot grazed between 3rd & 4th plate top from left, mashed first plate back slightly deflected upward top of target.

■ 2 November 1861
Brooke journal, BP

I have been so much occupied lately that I omitted noting incidents as they occurred, but shall try hereafter to keep at least the shadow of a diary.

The work upon the Merrimac is progressing as rapidly as could be expected with our limited means. My experiments at Jamestown Island proved that at three hundred yards a solid 8 inch shot could do no more than break three one inch wrought iron plates and bruise the wood to the depth of five or six inches—pine. Nine shots were fired and struck the target which was 12 by 12 and inclined at an angle of 36°. But we have increased the strength of the Merrimac's shield by placing two inch plates laid fore and aft under the two one inch plates laid up and down and breaking joints, using only those 1 inch plates already prepared, and for the remaining portion of the shield two 2 inch plates at right angles, the lower or inner tier lying fore and aft. I have been twice to Norfolk to consult with Mr. Porter and Engineer Williamson. When the iron was first prepared it was supposed that nothing thicker than one inch plates could be punched, but subsequently Mr. Haskins, foreman of the rolling mill, succeeded in punching 2 inch plates [cold] and I therefore proposed its substitution in the plan. About 200 tons of iron have been sent by R.R. to Norfolk and the plates are now being put upon the ship. Mr. Porter has placed upon the shield at the forward end of the opening a sort of look out house, a hollow cone of cast iron. It will I think break into fragments if struck by a shot. He has also so closed the aperture that there would be great difficulty in repelling a boat attack. He had in fact but two hatches, both nearly amidships, but at my suggestion he made two more, one forward, the other aft. The grating is composed of square bars of two inch iron, 2½ inches apart, the first or lower course, fore and aft, the 2nd or upper, athwart ships. It would have been better to lay it just the reverse. By order of the Secretary I designed two rifled cannon of 7 inch calibre for the Merrimac, one of them has been cast and is now nearly bored. Four others will be cast for the Mississippi river boats. I have also designed a rifle gun of 6.4 in[ch] calibre weighing about 9,000 lbs. The 7 inch gun weighs about 14,500 lbs. Twelve of the latter 6.4 inch are ordered at the Tredegar Works.[49]

■ **3 November [1861]**
   Brooke journal, BP

Fine weather. The enemy's fleet of over one hundred sail got off from Hampton Roads a few days ago. Since then we have had a heavy gale and I suppose their operations were retarded by it. We have heard nothing from it since it sailed, from which it may be inferred that its destination is the far south, perhaps Pensacola. The Secretary asked me today if I could think of an effective ram steamer. Our Evansport batteries have closed the Potomac above that point. Dr. [Robert] Archers shells or rather his fuses, percussion, which were fired a few days ago without being adjusted and failed, were tried properly since and exploded when they struck the water.[50]

I wrote three days ago to Com. [Archibald B.] Fairfax at Norfolk for dimensions of the shells made there but have recd. no reply.[51] I now propose a wrought iron solid shot, conical or cylindrical, to be fired red hot from rifle cannon [and] cupped at base with a groove an inch or so from rear end.

I think it will take the grooves easily—like lead. A flat headed shot fired in the same way would be effective against batteries—floating iron cased. I am writing a letter to the Secretary suggesting uniformity in the rifling of cannon and form and dimensions of shells. Shall direct my efforts to that end. He proposes to establish an experimental Dept. of Ordnance.

■ **4 November 1861**
   Secretary of the Navy Stephen R. Mallory to Brooke, Richmond, BP

Lieut John M. Brooke detailed for duty under the officer in charge of ordnance in the Department is required to take special charge of the examination of all propositions for the improvements of ordnance, ordnance stores, submarine batteries, hydrographic information, and all matters in the armament and equipment of vessels.

■ **4 November 1861,**
   Brooke journal, BP

It appears that the gale interfered somewhat with the operations of the fleet. It is reported that four of their vessels were stranded on the coasts of Carolina. If the storm was a cyclone it is probable that several foundered at sea. It is to be hoped that they were at least dispersed. . . . The 7in. rifle is bored out and will be sent to Norfolk in a day or two.[52]

■ **5 November 1861**
   Brooke journal, BP

Today I sent through Capt. [George] Minor a letter to the Secretary calling attention to the want of uniformity in the Rifled Cannon etc. and suggesting that a circular should be addressed to all or each of the parties now engaged in manufacturing rifled guns for the Navy etc. Capt. Minor forwarded it with a letter of his own suggesting that the present plan, which is no plan at all, should be adhered to. I stated verbally to the Secretary that there was no plan but that each contractor was following his own notions and he then wrote a circular letter as I desired. This afternoon I went to the Tredegar. The rolling mill is stopped in consequence of some breakage, or probability of one, for repairs. I showed a plan of my hot shot for Rifled Cannon to Mr. [Uri] Haskins, foreman of the rolling mill, and he thinks it will answer—take the grooves—perfectly. Ordered bands for the 7 inch rifle to be sent to Norfolk. Pattern for the long banded 32 [pounder] is progressing. A second 7 inch rifle is in the sand, will be out day after tomorrow. Mr. Haskins will commence on the port shutters of the Merrimac next week.

■ **6 November 1861**
   Brooke journal, BP

Today I have been married 12 years.[53] I went twice today to the Tredegar Works to hurry up iron for the Merrimac. Nearly or full half of the whole quantity had been sent to Norfolk, but there appears to be delay in the transportation, although it is sent by the Petersburg and Danville roads. I told the Secretary this evening that I thought it possible that very large guns cast to the dimensions of 9 and 10 inch and then bored to calibres of 24 etc. might be weaker than if bored to larger calibers in consequence of the inferiority of the core metal. It would be worth while to try the experiment. I measured today the rifling of an old 32 rifled by Mr. Scott at Petersburg. I got also from Tredegar some drawings of Navy guns. I propose to collect drawings of all guns for purposes of comparison. I suggested to the Secretary keeping a register and record of guns hereafter cast or made for the Navy. Wrote to Com. Fairfax in relation to shells etc. Also to Constructor Porter. Requested Secretary to ask Gen [Roswell] Ripley for sketch of busted 9 inch gun bored to 24 and rifled. Graham iron and cast by [Joseph Reid] Anderson at the Tredegar.[54]

■ **7 November 1861**
   Brooke journal, BP

Today made plan of shell for the 7 in rifle, weight about 120 lbs., 17in. long, .05 windage. Wrote to Porter [and] sent plans of iron for bow and stern as laid off by Hagan of the Tredegar Works. Wrote also to Lt. [John N.] Maffitt asking if he knew anybody possessing a copy of his survey of the lower James.[55] I have had employed in my office for some months Mr. Volck as Draftsman and Mr. Ost, the former drawing plans, making tracings, and copies etc., the latter compiling charts from Coast Survey reports as of Hampton Roads and its approaches.[56] It is reported that fifty-two of the enemy's fleet are off Port Royal.[57] Saltpetre is becoming very scarce. [Josiah] Gorgas, Chief or Ordnance—Army—offers 40cts. per pound for it.[58]

■ **8 November 1861**
Brooke journal, BP

Fine weather. The enemy have taken our forts at Port Royal, the Confederates evacuating them and making safe retreat to the mainland, less 40 killed and wounded. We are extremely impatient to hear more from that quarter. I saw [a] dispatch at the Dept. from Com. Tattnal[l] which contained the above. Good news from Kentucky, a victory over the Yankees by Pillow and others.[59] I went to the Tredegar today to arrange about boat guns rifled and banded. Decided to take a gun of the Tredegar pattern 6ft. in length, weighing 11,000 lbs., ratchet rifling, 5 grooves, depth 8/100 of an inch, instead of that just adopted by the Tredegar. On Monday the 1st 7in. rifle will be ready to ship by R.R. to Norfolk. Received a letter from Com. Fairfax at Norfolk N. Yard; says he has sent me drawings of shell for 7in. rifle. Have not received it. Shall write to him tomorrow. I am getting on very well, shall soon have the Ordnance classified with full accounts of every gun made for the C. S. Navy. The rifles of 6.4 inch are soon to be cast. Pattern will be done first part of next week. Cheeny [Cheeney] will be ready to start on his submarine expedition soon. I fear that Com: Maury will alarm the enemy by his attempts which have so far proved unsuccessful.[60]

■ **9 [November] 1861**
Brooke journal, BP

Today visited Tredegar, took preponderance of No 1 rifle gun, 7in. It was cast .35 of an inch fuller in cylinder or .7 greater diameter to admit of turning off to diameter of 27.2 inches. Its foundry No. is 1287; its weight now—unturned 13,879 lbs. Its present preponderance at cascable is 300 lbs. allowing 25 lbs. for square block of cascable which is left for convenience of turning. The vent will be bored at Norfolk through the bands. Lt. Catesby Jones arrived from Jamestown Isd. today. Ordered by Secty. Will probably be 1st. Lt. of Merrimac and Ordnance Officer. We had a talk; I described the guns now being prepared etc.[61]

■ **10 November 1861**
 Brooke journal, BP

Saw the Secretary this morning. Talked of Jones. I told him no officer better qualified could be found to serve as 1st Lt. of the M[errimac]—Ordnance Officer etc. Rec'd from Norfolk plan of shell for the 7in. gun. Shall probably use it and another also.

■ **11 November 1861**
 Brooke journal, BP

Went this morning with Jones to see Tredegar works etc. Attended to business there. The 7in. Rifle will be started for Norfolk tomorrow. I see by the papers that the North is getting up some iron plated vessels, one is soon to be launched on the Mystic.[62] I must get up my solid shot to be fired red hot from Rifled Cannon. It is questionable now whether we shall put only rifled guns in the Merrimac. We may put some 9 inch shell guns on board. Tomorrow I must write to Fairfax. Jones approved of the guns designed by me. Dr. Archer proposed to cast brass sabots or bands on shells, but it appears that they will not stand shrinkage. I suggested making them thick enough. I directed Mr. Dulaney [Matthew Delany] to move the trunnions of the pattern for rifled guns, 7in., forward 2/10 of an inch. Three of the 7in. guns will be cast with trunnions as before, 80.5in. from muzzle face after adding 1 inch to length of gun which [was] originally 79.5in. The three to be cast will therefore have axis of trunnions 80.2in.

■ **12 November 1861**
 Brooke journal, BP

Today the 7in. gun was started for Norfolk. Jones recd his orders as executive officer of the Merrimac and was ordered to prepare her armament. Spoke to Mr. Mallory about Mr Volck who wishes to make a bust of the President. Volck is now in my office where he has been sometime employed as a Draftsman. News came today of the bursting of a rifled gun at Columbus. No particulars. Colonel Dick Mercer of Maryland is in town; he has been to Jamestown Island for some time. Had some conversation with Dr. Piggot who is endeavoring to make some arrangements for the manufacture of acids etc. He proposed to make some gun cotton to be used in shells.

■ **20 November 1861**
 Brooke journal, BP

Yesterday found that the 7 inch rifled gun had not even started from the Petersburg depot for Norfolk. Today went to the depot and was told it would start probably tomorrow. Jones is here from Norfolk getting his arrangements for crew of the Merrimac perfected. The Secretary said he could not well spare me from the Dept. I remarked that one who remained out of the field went to leeward, he then said if I wished I could square up the affairs of my office and go down to Norfolk to join the ship. It is desirable that the officers and men should be thrown together and be exercised at the guns preparatory to going out in the ship. Now this will interfere with the prosecution of my ordnance work very materially. I proposed to perfect as rapidly as possible our ordnance for the whole Navy and I do not see clearly how I am to manage.

The Secretary says I may have one or two of the 7 inch guns bored to 8 inches—putting on an extra band or so. Two of the 32 pdrs. or rather 6.4 inch guns will be cast this week. There is delay in getting the castings for bending machine from Norfolk. I read this evening some extracts from English papers relating to the failure of large Armstrong guns to stand the test of repeated firing.[63] I called this evening on the Secretary. His daughter Ruby has a fever.

■ **21 November 1861**
Brooke journal, BP

This evening by invitation of Com: Maury, I attended a meeting of the Convention of Va. to give an opinion as to the utility of gun boats for river and bay service.[64] It is proposed to build about a hundred boats, steamers carrying one or two guns and of very light draft. I expressed the opinion that such a force would be the only one to effect the object—drive off the enemy's cruisers, frigates, tugs etc. Virginia will herself get up these boats if the Convention so decides, Lt. Jones and Com: [Joseph W.] Barney were there.[65] Ex President [John] Tyler was chairman of the Convention.[66]

I explained to the Secretary today my proposed spring wad to cut off windage in rifled cannon. It is said that our ministers [John] Slidell and [James M.] Mason have been sent to Fort Lafayette.[67] The first 6.4 inch rifle for the Navy of my design was cast today. I have concluded not to bore the large gun to 8 inches but will see about cutting it to 7½ inches. The Secretary also ordered 200 shells of my pattern—from Dahlgrens, they will be percussion shells.

■ **22 November 1861**
Brooke journal, BP

Today a dispatch was received by the Adjt. Genl. stating that firing had commenced at Pensacola. Genl. [Braxton] Bragg stated that we were replying to Fort Pickens slowly and carefully.[68] The cannonade began at 9:00 a.m. A second dispatch at 1:30pm stated that the enemy was firing rapidly but wildly. No one hurt as yet. This contest may be prolonged for <u>months</u>.

■ **23 November 1861**

Brooke journal, BP

Richard Garnett just promoted to Brigadier Genl. arrived from the peninsula today on his way to Manassas. Wm. Sharp and H[enry] K. Stevens of the Navy have arrived in Richmond after a sojourn in Fort Lafayette.[69] No news from Pensacola. It is said that yesterday the Niagara was roughly used by Bragg's batteries. I finished today overhauling estimates of cost of proposed iron plated steamer for inland waters by J. L. Kitchen. Saw Lt. [David P.] McCorkle who has been stationed at the Evansport batteries.[70] I shall propose to the Secretary to bore the large guns to 7 ½ inches calibre.

■ **24 November 1861**

Lt. John N. Maffitt, Coosawhatchie, South Carolina, to Brooke, Richmond, BP

I am with the Genl. [Robert E. Lee], as an aid . . . times are <u>squally</u>!—and the enemy are active—<u>We</u> are not in condition to meet them—<u>every thing</u> is "slip shod"—tis a hard case, that Genl. Lee, should be always, thus situated.

Powder is wanted—arms we are <u>suffering for</u>—where is our enterprise? our genius to overcome all these obstacles in the way of success? Naval men should be more <u>freely used</u>, for such matters—I am anxious for that kind of duty as it is in my opinion the most dangerous—and <u>most necessary</u>.

Genl Lee speaks of you with great regard.[71]

■ **27 November 1861**

Lt. Catesby ap R. Jones, Norfolk Navy Yard, to Brooke, Richmond, BP

Your Pivot Gun arrived to day. The Merrmac [sic] still lags in spite of the apparent efforts of those at the Yard. The narrow iron has not come down yet, and there is a hitch generally in the transportation which however I hope will be cleared by Mr. [William A.?] Webb who has been dispatched by the Com. to make all the necessary arrangements with, and explanation to all concerned. I have requested him to see you and the people at the Tredegar in order that all may work understandingly. Guns as well as iron may be brought in the same way.

No orders at the yard in relation to the crew. I hear of many good men (Volunteers) who are anxious to ship for the M I also hear that the officers may not be willing to give them up, and will throw obstacles in the way. I hope not I believe some orders in relation to the matter has [sic] been received by the Army, but the commodore has not been notified of it. It is of first importance that the crew may be drilled before the M is ready.

The Engineers have been ordered as soon as Mr. Williamson returns, he is expected tomorrow. I will consult with him. I think he is in favour of Mr. [Henry Ashton] Ramsey who is at this yard.

I think of going to Craney Island tomorrow and will examine where the ranges can best be obtained.

When will the target be ready? I should like to have some days notice. Let me hear from you—in great haste.[72]

■ **27 November 1861**
Brooke journal, BP

Have been busy by order of the Secretary getting regulations for uniform out. At my suggestion [blank] forms are being printed to contain notes of practise made with rifled cannon at the various batteries at which Naval officers are stationed. We have had no experiments of value as powder is scarce. Got the Secretary to apply to Ordnance Dept of the Army for 200 steel musket cones for percussion fuzes to be used in shells of 7 inch rifle. 200 shells are being cast at the Tredegar—of my design—Dahlgren pattern serving as a basis. The second 7 inch gun has gone to Norfolk. Saw H. Stevens yesterday; he went with me to Tredegar works. The Secretary has ordered some spring sabots of my invention to be made at Norfolk.[73] Read today in newspaper description of iron clad gun boat building at St. Louis. It may be destroyed by hot shot from Rifled guns.

■ **30 November 1861**
Brooke journal, BP

Employed today revising specifications for an iron clad gun boat for the inland waters of North Carolina by J. L. Kitchen, and arranging uniforms for the Navy, a task not to my taste. It is by the president's order to be gray, a color universally disliked by the Navy. I need must write to Mr. Porter for the calculated position of the Merrimacs center of gravity which I fear Mr Porter has placed too high in the construction of the ship. He has always told me that she would easily carry the shield.[74] Lt. [Charles C.] Simms was at the Dept. today.[75] He is ordered to the Merrimac. Lt. Terry Sinclair told me that he was going abroad.[76] A target is being put up at Jamestown by Mr JC Summers—section of the Merrimacs shield to be fired at. It will probably be ready by next Thursday. Richd. Garnett is still here. The enemy appears to be making very great preparations for an attack some where.

■ **7 December 1861**

Archibald B. Fairfax, inspector of ordnance, Navy Yard, Gasport, Virginia, to Brooke, Richmond, BP

I am in your debt for two letters of Nov. 13th & 27th both interesting. But both I and my workmen are so pressed for time that we can scarce give the attention to your suggested improvements which would be desirable at a season of leisure. I have <u>orders</u> from the Bureau to make <u>two different</u> sized "spring sabots"; each of which <u>seriously</u> interrupts important work in the shops, without being adapted to any class or form of the shells we are now making. I have been waiting for months past to make Presses for <u>Fuses</u> and Rockets, and have not been able to take the men off from other work, but have to drive them by hand. Therefore I beg you to spare us any more experiments till a season of leisure, if that ever comes.

The drawings sent by you cannot be fully understood by us. If these sabots be deemed important please send more minute drawings and directions or come and show us in person.

You did send me a tracing (without dimensions or scale) of your 32 Pdr. gun of about 9,000 lbs. weight, for which are making carriages.

I cannot advise a larger bore than 7 inches for a rifle gun. The projectile may be elongated to any required weight!

The Bars for banding your 7 inch guns are too short by nine inches. They measure only seven feet two inches, and should be seven feet eleven inches long. They will answer for banding the 32 Pdrs. of 9,000 lbs. The iron, however, is <u>very rough</u>! There will, or course, be much waste, as the bars for the latter gun need not be more than six ft. 4 inches long. Thus you see it is best not to reckon without your host. I hope that should delays occur they will not be charged to us

———————

I must say that it is not good policy in the Dept. so often to ignore the Inspector of Ordnance, and to make what might be a labor of heart seem a degrading burden!

But for the war I should be tempted to seek some employment in which I should not be a mere bridge for other mens advantage, and where any little credit I may have deserved would not be withheld, whilst others, for less service, are commended.[77]

■ **14 December 1861**

Brooke journal, BP

On the 6th and 7th fired at an iron target, at Jamestown. Lt. ap C. Jones and Com R Page witnessed the experiments which were quite successful.[78] The target represented a section of the Merrimac but was not quite so well put together. Solid 8 inch shot & 9 inch shells of 70 lbs did not penetrate to the wood. Yesterday by order of the Secretary met several officers at the Navy Dept. to consult with reference to the adoption of a certain model for gun boats armament etc. There were present Com M. F. Maury the originator of the gun boat plan on a large scale, Capt [Franklin] Buchanan, Capt. Geo[rge] Minor, Lt. Barney, Chf Engineer Jackson, Constructor Porter & myself.[79] We concluded to adopt a model 106ft. in length, 20ft. beam, 6ft draft—propellor—to be armed with one 9 inch Dahlgren gun and 1 rifle of 6.4 inch bore. At first Porter would not admit that his vessel would carry the IX inch gun but I insisted so strongly that he found a way to make her do it. Maury, Barney and myself were together on that question. The others would have taken the inferior 8 inch gun.

I propose now for the Confederate flag:

I suggested today to the Secty to construct a mortar of 24 inch calibre, on Longridge's plan with some arrangements of my own. He directed me to prepare my plan etc. and he would lay it before the President.

■ **20 December [1861]**
Brooke journal, BP

For the past ten days we have had delightful weather, clear and fine. Anna has been right sick—fever—we feared she had some severe disease.[80] Mary Selden lost her son Henry.[81] Uncle William arrived today from Lexington to see her.[82] Night before last news came of the attitude assumed by England in regard to the seizure of our ministers Mason & Slidell.[83] The whole South rejoices. The general opinion seems to be that the Yankees have shown themselves unfit to be republicans and that as far as they are concerned it is immaterial how soon Europe takes them in hand. They will find no sympathy here, some pity and great contempt. The wooden model of my 2 foot mortar was completed today, showed it to the Secretary who desires me to hasten the preparation of my letter to him on the subject in order that he may lay it before the president.

Capt. Buchanan has gone to Norfolk to see the Merrimac which vessel he is to command. I shall suggest to the Secretary to reprint the signal book and also Ordnance instructions.

I am projecting graphically the ranges and times of flight of shot and shells. Already perceive some curious and interesting relations.

The uniform of the Navy has been decided upon and I had the ungrateful task of printing it etc. I designed the button—a ship under sail seen from the lee bow, surrounded by stars in arch over sea. It has been much admired.

- **21 December [1861]**
  Brooke journal, BP

It is reported this evening that some 3000 of our troops had met some 12,000 of the enemy near Dranesville, that reinforcements had gone on.

Today Com. M. F. Maury asked me if I would prefer getting up some of the proposed gun boats with prospect of command of a division to going in the Merrimac. Said he had presented my name with others to the Secretary of the Navy but found several as well as myself detailed for her, that he intended speaking to Capt Buchanan as he thought that Buchanan had rather too much of a good thing. I replied that while I wished to serve my country as I best could a decision might only be arrived at upon careful deliberation, that being largely concerned in getting up the Merrimac and it being generally known to the officers going in her, my not going might be construed into a want of confidence on my part in her. That in fact I did not wish to stop in the middle of work but would like to see it through. I have great confidence in the Merrimac, in Jones, her officers and guns, and as much in Capt. Buchanan as I could have in any of the older officers. I showed to Maury my projections of ranges of shot & shells, also to Capt. Minor. Both were much pleased with the idea, particularly the latter. I bought today from the Government 1 English Revolving pistol, Tower [?] armory make, $20.00.

I feel the want of my books now in Lexington very much indeed.[84] Think of getting them down here and keeping them in a private case in the Department. Mr. Cheeney's crew prefer to be paid at the rate of $70.00 or $75.00 per month to receiving appointments as Masters Mates with pay of that grade. I hope his boat will soon be ready. Anderson has recd orders to manufacture a large number or IX inch guns and 32 pdrs of 57 cwt. to be cast and made in all respects like the guns made by U.S. Navy under contract of July 3rd 1857.[85] All founders object very strongly to turning the guns off, they wish to cast to the next size.

- **23 December 1861**
  Lt. Catesby ap R. Jones, Norfolk, to Brooke, Richmond, BP

Cannot something be done to hasten the iron of the Merrimack? If not, the ship will render us no service—she will not be ready this winter unless she progresses more rapidly than she has during the last three weeks, the fault lies principally at Tredegar. When I was there they said all the iron would be made before this—and yet the ship lingers for want of iron—not more than 20 ft. has been put on the stab-side, and the stern not commenced. There is also sometimes delay at the R Road.

The North expect to have their ironclad ships in January—hence the very great necessity of dispatch with us. Capt. Buchanan was under the impression there had been some change in our battery, is it so? and what is it?—

Will you please send me a naval list—I enclose 25 cts. Have you drawn up the report of the experiments at Jamestown? the first should also be on record.

■ **24 December 1861**

An act to authorize the President to confer temporary rank and command on officers of the navy doing duty with troops, *Register of the Navy of the Confederate States to January, 1864*

Section 1. The Congress of the Confederate States of America do enact, That the President be and he is hereby authorized to confer on any officer of the navy to do duty on shore with troops, such temporary military rank and command, and with such limitations and restrictions as he may deem proper.

Sec. 2. Any officers of the navy on whom military rank and command shall be conferred, in virtue of the foregoing section, shall retain his rank in the navy, and shall be entitled to only the same pay and instruments that he would have received if no such rank and command had been conferred on him. p. 72

■ **25 December 1861**

Brooke journal, BP

It is generally believed that the blatant, bullying Lincoln government will eat dirt. After talking most ferociously about humbling the British Lion, the Yankees are backing out and humiliate themselves before John Bull.[86] Thank God we are independent of Yankeedom. I really pity my old companions who remained with them. Congress—our Congress—has voted 2,000,000 for gun boats. I shall propose to so arrange the gun carriages as to permit of firing at high elevations, slope the chassis to diminish recoil—effect of recoil—am now making graphic representation of ranges and time of flight of shot and shells from guns of various calibres. Dahlgren's tables do not give elevations of more than 6°. A great omission. I must hurry up my mortar.

■ **26 December 1861**

Lt. Catesby ap R. Jones, Norfolk, to Brooke, Richmond, BP

Yours of the 26th was received yesterday. Thanks to the arrival of the iron the progress of the Merrimac has been quite encouraging for the last two days. I trust there will be no further delay. The Superintendent of the Seaboard R[ail] Road tells me that the flats he sends up tho marked "for Merrimac iron" are sent south by agents of the government—this should be prevented. The experiments for range etc. were deferred until the shells and fuzes were prepared. I went down on Friday to commence them at Craney Island with the banded 32 pdr.–they have there. The wind was too high to attempt obtaining ranges. Fairfax had requested me to fire a few rounds for him and endeavor to ascertain why the shell[s] so often break in or near the gun, he attributed it to the water cap in the fuze being loose, but we fired four shell charge 7 lbs. with the water caps loose and none of them broke. I think the iron was inferior in the shells that broke. Two of the four were Reed's, chips flew from the shell near the gun, from their size and shape, I thought they were part of the saucer, but did not at the time examine to see whether they were of wrought or cast iron, which I regret as they have been mislaid and Fairfax says that sometimes pieces come from the shell near the base–it did not prevent the range from being good, about 1960 yds–at 4°, not so with the other two having the lead band around the base, here called the banded shell.[87] I distinctly saw them tumble in the air–of course the range was very inferior–the lead became detached near the gun, we recovered some of it–these were the shells we were to have had in the Merrimac. The honor and safety of the country and the reputation of the Officers demand that everything should be rigidly tested before issued for service. Shells would not then jam and break in the gun–and if for no other reason it should be done for the sake of economy. I think there was not enough lead. Have you any ranges of rifle guns? It is difficult to get the times of flight with accuracy even with proper instruments and practised observers. I will endeavor to obtain them approximately–the other day [William] Parker could only give me two out of five–tho–he was endeavoring to make them for me. The only ranges I have for the IX^{in}, not in the book, are at 10½ ft above the water-level 340 yds, 1°–710 –2°–970–3°–1220 4°–1470 –5° 1710 –& 10° 2760–time of flight 11.5. Your proposed projection of ranges will be very interesting. I should like very much to see it–Dahlgren's are the only ranges that I know of that will bear scrutiny–you ask why the difference in graduation when the gun is level and 10 or 20 ft. above the water? It is because the sights are graduated for the point to be struck.–With the gun 10 feet above the water, and the sight down, aiming at a ship 306 yds. distant, you would sight the ship at the height the sights are above the water, but the shot would strike the water's edge, and you would have to raise the sight in order to see the point you would strike–of course you would have to raise it higher for 20 ft than for ten. [With reference to the last statement there is the following penciled insertion: "[John A.] Dahlgren's method is in error, J. M. B!"] The case you cite is complicated by the increased range due to the time the ball is falling the additional 10 feet.–The sights are marked with reference to the depression of the object, it is not appreciable at long ranges–We expect to get seamen from Magruder's command and from the

Potomac, we ought to have them now under drill—we can get plenty of lands-men here.—I am glad to hear of Minor's return, remember me quietly.

3

The *Virginia* in Hampton Roads

■ **5 January 1862**
Lt. Catesby ap R. Jones, Norfolk, to Brooke, Richmond, BP

Yours of the 28th, 30th, 32st Ult. were received on the 2nd and today yours of the 2nd has come to hand. I had intended to have written to morrow after firing the IX in at Craney Island, but have just heard the gun will not be ready for me—I expect to go down the day after to morrow to fire rifle shells and will at the same time if I can, fire the Ix^{in}, but I cannot obtain the ranges you desire as the carriage will not admit of it, and I cannot expect much aid from the Army if it troubles them—I will endeavor to obtain a carriage which will give the elevation. Since I last wrote I have fired other 32 pdr rifle shell and with the same result, all, except one, failed to take the rifle motion, I could distinctly see them warble [*sic*] and tumble in their flight, and the ranges also demonstrated it—Two kind of shells were fired, they were banded with lead thicker than the first, and in some of them, the bands were broader, and set further on the shell, but the result was not different, the bands were thrown off and the shell did not rotate. I have some hopes of the next as their base is also to be made of lead. One of the shell that tumbled fell on the beach, when [Hunter] Davidson found it, some minutes after it was fired, gas was escaping about the bouching of the fuse—the percussion fuse had acted and ignited the ounce of powder in the shell. In this and in another shell the plunger had been forced back with so much violence that its form was altered, having been shortened half an inch, by striking the rear of the shell.—I was very much pleased with your projections, all that is required is seen at a glance, they are admirable—I hope you will continue them, the difficulty I should apprehend would be in the impact data.—You may rely upon 11.5 seconds as the time of flight of the Ix^{in} shell at 10° elevation. You will find in Benton's gunnery a table of ranges obtained at West Point with the Armstrong gun which I think is reliable—Custis Lee has a copy.

The specimens of powder you sent look well, it might be very satisfactorily tested here by comparison of range with powder of known quality. It is known in Richmond that there is not half as much powder here as we require for the Merrimac, we have 2000 shells, 6000 lbs of powder will be required for them alone.—I am glad you have the 7^{in} shell cast in Richmond. I doubt whether those we require will be ready for us, as none of those now cast will answer—I do not see how we can fire the 7^{in} as the carriage has to be put together on board ship—I enclose the desired diagram of transverse section of 7^{in}—Mr. [John L.] Porter says the ship will be ready by the 1st of Feb.—Officers have been sent after men, 22 have arrived from [John] Magruders command, we will send 10 of them back if I am correctly informed that they have been sent because they could not be managed—(Magruder knows nothing of it)—I will find out tomorrow; so many are desirous of entering that we can choose—In case the ship will bear it, I should like to see the hull covered with iron some feet below the roof—the Armstrong gun has done execution after passing through 8 feet of water—I have not succeeded in getting the prow changed—We expect to get up steam in a few days.—The work was delayed yesterday evening for want of iron—I will send the ranges as soon as I obtain them. Regards to [Robert] Minor.

What have become of the revolvers and rifles for us that came (I think) in the Fingel, it is time they are here.

■ **8 January 1862**
James D. Johnston, Mobile, to Brooke, BP

Having learned recently that you are engaged in the agreeable duty of designing a uniform dress for the Navy, I have determined to write you a line asking the favor of a copy of the regulations that may be adopted on this subject, as soon as you have completed your labors. I am enlisting men for the service here daily, and as I have to purchase clothing for them, it would be preferable to have it according to regulation, if practicable, besides, the officers ought, for the sake of discipline, as well as appearance, to be dressed in something like uniform style.

■ **8 January 1862**
Brooke journal, BP

Three or four days ago I was ordered by the Secretary on a board to consider the feasibility of a plan proposed by Capts James Montgomery & Townsend of the Mississippi to destroy the Yankee fleet at Cairo. The plan was approved of and steps are being taken to carry it into execution.

Com M[atthew] F. Maury has asked me to aid him in getting up the gun boats. Said that he wished to speed the matter by appointing officers to command divisions of ten. I said I could not leave the Merrimac, as to a certain extent I was identified with the ship etc. He seemed to think I could render more service in getting up the steamers. He said that [Franklin] Buchanan had too much of a good thing, that is too many good officers.[1] I suspect that we shall be able to do something in the Merrimac and then go on with the gun boats. I must have a consultation with the Secretary on this subject. Jones writes from Norfolk that Porter says the M— will be completed by the 1st of February. Iron for her has again been delayed upon the road. [Catesby ap R.] Jones writes that the shells for rifled guns of the M— cast at Norfolk will not do. 200 have been cast here after my plan. I hope they will prove better. My diagram for ranges and times of flight for shot and shell is much approved.

Jones is to fire at different elevations to get ranges of guns.

■ **9 January 1862**

Lt. Catesby ap R. Jones, Norfolk, to Brooke, BP

Yours of the 8th is just received—Our experiments yesterday with the rifle shell promise well—The base of the shell was covered with lead—In each case the rifle motion was imparted, and we did not discover that any of the lead was detached—Unfortunately I have not been able to project the ranges as the officer who observed the angles has mislaid his notes—I hope however to recover them.—I expected to have fired the Ix[in] also, and an attempt was made to transport a gun for that purpose, but failed. The commanding officer now says he requires an order from Gen [Benjamin] Huger, this order has been given—I will send to morrow to see if the gun will be ready for the next day—A Navy officer would have transported the gun with its crew in 45 minutes. I will get as great an elevation as possible.

The VII[in] will I think be fired but doubt whether we can obtain ranges—in cas[e] we do not fire it, the same kind of shell should be fired from the 32 pdr. and it would be interesting to compare them with the others—We need very much an instrument, of greater accuracy than we have, for measuring the elevation—we only have a gunners quadrant of small radius. [John A.] Dahlgren's was graduated with all the accuracy and nicety of a sextant, hence he was always certain of firing at the desired elevation—I am well convinced of the great importance of your projections—they themselves will serve to detect errors.[2]

We fired some of the new powder and as far as we could judge with good results—when we find the ranges, can give a better opinion as to its force—we will apply other tests—ask [Robert] Minor if he knows whether the ingredients were pure, and how he knows it.

Having proper shell I shall now endeavor to obtain ranges for the Merrimac—We are now and have been for some days waiting for iron—Can you not send me a copy of the chart you were making of Hampton Roads and its vicinity—We expected to have received some 50 or 60 seamen from the Peninsula, but have only 9 and they are not all seamen. [John T.] Wood returned without any—I hope Simons[?] will be more successful—

The projection has just been received, I have not had time to examine it.

■ **16 January 1862**

An act to authorize the secretary of the navy to give a bounty to all persons enlisted as seamen who enlist for three years or for the war, *Register of the Navy of the Confederate States of 1864*

[T]he Secretary of the Navy is hereby authorized to give a bounty of fifty dollars to all persons enlisted as seamen, who shall enlist for three years or for the war. And the provisions of this act shall, in like manner, extend to all seamen heretofore enlisted and who will extend the term of their enlistment to three years or for the war, such bounty to be paid at the time of their enlistment. p.73.[3]

■ **18 January 1862**

Brooke journal, BP

Today Ex-President Tyler died suddenly. Such men can ill be spared. Mr. [A. Frederick] Volck asked me if I thought it probable that he could get a cast of the face. I saw Com: Maury who gave him a card of introduction to Gov [Robert L.] Montague and I gave him another to Gov [John] Letcher.[4] He went off to see them and I suppose succeeded in the object of his call. Mr. Fred Volck is a young man of genius who came south chiefly to model busts of our distinguished men. I employed him in my office. He modeled a bust of Jeff Davis. I carried it to Secty Mallory who exhibited it at a cabinet meeting. The likeness was considered excellent and the president granted Mr. Volck his request to sit for him. Volck had studied our president's features in church. Capt Maury is busy with his gun boats—tells me that he has addressed a letter to the Secretary requesting reconsideration of the gun boat model adopted etc.[5] I go for an armament of 1 9 inch and one 32 pdr. (6.4 inch), the latter rifled for each boat. Maury don't approve but desires to substitute an 8 in. gun for the rifle. I shall maintain my opinion and if a Board is ordered shall request that minutes be kept. Powder mills are now in operation.[6] The Merrimac progresses slowly owing to the delay in transportation of iron. Catesby Jones is experimenting on rifle shells at Craney Island. [Archibald B.] Fairfaxs shells failed and we are thrown back a little. I am having some made here. Our preparations are slow and I lost interest. Have no power to expedite matters.

■ **21 January 1862**

Lt. Catesby ap R. Jones, Norfolk, to Brooke, Richmond, BP

I have deferred writing hoping to give you the ranges etc. but I am not sure of our base. I have fired the IX^{in} at 8°–12°–15°–20°–I could not get 16° on the platform, so had to take 15°–I will send the result as soon as I can. Of course I cannot get ranges with the rifle 32 pdr–without a proper projectile, which we have not yet–We will fire the next fair day some with 14 lbs. of lead–which I think will answer, tho I think it inferior to the Dahlgren, of which it was supposed it to be an improvement–particularly in economising lead–tho from all such economy deliver us–I dont know how many had been sent out before our experiments. The bands were first thickened, & made broader, then the base covered with lead ajoining [sic] the band, (one casting) then the outer part of the base of the shell turned down little by little until it now weighs 14 lbs–with less lead it is fused–the best shell we have tried is an Army shell (inverted saucer) invented by a Tenessean [sic], at 8° the range was over 3100 yds–Our 7^{in} will be made after that manner.–I hope to fire the 7^{in}–I fired 5 of those shell, they were furnished with [Robert] Archer's fuse, not one of them could be screwed down–We sawed one of them in two the core was on one side, making the shell very unequal in thickness–they are very careless, you ought to keep an eye on your shell and have them inspected.–I was very desirous of having some IX^{in} shell cast with the X^{in} core, but Fairfax asked me to dispense with them, as he was much pressed, I assented as the iron here is bad. Can they be made in Richmond? I think we could use them with great effect.–A few would be better than none –Please attend to it.–Fairfax and I were ordered to test the NC powder–I am satisfied but F is not. It is deficient in strength, the range, recoil & time of flight all indicate it–the range is 200 yds–less than Dupont at 8°–The iron will all be on by Friday, but as I predicted the ship is not ready, her coal and stores are not ready aboard–nor have we a crew–some body ought to be hung,–There is not powder enough here for the Merrimac–her shell (2000) ought to be filled–cylinders–no revolvers yet–Capt. [Samuel] Barron sends word we should have two tugs, he may know their mode of attack. We have commenced exercising the men that we have, at the guns.–

The proposed sketch with angles etc. for sighting guns–would teach many what they are very desirous of knowing and what is very important they should know. The projections too will assist much.–I will write you as soon as I get results.

■ **24 January 1862**

Lt. Catesby ap R. Jones, Norfolk, to Brooke, Richmond, BP

The heavy storms now raging will prevent us from verifying the base this week–I will therefore give you such results as I now have–Should the base prove to be correct I would only regard the ranges as approximative and wish that they may be so considered—nicer instruments more time and a greater number of rounds at each elevation would be required for reliable ranges.

Ranges (approximative) of IX Gun—
Charge 10 lbs. shell unfilled 69 ¾—filled with rice

Elevation	Range	Time of flight	
8°	2167 yds.	8 seconds	) The mean of three rounds
12°	2939 "	12 "	) at each elevation shell
15°	3425 "	15 "	) weight 70 lbs. unfilled
20°	3742 "	18.8 "	

In proving the powder I selected 8° elevation so that we might also obtain the range, three rounds of the N Carolina and the same number of Duponts were fired alternately. You may be interested in the experiment I will copy the firings—I don't know why Fairfax delays the report—

10 lb. charges—Shell unfilled 69 lb. filled with rice

Rounds	Powder	Range (8° elev.)	Recoil	Time of Flight
No 1	NC Powder	1956 yards	36 inches	8 sec.
2	Dupont	2180 "	51 "	8 sec.
3	NC	1936 "	45 "	7.5
4	Dupont	2160	51 "	8
5	NC	1980	41 "	7.5
6	Dupont	2160	54 "	8
Mean of Dupont	2167 yds.	52 in.		8
NC	1957 "	40.7		7.67
Diff.		210 yds.	11.3 inches	33 sec.

Fairfax thinks the above is not sufficient, and prefers more data—I regard it as conclusive, since the range, recoil & flight accord.—

What charge do you propose for the VII in rifle gun? I expect to fire it on a rough carriage at the Hospital—Fairfax thinks 10 lbs. sufficient—I will fire it with both 10 & 12 lbs, should you wish other charges tried, let me know— I will not have time to obtain its ranges, and will therefore fire at 8° elevation, a comparison will enable us to estimate the ranges at other elevations. It will not be safe to fire at less elevations from the hospital, and 8° is about the extreme elevation the port will admit—the Blakely shell I think will answer, I will try them and at the same time would like to try those you have had made at Richmond, as well as those made here—But for the storm the iron would have been on today, I suppose it will be finished tomorrow—The coal and stores are not aboard and the crew is not here.—In my opinion the ship should have been ready for service as soon as the iron was on with a well drilled crew.

Yours of the 23rd has just been handed me—I received the english ranges and the chart of the roads also, thanks for them. You will find that the IX in curve drops much more than you had supposed—A Captain at Craney Island has taken a great deal of interest in our experiments and has assisted me more than any one there, I should like to have a projection by the Ix^{in} rifle 32 pdr for him, when you complete them. Who is to be ordered in place of [Charles C.] Simms—Carter is anxious it to go—Please say to Capt. [Franklin] Buchanan that we ordered six servants from New Orleans but could only obtain one—We will be badly off—If you can obtain one or more you had better do so.

We only muster three guns crews, exclusive of the firemen, coalheavers & marines they are drilled daily—The core of the X^{in} is the size of the 32 pdr shot—I hope you will be able it to have some of the Ix^{in} made with it—the difference in content is more than a pound of powder, a difference that might often decide an action. . . . Firing is occasionally done at the batteries with the rifle guns—but no record made—send me some of the forms.[7]

■ February 1862

Brooke to Capt. Albert S. Reeves, Topographical Engineers (copy), BP

As I am informed that there are several vacancies in the Corps of Engineers which should be filled speedily by competent persons, I beg leave to call to your attention an application of Mr. William Williamson, son of Col Williamson of the Engineers, which has been for some time on file.

Mr. Williamson has been for several months employed on engineering duty under his father and is now performing that duty under the command of Col Hill, at Leesburg. Mr. Williamson is a young man of excellent character, firm and intelligent, and has had unusual advantages in acquiring a knowledge of practical engineering in the field.[8]

■ 5 February 1862

Lt. Catesby ap R. Jones, Norfolk, to Brooke, Richmond, BP

I am sorry to hear that your family are so afflicted but trust ere this that they are improving—There has been much sickness here Davidson wife is quite ill and three of his children have the scarlet fever.[9]

I fired the VII^{in} gun today for the first time[.] All were much pleased with its performance.[10] The Britton shell (Fingal 63 lbs) and the shell made here with composition saucer called Tennessee 100 lbs—were fired at 8° elevation, with 7, 10 & 12 lbs. As was expected 12 lbs was too much for the Britton[11]— the others all went well—sorry the shells from Richmond were not down. The want of interest and energy in completing the Merrimac is disheartening—

We are threatened with a repetition of the previous delay. It certainly is desirable that iron should be put on her hull—but not if it occasions so much detention as our experiences made us dread—Iron clad vessels are shortly expected in Hampton Roads.[12] I do not see why the Merrimac might not be at work in a week from this time—She can be easily submerged to the desired depth.—Her Captain should be here and so I wrote him a month ago.[13]—Until he was ordered I was listened to, but of course that cannot be now. It is generally known that a mistake has been made in regard to the ship floating—It has been intimated to me, that advantage will be taken of this to deceive the Yankees, by inserting an article in the Day Book exaggerating and magnifying it very much. I hear several articles are to be written, the first to appear on Friday, let Capt. B. know it that he may be on his guard—One good effect anticipated, is that it will lessen the undue expectations of our own people.—We all here regard [James D.] Bulloch'[s] appointment an outrage.[14] It is very certain that a Lt. would not have been promoted for doing what he has done—and he has far less claim—against him personally, there is no objection, but the precedent is bad—We have sacrificed more than any other class and if we have not some chance of promotion—I am in favour of promoting for gallant conduct or highly distinguished services, but Bulloch'[s] is not enough so—That it is only for the War does not affect the principle—as it is better to promote a Lt. for the War than not at all.

If this cannot be done what can be done to prevent a repetition. . . .

PS—I am glad to hear that the IX in shell with the X in core are to be cast—It will be necessary to have them rigidly inspected—particularly the thickness of sides. There is so much delay in transportation that it would be well to send down the shell and other things for the ship without waiting until they are all completed—for example send fifty shell as soon as they are ready. What about those with incendiary composition? The men are drilled twice a day at the guns—unfortunately we have no pivot gun to drill at— . . .

It is rumored a Commander is to be ordered to the Merrimac, I hope not.[15] Please deliver the enclosed to Capt. Buchanan.

■ **10 February 1862**
A. Frederick Volck, Navy Department, to Brooke, Richmond, BP

After a five days unsuccessful inquiry into the state of your health, I heard with much pleasure yesterday that you were mending and would soon be out again. I trust it may prove true for your office looks desolate without your presence.

Capt. [George] Minor returned from Norfolk on last Saturday with the good news that your Seven Inch Gun is a complete success. They threw a shell of a hundred pounds weight four miles & half.

- **13 February 1862**
  Brooke journal, BP

Lately I have had much trouble. First Anna had the scarlet fever, then Matilda the nurse got sick and went to bed for a couple of weeks, the baby is right sick, and I am troubled to procure a nurse for her. Mercer William-son kindly came down from Lexington to aid us.[16] I was quite sick in bed several days. We have a nurse from Norfolk. Anna is convalescent now, and I have been able to go to my office the last three days. I have had solid shutters rolled for the Merrimacs ports, at least for the 3 bow and stern ports. Hope we may have all rolled as I do not believe the compound ports will stand. The ship has been floated in dock, draws less water than was anticipated, additional plating is applied on the submerged deck part forward and aft.[17] The 7 inch Rifle is a very fine gun and throws 100 [pound] shell admiredly, so Jones writes. We are short of lead here to finish the shells prepared. I have had special fuzes prepared for them. Wish we had the lead.[18] Roanoke Island has been taken by the enemy as was anticipated by naval men.[19] Mr. [William G.] Cheeney's boat is not ready yet. He proposes to go down on a preliminary trip in a row boat to try and blow something up. I have sent copies of range and time tables to several points. I shall try in a day or two solid wrought iron shot red hot from rifled gun. I propose it to meet the enemys iron clad vessels. Mr. [William James] Hubard will never get his incendiary shells filled, he is not steady to the point.

- **16 February 1862**
  Brooke journal, BP

Poor Hubard, on the very day I wrote the above, met with a fatal accident. An explosion occurred in his laboratory and he died last night.[20] I asked Mr. [Charles M.] Conrad, Chairman of the Naval committee, whether some relief might be obtained from Congress for his family—Wife, son, and daughter. He replied, not now but hereafter perhaps and certainly if the burning composition proves valuable. He said he wished me to prosecute the experiments.

Today I changed the numbers of our naval signals as it is feared by Capt. [William] Lynch that our signal books on board the "Ellis" and "Seabird" fell into the hands of the enemy.[21]

- **16 February 1862**
  Brooke journal, BP

Yesterday, Mr. Mallory sent for me and after asking me as to the condition of my family who are all sick, said he thought I could not go in the Merrimac, that he wished to send her out in a day or two, and that she could not wait for her shutters. I said I wished to go if possible. He said he knew that, but that under the circumstances he did not see how I could go. I told him if he thought it right I would stay. He said he did think so most decidedly, whereupon I said I would wait. He said also that there was plenty for me to do at the Dept. I regret exceedingly this condition of affairs, but leave it to providence, hoping for the best.

He also read me an extract from Com: [French] Forrests letters in which he reports as his own a suggestion I made to Lt. Jones in relation to dredging the channel off Sewells pt for Yankee torpedoes.[22] I had mentioned having written to Jones on the subject several days ago and the Secretary was much amused. I am designing an 8 inch gun after the Dahlgren pattern to weigh about 7,000 lbs.[23]

Today I met Capt. Reeves in charge of Engineers office. He told me that the fortifications at Hardy's [?] Bluff were to be much improved. He said that Capt. Myers had gone down the river to select sites for fortifications etc., that he had expressed a wish to have me with him but that he—Reeves—knew I could not go. He asked me where would be a good place to plant obstructions to prevent a dash up the River by the enemy's gun boats. I replied, that instead of obstructions, I would plant a battery of four heavy guns at Kennons on the James near Lower Brandon, that the only reason a battery had not been placed there was that the proprietor objected to having it in his front yard. He said he would place it there. Asked me if Fort Powhatan was not a better position. I replied no, as a number of vessels might attack Powhatan simultaneously, but only one or two could attack Kennons, the channel being long straight and narrow.[24]

We are all very impatient to hear from Fort Donaldson [Donelson], a battle has been fought there, the enemy were repulsed but have received large reinforcements.[25]

■ **17 February 1862**

Lt. Catesby ap R. Jones, CSB *Virginia*,[26] Navy Yard, Norfolk, to Brooke, BP

Yours of the 15th is this moment received. I have been unable to reply to the previous letter before—We went in commission today, tho strange to say the day has been lost in the yard as far as the ship is concerned, neither guns or coal have been put aboard, driving energetic officers are wanted here. The ship went out of dock yesterday, and took on board six broadside guns—she has most of her anthracite coal aboard and about 100 tons of bituminous, and will take 250 tons more, all the stores and some of the shell—and she floats about a foot below the eaves of the roof—there will be trouble to bring her down.—You have no idea of the difficulties in having anything out of the regular routine done, if the Captain were here it would be better.—I have been anxious to have guns above and think the plan you suggest very good. An order from Richmond would be necessary, as the Commodore here after consenting to it, hesitates, Capt Buchanan desires the gun—You[r] other suggestions are admirable, and if our Captain agrees, may be done—I have not been able to fire your shell for the VII in, the gun is at the Hospital, and cannot be fired on account of the wounded. The range of the Tennessee and Britton shell was very indifferently obtained at 8°—with 12 lbs of powder—I have mislaid the paper—I received the range tables, and sent one to Gen. Huger who said he would send a copy to each battery. Have you not the VIII in shell gun and 32 pdr—?—300 of the IX in would be sufficient, large core—please have 100 of them sent as soon as ready—Fairfax would not like to fill the carcasses here if there is danger in it.—The fuzes sent by Mr. Porter are the best I have seen. [William] Parker says he does not think a single rifle shell exploded properly at Roanoke most of them broke near the gun. We want about fifty men to complete our crew—For about the hundredth time I am interrupted and must stop—I am very sorry to hear of your bad health and that of your family, hope have improved, and that you may be soon be well enough to join us.

■ **17 February 1862**
Secretary of the Navy Stephen R. Mallory to Brooke, Richmond, BP

Report to Flag Officer William T. Lynch on the 19th inst for duty as member of a Board to prepare Regulations for the Navy.

Reported Feb 2, 1862
W F Lynch
Flag Officer

■ **18 February 1862**
Brooke journal, BP

All impatient for reliable news from Fort Donelson.

■ **20 February 1862**
Lt. Catesby ap R. Jones, aboard CSSB *Virginia*, to Brooke, Richmond, BP

Yours of the 17th was received yesterday. Fairfax thinks he cannot lead your VII in shells, says he is pressed etc. I wish you would send as many down as are completed. We are living aboard, and are as uncomfortable as possible—there has not been a dry spot aboard of her, leaks everywhere. Mechanics are at work at a thousand things which should have been done months ago, cooling also and receiving stones and drilling.

■ **21 February 1862**
  Lt. Catesby ap R. Jones, *Virginia*, to Brooke, Richmond, BP

I have only time to acknowledge yours of the 19th and express my great regret that you are not to be with us in the Virginia. I had hoped we would have had your advice and counsel and should have felt better satisfied if it were so, but know full when [well] how important your presence is both to the Department and to your Family. I trust indeed that you may be spared the great calamity threatening you, and truly hope your children may escape—I can appreciate and fully sympathize with you in your distress. I have not time to say more.

■ **25 February 1862**
  Lt. Catesby ap R. Jones, *Virginia*, to Brooke, BP

I wish you would send me the length of sight bar for the 32 pdr rifle [6.4 inch] VII in rifle & IX in guns up to 10° for muzzle sight and to 6° for reinforce sight—I am constantly occupied or I would not trouble you, and I dont know whether our officers are familiar with the calculations. The distance wanted is the length of bar above the level mark.—The water is now just above the eaves, we have yet to take [on] our powder and most of the shell, and 150 tons of coal which it is thought will bring it down a foot more—I should feel much better satisfied if the hull had six inches of iron where it now has but one, tis our most vulnerable part, and unfortunately for us, where a shell can easily penetrate.

From strange neglect, there is no coal here for us, I never saw anything so mismanaged—Powder is wanting to fill the shell, or we might take them aboard. What of the VII in shell ? and the IX in with the X in core? Do let us have those finished.—The ship is yet filled with mechanics, which prevents us from drilling, and keeps the crew in a disorganized condition—We are 50 short of the complement.—In great haste.

■ **27 February 1862**
  Brooke journal, BP

For the past two weeks I have done but little, domestic affliction ruling the hours. Yesterday evening I saw Muscoe Garnett and had some conversation with him in relation to our defences.[27] I remarked that Congress should appropriate $5,000,000 for the construction of iron plated gun boats for River & Harbor defense. He said Congress would readily give whatever the Secretary might ask for. He said that he would speak to Mr [William Porcher] Miles in relation to the formation of a proper heavy artillery corps to serve the batteries etc.[28] I suggested that as an important step, it is only a few days since the Engineer Corps was organized. Today I saw the Secretary of the Navy and mentioned what Mr Garnett said about the appropriation and again suggested to the Secretary the importance of constructing proper gun boats iron clad. Told him of a rolling mill which might be purchased in Georgia. He saw Mr[George] Minor, the person who mentioned the subject to me, and has ordered Lt. Sinclair to visit the works.[29]

I saw Capt Reeves of the engineers and suggested to him the importance of keeping a battery of field artillery on Jamestown Island on the lower part of which the enemy might land with facility as there are no guns there, the batteries being all at the upper end of the Island. I urged also the establishment of a battery at Kennons or Wilsons opposite Brandon. I had already urged it. He said the order had been issued and that 8 in guns would be mounted there. I recommended guns of heavier calibre and <u>Rifled</u> guns particularly.[30] Wrote to Lt. Jones, sent him as he requested graduation for sights of cannon. Went to Tredegar works. 6 prs. of rolled iron shutters have gone to the M–3prs of built up shutters also, which are good for nothing.

The wrought iron experimental shot for 3 inch rifle are ready. On Saturday I propose to fire them, some red hot .50 shells have gone down for my Rifled guns on the Merrimac.

■ **5 March 1862**
Lt. Catesby ap R. Jones, *Virginia,* to Brooke, BP

The VII[in] shell have arrived, but are condemned by the Ordnance here, I have not had time to examine them. It will not incommode us much, as we will take the Britton shell instead of them.

There is some discrepancy between your drawings and your table for tangent sights, we will however investigate and find out which is right—I fired on Saturday six of the Richmond VII[in] shell—I will send you the results, and also the firing of the other shell—I regret that the observations were not such as to make them valuable, the position of the observers was bad. I hope we will get off on Thursday night—The ship will be too light, or I should say she is not sufficiently protected below the water—Our draft will be a foot less than was first intended, yet I was this morning ordered not to put any more ballast in, fear of the bottom—The eaves of the roof will not be more than six inches immersed, which in smooth water would not be enough—a slight ripple would leave it bare except the one inch iron that extends some feet below—We are least protected where we most need it, and may receive a shot that would sink us, a 32 pdr. would do it—The constructor should have put on six inches where we now have one—We have taken on board a large quantity of ballast—The ship has been in possession of the mechanics, they are still at work—The shutters for bow and quarter ports are fitted temporarily, t' would take a week longer to fit them. The crew and officers are nearly all sick with colds etc.—our reliance is upon the intelligence of the officers, as the crew are very green, we will have a Lt. or mid. at each gun—Buchanan hoisted his flag yesterday.[31] I think he prefers close quarters, and has faith in the ram—It is unfortunate that so much is expected of the ship—As we know that she may fail completely, either from receiving a shot between wind and water, or from grounding—to speak nothing of the devices rumour says they have in store for us. I can only say for the officers that they are willing and anxious to try.—I write in haste and am constantly interrupted. Goodbye.

■ 6 March 1862
Brooke journal, BP

Several days ago I said to Muscoe Garnett that we ought to have $5 000 000 for iron clad gun boats. He said Congress would give whatever the Secretary would require. I mentioned this to the Secretary the next day. Our chief trouble arises from the want of rolling mills.

Several days ago I found that 2000 loaded shells were stored in a tobacco ware house in the city; after urging their removing Capt. [George] Minor issued the order. Last night called on the Secretary, proposed formation of a boat corps, 8 12 oared boats on wagons drawn by 4 horses each, boat howitzers by one horse each, and two 1100 lbs. rifled guns, tents etc. the question is whether we shall hold the bank of the Potomac during the Summer if so we could capture many vessels. the Merrimac is reported ready with the exception of some port shutters.[32]

I suggested to the Secretary the establishment of a laboratory on a proper scale at or near this city.

■ 7 March 1862
Lt. Robert D. Minor, CSS *Virginia*, Norfolk, to Brooke, ordnance officer, Richmond

I have read your letter to Jones, and he desires me to say to you that he has not seen the shells complained of, that they have not been sent on board the ship, and that the "Britton" shells have been substituted for them—and furthermore that he is inclined to believe that it is not the 7 in shell—but the 32 pdr—which has been found defective.

We are ready—and you may look out for some tidings of us soon.

Signal books are very much needed, and I wish you would send a package of them to the Ord Dept here—for I have had to deprive Billy Parker of his in order to have one for my own use as Flag Lieut of the Squadron. Please give your special attention to this!

What is it about the rumored changes in the Ord Dept at Richmond? Is Capt Fairfax to have charge of the office, and what duty will Bro George have?—The edges of our plates are only five inches below the water. The ship is exceedingly formidable and I believe she will be a success, on which you may be most heartily congratulated. I made a reconnaissance of the enemys ships a day or two since and was glad to be able to report them in less force than I had been led to suppose. Goodbye until we meet, which I hope will be soon, when I go up with the announcement of our victory and with the hope that Mrs. Brooke & your family are improving in health.[33]

Merrimac's Victory

■ **8 March 1862**
   Brooke journal, BP

This afternoon while taking a nap I was awakened by cousin Hen Brooke who came to my room with the glorious news that the Merrimac had sunk the U.S. Frigate Cumberland and driven the U.S. Frigate Congress onshore and was shelling the enemy's battery at Newports [*sic*] News. Lizzie understood him to say that the Merrimac was sunk but was quickly undeceived. I went immediately to see Mr Mallory whom I found in the parlor of the Arlington. He told me that the telegraph recd was as follows. The Merrimac and gun boats are doing nobly, the Cumberland is sunk, the Congress is onshore and the Merrimac is bombarding New port News, the Patrick Henry and Jamestown are in sight coming down the river. I left Mr Mallory and went to the Dept. Near the door met brother William who told me that a second dispatch had been received as follows:

The Cumberland is sunk, the Congress ashore has two white flags flying, the US Frigate Minnesota is ashore, the Jamestown and Patrick Henry—two gun boats—are firing vigorously upon her. The U.S.F. Roanoke has run under the guns of fortress Monroe. The Merrimac is bombarding Newports News. The battery responds feebly.

That is glorious news, all honor to the brave and skilful officers & men who achieved the victory.[34]

Today I was consulted by the engineers as to the best plan of boom to obstruct channel at Fort Powhatan. . . . I proposed salients and beams or spars projecting to prevent forcing by steamers & diagonal timbers, two tiers on the parallel timbers breaking joints below. Also coincided with opinion that boom should be within grape range. Suggested that piles & buoys should be placed to catch torpedoes [mines]. Also that single timbers moored would annoy steamers. Proposed tripping lines to impede troops disembarking and stakes in [rows?] to prevent boats landing readily.

I maintain that works should be erected at both Fort Powhatan and Kennons. Engineer [Isaac M.] St John coincides with me.[35]

■ **9 March 1862**

Alexander Tunstall, Norfolk, to Brooke, BP

Yours of the 6th inst was received yesterday. I have been pained by the recent afflictions in your family, and regretted them the more because of their occurrence at a time when the mental and physical energies of every man were required in the Service of our Country. Whilst I write the house is jarred by the renewal of the battle this morning, between the Virginia (Merrimac) & Minnesota. It is greatly to be regretted that anything should have occurred to prevent your joining the former; however important your agency may have been in the planning of her, and her armament, the glory of participating in the fight would have been far greater, or added materially to the credit you may otherwise get. A man must occupy a very high position, one reached by few, to justify him in disregarding public opinion. We all know the effect on the public mind, of <u>courage</u> & <u>skill</u>, successfully exerted in battle. A victory may be the result of profound study & inventive talent in one who has cont[r]ived a new implement of war, but the fame of the victor who uses the implement, will transcend that of the inventor in public estimation. He who seeks fame in this world, can't wait for the dispassionate & disinterested judgement of the most enlightened portion of mankind, Post humous fame, as a legacy to ones descendants, has its value, but the fame which gives a man power influence and wealth whilst living, and which is not incompatible with virtue, is worth more in the market; and will enable one to benefit himself and his fellow man, which ought to be the motive of all our actions. You are aware, I presume, that the position you occupy in the navy renders you unpopular with those of your rank, and probably with some of higher rank, and that that feeling is increased, by your exclusive & seclusive habits—this is unfortunate. You know that the same feeling exists towards Maury:—and though not founded upon any just ground, is nevertheless to be deprecated. A man should have as many friends as possible in his profession; not however at the sacrifice of ones self respect. Every man has <u>some</u> influence; and we cant tell what day that influence may be exerted either for our benefit, or injury. Therefore it is desirable that we should make enemies of none. We are not justified in treating a man contemptuously, or with disrespect, because he fails to appreciate us, as we appreciate ourselves—It is wrong to <u>underrate</u> others, especially our enemies.

May you not have committed an error in over taxing your mind, at the cost of physical energy & health, which are necessary to sustain mental vigor. Leading a sedentary life begets an indisposition for action, which grows upon us—this I know from experience. You should ride or walk <u>rapidly</u> an hour or two every day. You will pardon the liberty I have taken in making these remarks, for the sake of the motive which prompted them.

You talk of selling a Confederate bond, to raise money to meet current expenses. Confederate bonds will be worth $120. soon after the war ends. You can borrow as much or as little as you require from any of the Banks, at 6 per cent, and pay it at your leisure or convenience. You get 8 per cent interest on your bonds—the banks will lend the money on your depositing a bond.

Virginia stock was worth $40. When I advised you to invest your money in it, last week it sold in Richmond at $91. You will get by tomorrows papers accounts of the glorious achievements of the Merrimac. The officers will get more credit than the contriver of her.[36]

■ 10 March 1862
Brooke journal, BP

This evening I saw Lt. Wood who was onboard the Merrimac in the two engagements.[37] The ship stood the hammering exceedingly well.

I am now having VII and 6.4 Inch wrought iron shot, solid, made for the M or rather the Virginia to be used on the Erickson which vessel is in the road.[38] She and the Merrimac had a long fight, neither being able to hurt the other, although they were with[in] 30 yards and touched each other. I must hurry up those shot and the plating iron.

■ 10 March 1862
Brooke, Richmond, to Lt. Robert D. Minor, CSS *Virginia*, Norfolk (copy), BP

You can not imagine how intensely interested I have been in the progress of the conflict which will hand your name down to posterity as one of the gallant band that struck our powerful enemy so fatal a blow. It is said that you are slightly wounded. I hope you are not seriously wounded. Yesterday I was about to call on Mrs. Minor but was informed that she had left for Norfolk. If you can, drop me a line.

I am hurrying up iron plates & some projectiles.

■ 11 March 1862
George T. Sinclair, Norfolk, to Brooke, BP

As you were the originator of the idea of altering the Merrimac into a battery, I know you will be interested in what I am about to say [to] you. I witnessed the action of both days, from a very near point of view, I may be prepared to venture an opinion. If the Virginia could have got off a few weeks sooner her success would have been far more complete, for she has met much more than a match in the Erickson, from the fact that she is much faster, more easily managed, runs with either end first, and is invulnerable to any gun we now have & at the same time has the most powerful gun or guns I ever saw. One of her most striking features is, her apparent light draft of water, with power to increase or decrease it, by means of compartments (I presume) which she can fill or empty at her pleasure, raising or lowering herself several feet. If the Virginia were fitted with a properly cased prow & could run into her, I think she would cripple her, she did run into her once & I doubt if she will ever be allowed to do so again "a burnt child fears the fire"—she has the speed & advantages of draft & can keep out of reach & will do it. The Virginia is cut up a good deal, almost entirely by the Erickson, the projectiles from the other guns having done her apparently but little harm. The Erickson appears to have Engines & propellers in both ends, no smoke stack & only a very small steam chimney. If she could be grappled & boarded, she might be destroyed by covering these up and stifling those below—she seems in all other respects to be so perfect a success, that I have no doubt she is prepared, even for such an event—but as I said before, her draft & speed will keep us at her own distance. She was splendidly handled, and I am confident that two like her, would capture the Virginia, as she now is & no doubt they will soon have a dozen—What I would now propose to you, is at once to prepare for the Virginia some solid wrought iron shot, with heads of steel, fitted like those punching machines in the factory—These fired from her VII inch rifle gun may penetrate the Erickson, tho' I doubt it, for I saw her receive the entire broadside of the Virginia, within a few yards, striking her fair on the revolving tower & on her deck without injury—In my judgement, she can only be reached by the momentum of a solid wrought iron bolt of 300 pounds weight, fired from a rifled gun at short range. Two such guns should be made for the Virginia as soon [a]s possible & preparations made to cover her with two inches of additional iron & to extend the heavy plating, at least three feet below the water line, which would not more than bring her down to her draft, leaving out the kenledge & other weights now onboard. Her two bow & quarter ports should be closed permanently & opened further aft & forward so that the bow guns could be used in broadside also—the ports to be shut when not in use. The Virginia has had not only the iron destroyed, but the frame work broken in, by the heavy solid shot of the Erickson, in two places, so you can imagine the force used.

As to the wooden gun boats we are building they are not worth a cent. The death knell of the wooden ships for war purposes, was sounded last Saturday.[39]

■ 11 March 1862

Lt. Robert D. Minor, Naval Hospital, Norfolk, to Brooke, Richmond, BP

Many thanks my dear Brooke for your very kind letter which reached me by to-days mail.

You richly deserve the gratitude and thanks of the Confederacy for the plan, of the now celebrated "Virginia," and I only wish that you could have been with us to have witnessed the successful operations of this new engine of Naval warfare, fostered by your care, and watched over by your inventive mind.

It was a great victory tho: the odds were nearly seven to one against us in guns and in numbers—but the <u>iron</u> and the <u>heavy guns</u> did the work, handled by such a man as glorious old Buchanan, and with such officers and men as we had. The crash into the "Cumberland" was terrible in its effect, tho: hardly felt by us and in 30 minutes after the first gun was fired by us, she was at the bottom, with her topsail yards just clear of the water. The "Congress" gave us her guns as we passed, but tho: the shot fell like hail stones on our roof we passed on, and settled the "Cumberland" in short style. By this time our dear old beauty was in shoal water with her head up stream and twas fully twenty minutes before we could turn her—to fire well & rapidly on the Congress, meanwhile running the fire of the battery on the Point, tho I cannot vouch for this exactly for in such a row, twas hard to say where [in] thunder all the licks came from. Very soon the Congress ran ashore, purposely I suppose, to save herself from such a fate as the Cumberland, and we had not given her many shots before she hauled down the stars & stripes, and soon afterwards hoisted the <u>white flag</u> at her peak— [William] Parker & Alex [Joseph Alexander] in the "Beaufort" & "Raleigh" were ordered to go to her—send her men on shore, bring the officers on board & burn the ship—but on going alongside—Pendergast (Austin) surrendered the ship to Parker and told him that he had too many wounded to burn the ship. Bill told him to have the wounded removed at once, and while the Raleigh & Beaufort were at this <u>humane</u> work, the Yankees on shore opened fire on them, killing some of their own men, among them a Lieut. Parker & Alex then left her with some twenty or thirty prisoners—the fire from shore being too hot, and as [Joseph] Alexander backed out in the Raleigh he was fired at from the ports of the Congress, tho: she had surrendered to us—a dastardly cowardly act! Buchanan not getting Parkers report and the frigate not being burned he accepted my volunteered services to burn her, and taking eight men and our only remaining boat, I pulled for her with [William A.?] Webb in the gallant little Teazer, steaming up soon afterwards to cover me. In the meantime the P Henry Jamestown & Teazer had come splendidly into action just about the time or a little before the Congress struck, and when I left the old beauty they were doing grand work with their guns on the Minnesota & shore batteries—I did not think Yankees on shore would fire at me, on my errand to the Congress—but when in about 250 yards of her they opened on me from the shore with muskets & artillery, and the way the balls danced around my little boat & crew was lively beyond all measure—Soon two of my men were knocked over and while cheering them on I got a clip through my side, which keeled me up for a second or two—but I was soon on board the "Teazer" Webb very bravely having come to my protection—Old Buck [the commanding officer Franklin Buchanan] seeing what the scoundrels were doing, made our recall, and deliberately backing the Virginia upstream, poured gun after gun, hot shot & incendiary shells into her stern & quarter, setting her on fire—and while doing this he was knocked over by a minnie ball through his left thigh and the Medicos laid us together in the Cabin, while brave, cool determined old Jones fought the action out in his quiet way giving them thunder all the time—as you supposed—the Minnesota & Roanoke came to the assistance of the two sailing Frigates, but the former got aground, and the latter, ran, actually turned tail, and as the sailors say "pulled foot" for Old Pt. The "St. Lawrence" got a dose & cleared out, leaving the Minnesota alone in her sad plight, hard & fast aground, with some tugs trying to lighten her, and taking fire from our squadron, to which she replied as well as she could generally from her forward pivot gun—She being aground & night coming on, of course Jones could not carry on the fight and after a hard night of it the Commo. and I were landed early on Sunday morning at Sewells Pt. and Jones took the ship into action that day, fighting her like a bold seaman as he is. He must tell you of his tussle with the "Ericsson"—a very devil of a iron battery, for he has just come in and said he had a letter from you. God bless old Buchanan for a true hearted patriot and bold dashing sailor—as brave as brave can be—but he exposed himself entirely too much, and was struck by a musket or minnie ball while on the upper deck I believe—for I was under Doctors' hands then, and could not be with him at the time! I am writing in bed and by "fits & starts"—so excuse all inaccuracies and want of details of which I will tell you when we meet. Mrs. Minor is with me and I am decidedly comfortable, tho my wound is a severe but not dangerous one. The ball struck a net & glanced coming out over the heart. It knocked me down for a second or so—but I got up and cheered my men, some of whom were panic stricken by the shower of balls, tho: they rallied when I got them to the "Teazer"—Send the signal books—!

N.B. There will doubtless be an attempt made to transfer the great credit of planning the "Virginia" to other hands than your own, so look out, for to you it belongs and the Secty should say so in communicating his report of the victory to Congress.

By no means must any Capt. or Comdr. or even Flag Officer be over Jones. In old Bucks sickness from his wound, Jones must command the ship.

■ **11 March 1862**
Brooke journal, BP

I have been very busy today. Went to the Tredegar and fired wrought iron shot from one of the Navy boat guns at a target, composed of two pieces of oak, each 18 inches in width by 9 inches depth faced with iron plates—rolled—6X2, with a punch headed projectile weighing 8½ lbs. and a charge of 1¼ lbs. The plates were penetrated, the shot lodging. I fired also a red hot shot. The first probably ever fired from a Rifled gun. It struck a seam; a portion of the iron entered the seam between two plates another rotation of the shot caused it to split in two parts. It presents a remarkable appearance. I am having wrought iron shot made for my VII inch and 4.6 [*sic*] in Rifles to fire against the enemys iron plated vessels, particularly the Erickson. Tomorrow I shall try it again. The shot take the grooves, not only in the rear but even half way to the forward end. The rifled gun fired is 3 in bore, weighs about 1100 [lbs.], is banded and rifled [with] 3 grooves 5/100 of an inch. This evening went to the Dept. by order of the Secty., met Mr. [Robert M. T.?] Hunter and several officers, also Mr. Tanner and Robt. Archer of the Tredegar, to consult with reference to supplies of iron gun boats etc. Showed one of the shots I had fired to the Secretary.[40]

- ■ **12 March 1862**
  Acting Master William G. Cheeney, Norfolk, to Brooke, BP

I send you this note by Mr. Steadman. He goes to Richmond to bring back my armor. I have not yet made any attempt against the enemy's vessels. . . . I have not yet overcome all troubles and hindrances occasioned by Military regulations, Martial Law etc. I had great trouble in obtaining any kind of boat to suit my purposes. I tried one but it would not do. I have applied to Com. Forrest, and am now having a little sheet iron cigar boat made—only 12 feet long and 2½ feet diameter. It will cost very little and will require only about one week to complete it. When done I shall make the first trial on the "Monitor" which is the only enemy our noble "Virginia" has to fear. I believe I shall succeed. I would return to Richmond and get my sub-marine boat in order, and I should need to experiment so long with that that I consider this much the speediest way of effecting the desired object.

Do not get impatient—I assure you that if I am slow I am at the same time persevering and doubt not that I will yet fully succeed.

If you desire, Mr. Steadman will explain to you the manner of operating with the little boat I am getting here.

- ■ **12 March 1862**
  Brooke journal, BP

At my suggestion Muscoe Garnett introduced a resolution to inquire into the expediency of organizing heavy artillery for service in the batteries, to be instructed etc.

■ **13 March 1862**
  Brooke journal, BP

Today ordered several forms of solid wrought iron shot to be made at the Tredegar, also a target for experimental purposes. The following are the forms. Reported result of yesterdays experiment to Secty. Asked the Secretary to order shot to be forged at Norfolk which he did. Drawings were sent. Some are making at the "Tredegar." I wish to have the rolled iron  hammered. I think we shall manage it. I am informed by Major [William P.] Williamson that two of the rolled port shutters of the Virginia will be welded together and placed on the stern of the Virginia, a bar of steel in the angle. It will also be carried well along the bow by iron fastenings. The Virginia's bow penetrated 8 feet into the bow of the Cumberland, speed about 4 knots. I shall make a very strong double banded gun [with] strapped trunnions to throw heavy bolts very long.

■ **13 March 1862**
  William Garnett [Lexington?] to Lizzie Brooke, Richmond, BP

We have heard of the glorious achievement of the Merrimac, alias the Virginia; and from the handsome compliment, paid to John, in the Enquirer, for his construction, I presume, that he is now satisfied, that a man may obtain reputation in the navy, on shore duty, as well as at sea. Nay, from the very narrow limits, in which our navy is compelled to operate, I am persuaded, that a navy officer, possessing the mechanical genius of John, has a much better chance of acquiring reputation, and of rendering valuable service to his country, than if in active service in a subordinate capacity, as he would be in such service. In all such cases, if the principal, does not monopolize the whole credit of any thing he may achieve, he at least obtains the lions share, whether he merits it or not, and the merits of the subordinate are overshadowed if not entirely obscured. No one ever hears of the subordinates now, who served under [George] Hollins at New Orleans. Whereas the man, who in the words of the Enquirer, "inaugurates a new system of successful naval warfare," spreads his fame at home and abroad. It must be manifest to John, and to every body else, that as a Lieut in active service, he never could, by any possibility, have rendered, I was about to say, a little of the benefit derived from the Merrimac; but in fact, there is no computing the difference between any advantage the service could have gained, from his active employment, and the benefit, which has already accrued from the destruction achieved by the Merrimac. For my part, were I an officer, and could confer upon my country, so substantial a benefit, others might seek the bubble, military glory, at the cannons mouth for me; I would be content to know, that I had most essentially served by country, a reward far more highly to be prized, by the true patriot, than the mere boast of having hazarded your life, without reaping any other fruit from the danger incurred than to be compliment[ed] for bravery, possessed in common by thousands in the ranks of an army, or the crew of a ship of war in an eminent degree, as in the officers.

■ **13 March 1862**
    Henry K. Stevens, Charleston, South Carolina, to Brooke, Richmond, BP

The glorious success of the Virginia has set every one here in the notion of having an Ironclad vessel constructed at this port. You I know have had a good deal to do with furnishing the iron for the "Virginia" and am conversant with the manner in which it was put on. If any new suggestions have occurred to you since her Triumphant trial, will you be kind enough to give me your ideas on the subject. As iron is scarce, I think Rail Road iron might be rerolled for the purpose.

We can easily raise the money and I believe we can get a ship that may be cut down for the purpose, but a suitable Engine is not so easily found. Two Engines however of less power may be used.

As you are in the gun line, I wish to suggest the trial of elongated expansive shot & shell from smooth bore guns of heavy caliber. For short distances, such chambered guns of 12 or 15 inch bore might be used with terrific effect.

■ **13 March 1862**
    Secretary of the Navy Stephen R. Mallory, Richmond, to Lt. Catesby ap R. Jones, Papers of the Jones Family of Northumberland County, Virginia, 1649–1889, LC

I deem it but just to you to thus place on record my high appreciation of the service you rendered the Confederacy by the care and attention by you in the preparation of Ordnance and ordnance stores for the Virginia. Her admirable practice in her recent engagement under her trained and gallant officers was in no small degree the result of the skill, diligence and investigation of those to whom this branch of her equipment was committed, and with whom you have been associated as the ordnance and Executive Officer of the ship. Special service of this character upon which victory so often depends are rarely named in reciting and recording the triumph, and usually meet with no public recognition. I know and appreciate their importance and hence I deem this acknowledgement which I hereby tender no less due to your high professional ability than just to the service and agreeable to myself. [true copy]

■ **14 March 1862**

Brooke journal, BP

Today the Secty. had a consultation with Chief Engineer [William P.] William-son, Constructor Porter and myself with reference to building iron clad gun boats.

He ordered us to report on the feasibility of sending the Virginia to New York. We reported that the ship could not be rendered seaworthy without rendering her inefficient as a man of war.

Went to Tredegar to hurry up shot and target. Made arrangements with Samson [Sampson] & Pae to make 50 large ones. Suggested to Mr [Charles A.] McEvoy a fuze for shells filled with turpentine or liquid fire.[41] The fuze is filled as usual but is stopped at lower end by a plug, so firmly fixed as to withstand the shock of discharge, but which is blown out by a small charge of powder above it, a powder b plug. The plug prevents liquid from moistening fuze charge. Capt [Albert] Rives asked me to think of some way of obstructing the river to prevent the Monitor-Ericson from coming up. Now is the time for big guns.

■ **14 March 1862**

Brooke journal, BP

Today furnished Samson [Sampson] & Pae with drawing of wrought iron shot to work from. Capt. Fairfax came up from Norfolk. He says that one of the 7 In Rifles (Brooke gun), bow gun of the Virginia, was accidentally charged during the battle of 9th. and 10th. with 24lbs. of powder. It threw a hundred pound shell without the slightest injury to gun or carriage. The mistake occurred in consequence of the death of loader & sponger; those who took their places not knowing that a cartridge had been put in.

In the evening I suggested to the Secretary that the iron prow of the Mer-rimac should be square on cutting edge to ensure taking the wood of[f] an enemy's side if struck quartering, not an acute angle. Constructor Porter pro-posed and was making the edge sharp. The Secretary telegraphed to make it as I suggested. Capt Lynch & Fairfax approved the change.

■ **15 March 1862**

Brooke journal, BP

Rainy day. Reported on Cowdons plan, cotton wood & iron for gun boat shields. Also a plan of Mr. Jones of Mississippi for iron cased dome on rotat-ing shield. Shall recommend the building of one. Went to the Tredegar to hurry up work. Saw Sampson and Pae who informed me that the rolled iron sent by Tredegar to them was not fit to make shot of. Said they could fuze them, weld bands of 4½ inch iron up to size of 7in & 6.4 bore. Say they will also cast solid cylindrical bolts and fit the Tennessee cup to them.[42]

Lt. [Catesby] Jones called this evening, had a long conversation with him. He thinks the 7 Inch guns of mine (Rifles) might be bored to 8 inches, but will probably be more effective for bolts as they now are. Says he would like to have the boat Rifles, 2 of them, to put on the M[errimac]'s shield.

■ **16 March 1862**
   Brooke journal, BP

Today went to the Department saw the Secretary with Lt. Jones who drew up a letter suggesting the completion of the Merrimac. I described a new gun which I propose to make. The Secretary desired me to go ahead with it [at] once. Also to give the proportions etc. of a light draft vessel that could enter Pamlico Sound, pass through the canal. Secretary asked me if such vessels were, iron plated.

■ **17 March 1862**
   Brooke journal, BP

Went to Tredegar with Lt. Jones, Mr Minor and a Mr [Alfred T.?] Jones from Mississippi who proposes to run in rolled iron in exchange for cotton. Lt. Jones presented me a cane made of live oak from the Merrimac. Chas Garnett called at my office to get notes for an article on the Merrimac, furnished them. The Secretary desires me to make the computation of weight etc. for small gun boats iron clad. The wrought iron shot progresses very slowly. I must have some of the bolts cast and fitted with the Tennessee sabot or cup. This evening I saw Capt Rives talked about the defences of the Rappahannock River. I recommended the Mississippi or Western torpedo, as an auxiliary.

■ **18 March 1862**
   Justice [Charles Garnett], Richmond, to the editor of the *Whig;* copied at the Whig Office by John B. Purcell and sent to John M. Brooke on 22 July 1887, BP

As the brilliant success of the Virginia has attracted the attention of all the country and is destined to cast much glory on our Infant Navy, it may be of general interest to publish some account of the origin of this magnificent ship. On the 23rd of June a board consisting of W[illiam] P. Williamson, Chief Engineer, John M. Brooke, Lieutenant, and John L. Porter, Naval Constructor, met in Richmond by order of the Secretary of the Navy to determine a plan for the construction of an Iron Clad vessel. The Secretary of the Navy was himself present at the meeting of the Board.

After full consultation, a plan proposed by Lieutenant John M. Brooke, was adopted and received the approval of the Secretary of the Navy.

The plan contemplated the construction of a light draft vessel; but the means at our command being limited, many reasons induced them to take the Merrimac and alter her according to the plan adopted. Her boilers were good, and her engines were only partially destroyed, and could be repaired in less time than would be required to construct an engine for a new vessel of light draft.

It was found that the plan of Lieutenant Brooke could easily be applied to the Merrimac, and in fact no other plan could have made the Merrimac an effective ship. Her guns now command every point of the horizon.

A report was made by the above named officers to the Secretary of the Navy on the 25th of June, in accordance with these facts and the Secretary ordered the work to commence forthwith.

Experiments to determine the mode of applying the armor and to fix the dimensions of its parts, were conducted by Lieutenant Brooke.

From the moment the plan was adopted, the Secretary of the Navy urged the work forward with all the means at the command of the government and without regard to expense and from this date to the day of the Virginia's egress from the dock, there were 1,000 to 1,500 men employed on her.

The four rifled cannon used so effectively on the Virginia were of a plan entirely new, designed by Lieutenant Brooke.

Most of the foregoing facts came to my knowledge long before the completion of the ship—others I have obtained recently from reliable sources.

I am a private citizen wholly unconnected with the Confederate or State Government but think that the public ought to know these particulars, which reflect so much credit on the Secretary of the Navy and his officers.

■ **19 March 1862**
David P. McCorkle, ordnance office, New Orleans, to Brooke, Richmond, BP

I have received your two rifle guns (seven inch) and also the drawings for the new 32 pdr rifle gun, which I am sorry to say, I cannot have cast here, the Founders refusing to have anything to do with banding guns as they do not approve of it. . . .

[Charles] McIntosh has arrived to take command of the Louisiana <u>he</u> does <u>not believe in rifle</u> guns or <u>rifle shells</u> or any thing else, that is new.

The L draws five and a half feet, and is being completed fast. We have no guns for her. You will have to send 14 inch guns to us.

Tifft's [Asa and Nelson Tift's] vessel is more powerful than the Virginia, has twenty guns, she will have two seven inch rifles forward, and two aft. . . .

We want here a sharp prompt, driving man, to command. [John K.] Mitchell is excellent as far as he goes, but too slow, he holds audiences one at a time, he cannot talk to but one, and business men cant wait for him.

The credit of the Navy is bad. No bills have been paid until lately, and the consequence is the army can purchase at one third of the price we do, because they have always paid promptly. If a merchant has to wait for his money he puts on the interest at a high rate. We have money now but our reputation is gone. I am driving ahead as well as I can. I found every thing behind hand. I am getting ahead slowly. I wish you would send me all the information about seven inch guns. You know I have to combat old fogies. Also strengthen me in the position I have taken here; not only by my own conviction, but by authority of Bureau, "that no rifle guns should be without bands."[43]

■ **20 March 1862**
   Brooke journal, BP

Several papers have published articles from the Norfolk day book giving the credit of the plan of the Merrimac to John L Porter. Maj. [Charles E.?] Thorburn called at my office, was glad to see him.[44] This evening saw Mr. Mallory at his house. We devised a plan of iron clad gun boats to substitute for the wooden gun boats.

■ **21 March 1862**
   Brooke journal, BP

Went to Tredegar to hurry up shot for Merrimac. The Secretary will or has sent for ship architects to construct iron plated gun boats. I computed this evening weights of shield for one. We can build them rapidly.

■ **28 March 1862**
   Brooke journal, BP

On the 24th [March] designed a shield for a gun boat building by N. Nash at Norfolk. Am now at work on one to be built by Mr. [William A.] Graves who is to start a ship yard at Richmond. Gave the plan of 7 In. gun to Mr. Matthew Delaney [Delany] at Tredegar works for pattern maker. It will be treble banded and 13 ft 3 in in length from cascable to muzzle face. I hope to fire 240lbs bolt from it, perhaps 300lbs. The wrought iron shot come on slowly, about 20 have gone to Norfolk for the Virginia. Chiefly for the 6.4 bore. The Army Ordnance Department is still opposed to banding guns. Robt. Minor is in town, is slowly recovering from his wound.[45]

■ **28 March 1862**

Hunter Davidson, CSS *Virginia,* to Brooke, BP

Why not have the Engines taken out of the "Fingal" & the "Economist" & sent here immediately for the Plymouth & Germantown?

They will make two first rate iron Batteries. I am informed by our Chief engineer that the Engines will answer, giving a speed of five or six knots to those vessels—We have not a day to lose at our Navy Work, the enemy are rapidly ranging ahead of us.[46]

■ **31 March 1862**

William H. Murdaugh, Portsmouth, Virginia, to Brooke, BP

It has doubtless occurred to you, but I will nevertheless make the suggestion that there are large quantities of wrought iron in the way of fences or railing around the grounds of public buildings in the southern Confederacy which might be obtained with ease and dispatch. The Court Houses in these two towns have wrought iron railings around their yards the State House in Raleigh has I know, so also with the one in Richmond I believe. Like the moves of a special committee I will undertake to get this iron if no more serviceable individual can be found.[47]

■ **3 April 1862**

Brooke journal, BP

Today an article appeared in the Examiner signed by Constructor Jon. L. Porter in which he claimed the credit of the construction of the Merrimac. I requested the Editor of the Examiner to publish the Secretary's reply to the resolution of Congress calling for information as to the construction of that vessel—Virginia. I trust that it will settle the matter.[48] Saw Com. Forrest at the Spotswood this evening. The Virginia is I believe ready for a second attack upon the enemy.

■ **3 April 1862**

Lt. Catesby ap R. Jones, CSS *Virginia,* to Brooke, BP

I fired day before yesterday from an altered rifle gun at Craney Island wrought iron shot of each kind that we have—Results very unsatisfactory— Those marked—R from Richmond and those made here, (one of each being fired) tumbled—the one marked—R—was recovered, having the very faintest trace of the grooves—Two were fired made in Richmond without marks which I beleive [sic] were forged—one went tolerably well, the other warbled and was distinctly seen to deviate in its flight, it was recovered and had taken the grooves very well. I had the cups of six thinned and deepened, two of each kind, all took the rifle motion, tho some of them wobbled, they will

I think answer our purpose, the ranges at 8° with 7 lbs. were 2700, 2940, 3050, 3050 yrds—Five were fired, at the second round the band next to the rear band broke, the three other discharges did not appear to affect the other bands. This occurred yesterday. Two were recovered the rifling was perfect, small portions of the iron that was forced in the grooves were broken probably from imperfect welding, it so happened that the two recovered were made here.

I send you a tracing of the cups as when fired—I think all should be changed VII in as well as 32 pdr—

Of the two fired on the first day, one without mark, made in Richmond, had a thick cup, the other made here was thin; tho not near as thin as those fired yesterday. I notice that some of the VII in and perhaps some of the 32 pdr—take much more than others, having a smaller head, why is this? Made as the two kinds of shot are, the VII[in] being so little heavier than the 32 pdr— I think the smaller calibre would penetrate deeper—Let me have your views in detail.

I cannot persuade myself that the work on our ship is pushed as it should be, I think the authorities here are laboring under a delusion. About one half of the ship is now covered with iron below the eaves, making three inches. I don't know when we are to come out, or what we are expected to do—Our crew have become very disorganized, living on board the "States"—

Buchanan is improving. How is Minor?[49]

- **7 April 1862**
  Brooke journal, BP

Stirring times, the Army of the West under A. S. Johnson [Johnston] my good friend won a splendid victory, but to my sorrow he fell on the field of battle.[50]

His death may be attributed to needless exposure. He was goaded by the taunts and insults of such men as [Henry S.] Foote of Congress, who puffed up and conceited, ignorant of all that pertains to nobility of character, open their mouths only to emit venom.[51] In Johnson [Johnston] the country loses a patriot and gentleman. If foot [Foote] were to die the country would lose a slanderer and a conceited ass.

The Virginia went out today in the afternoon. A large army of Federals is on the Peninsula. [Gen. George Brinton] McClellan is said to be in command.[52] Magruder has held them in check since the 5th, Saturday.[53] I trust that the Virginia will destroy his transports and supplies. Our army of the West under Beauregard is pursuing Grants Division. Have captured its camp's equipage, 18 batteries and many prisoners.[54] I have been today on a board to furnish some plans etc. for defence of rivers.

■ **8 April 1862**

Brooke journal, BP

This evening rain. The Virginia went down to Craney Island but owing to bad weather and some temporary derangement of the machinery returned to the city. The board consisting of Flag Officer Forrest, Capt Maury, Capt [Robert G.] Robb, Lt. [Robert B.] Pegram, Minor, Capt. Farren [Ebenezer Farrand], Lt. [John R.] Hamilton, Chief Engineer Williamson and myself met again today.

I proposed that we should increase the power of our guns to the maximum, which was adopted. Also made known my plan for the capture of Fortress Monroe by means of iron clad batteries to be built on the James and at Norfolk. Introduced Mr. Leavitt to the Board.[55]

■ **12 April 1862**

Brooke to Secretary of the Navy Stephen R. Mallory (copy), BP

I observe in the recent letters published by John L. Porter Naval Constructor reflecting upon me and claiming for himself the credit of originating the plan of the Ironclad Virginia that he quotes as evidence orders issued by you to Flag Officer Forrest: The following is published by Mr. Porter.

Navy Department
Richmond July [?] 1862

Flag Officer F. Forrest

Sir you will proceed with all practicable dispatch to make the changes in the form of the Merrimac, and to build equip, and fit her in all respects according to the design and plans of the Constructor and Engineer Messers. Porter and Williamson.

S. R. Mallory
signed Secretary of the Navy

Mr. Porter referring to the above order, says, "What, I would ask could be more explicit than this letter or what words could have established my claims any stronger if I had dictated them."

Now I have always been under the impression that the plans referred to in the above order were simply the drafts or working drawings made by Mr. Porter in accordance with the plan of construction proposed originally by me and which Mr. Porter was directed by you to apply to the Merrimac. In view of the impression which Mr. Porters letter is calculated to make I request that you will inform me if I am not right in so construing the expression "according to the design and plans of the Constructor and Engineer."[56]

■ **20 April 1862**

Brooke journal, BP

Rainy weather. 20 guns passed by today field artillery. Yesterday I tried burning fluid in 1X inch shell. With some change in form of fuze the shells will answer admirably. I propose to break them on iron clad vessels, thus enveloping them in sheets of flame which will draw through the ports. I think it would be well to have some of the fluid at hand onboard our vessels to set fire to vessels situated as the Congress was.

A thin stratum of the fluid burns well on iron plates. Shall send full description to Jones onboard Merrimac.

The Board has adjourned. We all agreed except on the following [blank]. Capt. Maury and I voting aye the others no.

I am endeavoring now to have projectiles made for Rifles from charcoal blooms, forged into shape at the blast furnace. The iron is magnificent but so far too hard for the tools and containing some grit.

I have proposed, and it has been adopted, a system of plating for iron-clad vessels by which the courses or layers may be bolted independently.

The present is a critical period. The Army is nearly concentrated on the peninsula and we must either attack or eventually be outspaded.[57]

■ **23 April 1862**

Brooke journal, BP

It appears from the movements of the Army that the government has determined to hold this city at all hazards. Today the Tredegar battalion paraded to the great delay of iron plates for gun boat at Norfolk. I suggested today to the Secretary the propriety of substituting heavy rifles for 1X guns of the Merrimac-Virginia. He telegraph[ed] to Norfolk in relation to it. Promotion by merit has been established by Congress.[58] The blast furnace which was to finish blooms for shot has suspended operations, the enemy approaching it.

■ **26 April 1862**

Brooke journal, BP

New Orleans has probably been taken by the enemy.[59] The only chance after the batteries failed was to board and run down the enemy's vessels on the way up.

Today proposed to Secty to get timber for floating battery here. Suggested sending [Henry H.] Lewis, Lt. to get the timber. Proposed also to rifle a number of 32 pdrs 61 cwt and band them.[60] Secty will apply to Gen Lee for them.

John M. Brooke. Photograph in possession of the editor.

Catesby ap R. Jones in
later life. Photograph in
possession of the editor.

Lizzie Garnett Brooke,
first wife of John M.
Brooke. Photograph in
possession of the editor.

4

James River Defense, Inventions, Personal Woes, and Promotion

■ **29 April 1862**
  Brooke journal, BP

Today succeeded in getting the 32 pdrs 61 cwt. Went to Tredegar, started the work of banding and rifling. Had some conversation with Secty of war Genl. [George Wythe] Randolph. I shall try my best to start the authorities in regard to proper ordnance to repel an attack on Richmond by water.

■ **1 May 1862**
  Brooke journal, BP

Very busy today as well as yesterday urging preparation for defence of Richmond on the James River. Having guns rifled & banded etc.

The Secretary seems impressed with the feasibility and importance of my plan of attack of fort Monroe by floating batteries. Steps are being taken to construct vessels or floating batteries as I suggested. Visited the Tredegar. Read today account of experiments in England to test iron plates. Sir Wm. Armstrong has constructed a smooth bore gun throwing shot of 156lbs, charge 51 lbs. Broke Warriors plates at 200 yds.[1] I have anticipated the advantages arising from high initial velocity and propose obtaining it with the gun now making in accordance with my designs. It is long and strong and will bear a 50lb charge.

■ **2 May 1862**
  William G. Cheeney, master, Confederate States Navy, Norfolk, to Brooke, Richmond, BP

I have the honor to inform you that I have passed nearly all of the two weeks past below Sewells Point. I have made several reconnaisances by water, besides such observations as I have made on land with the aid of good day and night glasses. I made several trials with my apparatus, but as yet have not made any attempt upon the enemys vessels. There has been an easterly wind constantly prevailing, which has caused the water in the Roads to be constantly rough and rolling. My apparatus worked well, except that in water rough or rolling, we were unable to guide it as desired. Slight changes were needed for which I returned here. I shall soon make a determined attempt, in which I believe I shall succeed. I cannot explain all the causes which have delayed me so long. I am doing what in my judgement seems best, and I only ask that the confidence which has been so generously accorded me heretofore may not yet be withdrawn. . . .

Like all first trials it [his submarine boat] has some defects which may be very much improved upon. Its chief defect I fear will be its propelling power in a strong current and inability to handle well in rough water.[2]

■ **4 May 1862**
   Brooke journal, BP

Today I heard with astonishment that orders had been issued to evacuate Norfolk without the slightest effort to save ordnance or indispensable tools. The loss of Norfolk is bad enough but worse is the management. I suppose that our leaders are trying to bring on the condition which it is said must eventually occur: concentration of troops in the interior, the whole coast being in the hands of the enemy.

Without ordnance I dont clearly see how we shall defend Richmond.

■ **10 May 1862**
   Brooke journal, BP

On the 8th the authorities were considerably exercised by the report that an iron clad vessel was on the way to Richmond, and well might they be so as there were but three guns in battery on the whole river and the obstructions were not completed.

■ **12 May 1862**
   Brooke journal, BP

Today it is reported that the Virginia was abandoned and blown up with loss of everything.[3]

If the cause of the Confederacy is in danger, it is in consequence of execrable management, not on the part of executives but on the part of directors who act without concert.

When the news of the approach of gun boats on the 8th. was recd. the Naval officers at hand were set to work and Bob Minor and myself were at work until three o'clock in the morning. Got off shot, shell, powder etc. On the 9th the Secretary at my request permitted me to undertake the construction of an iron shield to be placed on the Bluff commanding the river below Mrs Chapins [Chaffin's Bluff].[4] It is progressing rapidly.

Ap Catesby Jones arrived today with the Merrimac's—Virginia's—crew. He will command the battery. I recommended him for the position.[5] Today got Capt [George] Minor to take 50 tons of Liberty iron from Dr. [Robert] Archer to cast guns, Rifles, at the Tredegar.

■ **17 May 1862**
Brooke to Secretary of the Navy Stephen R. Mallory (rough draft), BP

I am informed that the 9000 lbs Rifle bore 6.4 inches is to be placed on Mr. Nashs boat. As this is the only 32 pdr. still in our possession, well adapted to throwing solid wrought iron shot it appears to me that it would be better to substitute some other gun.

The cannonade given by the height of the bluff would enable it to render far more effective service onshore.[6]

■ **19 May 1862**
David P. McCorkle, Atlanta, Georgia, to Brooke, BP

I have seen a drawing of the Prussian fuze, percussion, which I think is worth trying. Make the Archer fuze of steel with a point to it so and I am told it will penetrate (before it explodes) through the iron plates. Let me know what you think of it. I am [sic] just succeeded in getting a house for temporary use and they are moving the inmates out to day. I have had great trouble in getting along with the stores, from New Orleans. If that Chalmette Battery and the one opposite had been properly supplied and manned, New Orleans would not have fallen—even if the men at Fort Jackson had not mutinied, Com [David G.] Farragut would have been in a bad way—

I hope you will whip them again on the James River—what in the world did they give up Norfolk for. New Orleans was bad enough, but Norfolk made me sick—Write me if you have time—[7]

■ **21 May 1862**
Brooke journal, BP

For a week after the 8th I was sick, having the mumps and taking cold, was in bed several days.

The enemy attacked the batteries at Drury's [Drewry's] Bluff was driven off. Since then the obstructions have been strengthened and several guns added to the battery. There were no rifles mounted at the time of the attack. If the 7 inch rifle had been up the Galena might have been sunk.[8]

The shield I planned has been finished but it is not yet erected. It will be placed below Drury's [Drewry's] Bluff on the left bank at Mrs. Chapin's [Chaffin's Bluff] commanding the reach below, 3 rifled, 6 4 will probably be mounted on it.

A second shield also for three guns is nearly ready. I think we have nothing to apprehend now from the water. But 36 hours before the gun boats came they could have taken or burned the city. Riflemen were found, very effective on the banks. Naval sharpshooters commanded by John Taylor Wood. Capt. [Ebenezer] Farran[d] commanded the batteries. Since then he has been superseded by Capt. S[idney] S. Lee.[9] The Officers of the Navy are very much dissatisfied, the Army steps in to take all the batteries etc. after the Naval officers get them into condition. Our old officers are ranked by ignorant volunteer Generals who interfere.[10] I trust the Secty will now build iron plated boats, clear the river and take Fort Monroe. I have been computing graduations for gun sights etc. Range tables also for the battery.

The Navy is being ruined by the Seniority System. The officers—effective ones—are all very much dissatisfied, but keep quiet in consequence of the approach of the enemy. Whilst I was sick, Capt Minor Chf of Ordnance sent off all my papers, computations etc. to Charlotte, N.C. which is a serious drawback. The Navy Department is about as poorly officered as possible, and I see very little hope for improvement. The Army is now near the city and will I trust have an opportunity of fighting. If [Gen. George Brinton] McClellan is allowed to dig he will drive us out in time. We are rifling and band[ing] 32 pdrs. of 61cwt. they make splendid guns.[11]

■ **23 May 1862**
   Secretary of the Navy Stephen R. Mallory to Brooke, BP

You are appointed upon the part of this Department a member of the Board of Officers detailed by the War Department to list and report upon the condition, and assess the value of Mr. Charles E. Stuart's instrument for adjusting cannon sights. Captain T. D. [Thomas S.] Rhett and Lieut. E. Webster have been detailed by the War Department as members of the Board.

■ **5 June 1862**
   Gen. Robert E. Lee, Headquarters near Richmond, to Capt. George Minor, chief of ordnance and hydrography (copy obtained from U.S. Naval Institute), BP

The Armstrong Gun, if mounted, on a field carriage, with its supply of projectiles, will be of immense importance to us. Can we not have it in the morning? The smaller guns (Parrott) I think we have enough of at present. I am very anxious to have a railroad battery. I wrote to Colonel [Josiah] Gorgas on the subject this morning and asked him to get you and Brooke to aid me. Till something better could be accomplished I proposed a Dahlgren or Columbiad, on a ship's carriage, on a railroad flat, with one of your navy iron aprons adjusted to protect gun and men. If I could get it in position by daylight to-morrow could astonish our neighbors. The enemy cannot get up his heavy guns except by railroads. We must block his progress.[12]

■ 6 June 1862
Gen. Robert E. Lee, Headquarters, Dobbs House, Richmond, to Brooke, BP

I am informed by Capt Minor that you are busily engaged in arranging to mount & protect a gun on a RR flat. I am glad to hear that you are thus engaged & hope you will soon have everything prepared and ready for work. As it may take some time to construct the shield, I would request that the gun & platform be prepared at once, so that it may be used against the enemy & sent to the R.R. depot with directions to be forwarded to Genl [William H.] Whiting and Vaughns farm.

■ 11 June 1862
Catesby ap R. Jones, Columbus, Georgia, to Brooke, BP

I regretted not having seen you before leaving Richmond to join the "Chattahoochee"—I could learn scarcely anything of her there, the Secy. appeared to know more than anyone else and he told me that she was at Chattahoochee Florida, some forty miles below where she was built, and I was under that impression until arriving here when I found that she was at Suffolk the plantation of the contractor 175 miles below this, and not hav-ing any houses for miles about it. It may almost be said to be in the wilder-ness there is only weekly communication with Columbus, it took me 36 hours to come up. The difficulties have been very great; they can only be appreciated here, mechanics and materials had to be collected; the whole vessel was several times submerged from freshets; latterly it has been so sickly that most of the mechanics have left. Four of the ten men brought from Drury [Drewry's] Bluff are quite sick and an officer also. I intended to have removed the vessel to Chattahoochee fearing the river's falling, but the contractor would not permit the mechanics to leave the yard, and as no oth-ers can be obtained she had to remain and run the risk of low water. I found the vessel to be substantially built model not at all calculated for speed . . . she has nothing but her hull and decks—is not equipped in any particu-lar, nor is there any material here to equip her with, the masts are uncut, the sails & awnings unmade & no canvass to make them—there are no stores of any kind no rigging, no crew—and yet under these circumstances I am ordered to assume command of her. It might be supposed that some discre-tion would be allowed me in fitting her out, but no—everything must be referred to Richmond, that was bad enough at a Navy yard, judge what it is in a wilderness. With every possible facility in the power of the Dep. the difficulties and annoyances would be great—without them it is all most impossible. I have not yet been ordered to fit her out, is this not trifling?—it is provoking for if she were speedily completed I see some chance of effecting something.

■ 21 June 1862

Gen. Robert E. Lee, Dobb's House, Virginia, to Secretary of the Navy Stephen R. Mallory (copy obtained from Naval Institute, 1883), BP

I have been informed by Colonel Gorgas that the railroad battery will be ready for service to-morrow. Inasmuch as this battery has been constructed by the Navy, I would be pleased if you would assign an officer and a requisite number of men to take charge of and operate it. If you desire to do so, I request that you designate the officer at once, as I wish to place the battery in position to-morrow. I am very much obliged to you for your kindness as well as promptness in its construction.

■ 24 June 1862

George Minor, commander in charge, Office of Ordnance and Hydrography, to Gen. Robert E. Lee (copy obtained from U.S. Naval Institute, ca. 1883), BP

The railroad iron-plated battery designed by Lieut John M. Brooke, C. S. Navy, has been completed. The gun, a rifled and banded 32 pounder of 57 cwt., has been mounted and equipped by Lt. R. D. Minor, C. S. Navy, and with 200 rounds of ammunition, including 15 solid bolt shot, is now ready to be transferred to the army.

■ 2 July 1862

Brooke, Richmond, to Lizzie Brooke, Lexington

There are several persons lodging in the house, the provost marshall is one the others I do not know. . . . The new post stamps are out; I dont think the 5 cts or rather 10 cts difference will induce me to go without a letter from my Lizzie. But I think the government has made a mistake in raising the postage to so high a figure. The self sustaining principle ought not to be applied to the post office. I hope its receipts will be less with the present arrangement. . . . I shall try right hard to keep within my 3500 as I must have at least a cottage. I will certainly secure something. As to boarding I have a perfect horror of it; the last trial being the worst of all. . . . Wish I could see you every week and stay two days or more, as you say it would be well if you only lived on a Rail Road line. . . . I do long to see you I have so much to say that I can not write about the past about my own dear little Lucy, the only comfort I have is that she is in Heaven and can suffer no more. . . . Tell Thomas I will hurry up the map for him and that I will examine carefully the shrapnel he sent, will show it to Col. Gorgas also.[13]

■ **3 July 1862**
Brooke, Richmond, to Lizzie, Lexington, BP

I have read your letter in which you speak of the Merrimac etc. I am somewhat surprised as to what you say in relation to the opinions of people, but time will put all right. Thomas was misinformed. I had a drawing etc. Mr. [John L.] Porter has simply lied in his letters and I suppose that [Stephen R.] Mallory thought his services were so important to the government that it would be injurious to convict him of it at that time. The order sent to Norfolk related simply to the plan as measurements of the ship would require. Porters plan or model at the Dept is simply a shield (not original) with a box like boat under it the shield ends are the ends of the boat, blunt etc. thus

My plan was different and possessed the only original features, <u>prolonged submerged ends</u> which enable the attainment of speed etc. and render the application of a heavy shield practicable when wooden vessels of the

usual model are to be altered. Any ships carpenter could apply my plan to a wooden vessel just as did Porter. I will have it fixed all right. If this is not clear to Thomas tell him, when the proper time comes it will be made clear to all. I went up to see Mallory after I read your letter, he was out. . . . Dont write me anything more about the Virginia calculated to worry me. I am actually sick of her. . . . You must try to imagine some happiness, think of seeing me etc. <u>if that is</u> a pleasant idea. . . . Did you see how the English parliament regarded the Beast [Benjamin] Butler proclamation/ Thank Heaven Europe will see what demons there are in the North. I think we shall have intervention soon, but the South should strike while the iron is hot. I have not heard whether the R.R. to Staunton is yet open, but perhaps tonight I shall tell Mr. Mallory that in a few days I wish to visit you. . . . I shall not worry myself about Porter. I wish I could get over my excitability in such cases. You must be careful how you start me for I am sometimes right rash in my expressions and actions. Porter is here but don't seem at ease in my company he feels badly no doubt, as he knows I still claim the origin of the plan. He is entitled to the carpentry nothing more. . . . How is that little <u>baby</u>?[14]

■ **4 July 1862**

Brooke to Lizzie, Lexington, BP

There is no news from the battlefield today [aftermath of Seven Days' Battle, 25 June–1 July]. I am as you may suppose right impatient. There are many rumors but one can not sift the truth from them. I still hope that we shall capture a large portion of McClellan's army. . . . This is the 4th of July, the Yankees will hardly feel disposed to celebrate it. The long gun progresses slowly as of late my attention has been drawn from it, the fact is I want air and a change, am tired of my nondescript duties, Jack of all trades, but I hope master of some. . . . you have no idea how anxious one becomes when so near the battle field without hearing of results. . . .

You must try and cheer up my darling.

■ **4 July 1862**

Brooke to Secretary of the Navy Stephen R. Mallory, Jefferson Davis Papers, Flowers Collection (copy), Duke University

I have examined the rough drawing of a Steam battering Ram proposed by Mr. Wm R. Scott of Algiers and have heard his explanation. No similar proposition has yet been made to the Department—Mr Scott claims to be the originator. The Ram as heretofore constructed to be effective requires considerably [sic] headway and must strike at an obtuse angle in naval Engagements particularly in narrow channels the hedway [sic] nessessary [sic] to strike effectively cannot always be obtained and if the blow when struck fails the ram must withdraw to a distance prior to makeing [sic] a second attempt.

To render rams more efficient various plans have been proposed: submrine [sic] torpedos and guns placed on the bows etc But it appears to me that Mr Scotts Battering Ram would be more effective, the blows being given with great rapidity and power. I therefore suggest that steps be taken to add this Engine to the other means of offence we now possess. [William P. Williamson, chief engineer, Confederate States Navy, concurred in Brooke's opinion.]

■ **5 July 1862**

Brooke to Lizzie, BP

I have just returned from the Tredegar where I went to hurry up the rifled cannon. But I am getting tired of the positions I occupy, old fogyism is in the way, I cant help thinking how much more pleasant my former pursuits were, I had cleared myself of old fogies in that and it was an open field in which I had full swing, personally I have sacrificed everything and gained nothing by the change. Well better times may be coming. There is no news from the army today. My opinion is that we shall have a long struggle everything depends on its result, the North will make great efforts to take this city. But if we also do the same amount of work in preparing to defend it we shall succeed. We have many arms now and plenty of powder the Southern people should turn out for now is the critical period so far as a speedy end to the war is concerned. . . . There has been some delay in making out commissions for army officers, but I got possession of Willies today and will forward it to him as soon as possible. . . . for the last week I have been a state of perpetual anxiety and suspense waiting for the battle to end. The gunboats always come in to prevent a total rout of the enemy. I wish our cities were in the interior. But we have given McClellans Army a taste of what they may expect if they try it again. As to our Navy, I never felt as little interest in it before. No promotion and the talent in it is unappreciated, old fogies at the head of every Department. Its prospects are decidedly bad at this time. . . . I wish the war was over and I could find some opening to advance. Our Navy is worse than the old navy was before the retiring board acted. . . . I have just received your letter of July the 1st. The mails are very irregular indeed this is the 5th.

■ **5 July 1862**

John Taylor Wood, Drewry's Bluff, James River, to Mrs. John Taylor Wood, John Taylor Wood Papers, Southern Historical Collection, University of North Carolina at Chapel Hill

Yesterday I was down the River the greater part of the day with Capts. [John Randolph] Tucker & [Joseph W.] Barney at Chapin's [Chaffin's] Bluff, the place where I had my sharpshooters, a strong battery has been put up there now, mounting ten guns which the enemy will have to take before they can get at us. . . . Yesterday [Hunter] Davidson went down the River in his steamer the Teazer to reconnoitre having onboard Maj. [Edward] Alexander with a balloon; unfortunately running aground, the enemy came up & took his vessel he with the crew barely escaping to the shore, he lost everything, $200 in money clothes etc. but what is far worse all his papers, which will inform the enemy of the submarine batteries their positions etc. Davidson for some time has been engaged in the duty of placing them in the River, ready to blow the Yankees up. Really our little navy seems doomed. They got his wifes letters also. . . . I would not have you go to Richmond; it is very unhealthy now & again the expense is enormous, beyond dear our means.

■ **6 July 1862**

Brooke to Lizzie, BP

Mrs. Bidgood has two tables now so great is the press for meals on the part of visitors to Richmond. There is one right agreeable-looking young lady there who came to attend her wounded brother, she dresses generally in pure white which becomes people so much. I have never spoken to her however.

There are very few ladies in town nearly all gone to the country, a few are seen on the streets. If there were no women in the world I should prepare to leave, for although I am not a ladies man in the common acceptation of the word I do think very highly of them. . . . I do most cordially hate the north, I know you do. . . . I think I will now take a bath. Bathing clears the complexion and is in my opinion one of the best things in the world for health. I do wish you could stand Jordan's Springs if you could I would go there with you.

■ **6 July 1862**
Brooke to Lizzie, BP

As we have shown Europe that we can protect our capital there is nothing now to prevent recognition of the Confederacy. But I shall not expect much from Europe. I was struck today with the fact that people soon become accustomed to the sight of suffering, the ladies in the hospitals are as gay as birds which is all the better for the patients. I see Yelverton [Garnett] very rarely. He looks very badly indeed, ten years older than he did. . . .[15] Capt or Lieut Barry of Norfolk commanded that gun, he had men of his company, United Artillery of Norfolk, all sailors. He came to take charge long before it was completed. Old George M—interfering and reporting it ready without knowing anything about it. I told him afterwards I was told to get it up by the secretary etc. But the fact is that old George serves as a very effectual check on me. Kills the interest I take in the Ordnance Department generally. I wish I was at work on my surveying reports instead of the work I do here. It is well enough for war times. But I would sooner be known in my old vocation, than as the first ordnance officer in the world. Mallory certainly has singular notions as to the efficiency of his department. But you need not repeat this.

■ **7 July 1862**
Brooke to Lizzie, BP

The papers say that Abe is calling for more men 300,000 and well he may, the hour of retribution is drawing near. He and his miserable agents and prompters will reap the reward of their crimes. We have now an abundant supply of arms and powder, providence has favored us in that respect. There are various rumors about recognition etc. but none we may rely upon. Lincoln's call will astonish Europe. He said the rebellion was on the wane but he and his scoundrel crew will I believe grace the gallows yet, then the rebellion will wane and not much sooner. I shall be curious to know the finding of [Josiah] Tat[t]nall's court. . . . I am quite tired of suggesting and running about to get new things up. Our department is I suppose as good as that of the Army. This system of making no promotions and filling all the positions which require information and activity with men according to their age, leaving to the younger officers the task of mending bad work has disgusted me thoroughly with the Navy, there seems to be no such thing as advancement in it, personally I am very comfortably situated and very kindly trusted but I do not advance. I only wish I could find something to do which would be done for the love of it. The feeling of which I speak is not confined to me, it extends to all the officers in the Service. Well I will drop the subject. You must not talk of it. . . . Jones and Wood were in town for the court martial. I think the court will do justice, I do hope so, as I believe that Tat[t]nall acted properly under the circumstances, the whole trouble arose from not giving the command at once, after [Franklin] Buchanan left, to Jones; a month elapsed before even old T– was ordered. . . .[16] I have implicit confidence in Lee, more in fact than I could have in any man I did not think chosen by providence to command our armies. Lee is a second Washington.

■ **7 July 1862**
First Lieutenant Barry, United Artillery, Virginia Volunteers, Redoubt No. 2, to Brooke, BP

The Iron Clad Rail Road Battery planned by yourself and which I had the honor to have charge of, has in my judgment proved a complete success, and with the improvement suggested by you, would be a formidable battery for attack or defence.

It was severely tested on the 29th June and gave me the utmost confidence in it, and I flatter myself that it did good service. [There was a locomotive attached, and it was used on the York River Railroad.]

■ **7 July 1862**
Brooke to Lizzie, BP

I must dress for breakfast and try to complete today the plan of my big gun which is now being bored out. Afternoon. I have been at work all the morning in my own room on the calculations necessary to complete the gun. . . . Have been reading travels in Europe by Prince tolerably good. But I prefer the old voyagers. After this war I intend to make a collection of books of travel particularly those written by navigators. I do love exploration, only it separates me from you. I can not bear the Sea unless I am engaged in that way, then it ceases to be unpleasant.

■ **9 July 1862**
Brooke to Lizzie, BP

Last night I was at Mr. Mallory's he kept me there until after midnight talking of ordnance, torpedoes, etc. Mrs. Bidgoods charges are remarkably moderate considering the high prices of articles, $25—and she keeps a very good table I like it better than any I have seen in Richmond. The Yankees are a long way below Richmond and will find the road up a hard one to travel. You must my darling take a more hopeful view of our affairs. The flogging of McClellan out of his strong entrenchments was a wonderful achievement and satisfies me that he has lost the only chance he ever had of taking this city. . . . I cant say I wish you were like me, but I do wish you could experience more happiness and pleasure than you do experience. Then I should be happier because you would share my pleasures with me. Still there are times when you are all I could desire. . . . There are now two ladies at Mrs. Bidgoods nursing wounded brothers. You ask the price of tea, the last I heard of was $16 pr pound. Tea drinkers may as well give it up as an extravagance. . . . Willie [Williamson] says his company will be near the city this evening, he will start soon for it he is anxious to visit Lexington but I doubt very much if he can stay more than a day or so there as Engineers are very much wanted in the field, I think he will be able to get a short leave, will try to get it for him. Gen. Lee has pitched into the papers for publishing information about the positions of troops etc. It is time, the Federals in Norfolk say they get all the information they want from the Examiner & Dispatch. With all their professed patriotism some editors sell their countrymens lives for a few pennies. . . . I hope darling that your health improves I wish you could find some means of cheering up. Your despondency does you harm.

■ **10 July 1862**
  Brooke to Lizzie, BP

Yours of the 8th & 9th I recd today. You [must] not listen to the reports carried by croakers from Richmond. The affairs of the Confederacy are in excellent condition. Its all humbug to tell of what ought to have been done etc. The victory is far more complete than anyone had a right to expect, McClellans Army was whipped under most disadvantageous circumstances to us, he was driven from his stronghold baffled and defeated. Its all nonsense to talk about the failure of [Benjamin] Huger & [John] Magruder, their forces were required where they were, if they had moved it is very possible that McClellan instead of being forced down the river would have entered Richmond on the south side. His army was more numerous and better equipped than ours. He has now but little chance of doing anything. As to Beauregard the complaints are all based upon what the Yankees have since said, but the fact is his men went to plundering the enemy's camps etc. I do not however think him a great general. Lee is the only one great one and for actual results [Thomas J.] Jackson next. The latter fights if he don't plan. . . . Dont worry yourself about money or war. I will look out for the first and providence will look after the latter and help me in regard to the money I hope.

■ **11 July 1862**
   Brooke to Lizzie, BP

As I buy no papers now the extra postage is balanced on my side. I smoke no segars which more than doubly compensates for yours and I drink no juleps or cobblers or any other kind of liquors which balances against the whole postage so you need not worry about it. I hope this statement will help to cheer you. McClellan is the prince of liars. The Louisianians give no quarter. Butler's infamous conduct is fully appreciated abroad as well as in the South. Our Army is not inactive now Lee is fully warmed up to his great work, has the responsibility and the power and you may rest assured that he will prove himself our Washington. Willie Wmson appeared to be much pleased with his commission. . . . I can not get up any feeling of interest in my work, it is all a task, Mallory asked me about getting up some iron clad vessels. I told him I had not thought of it lately that in fact my interest in them was not what it was before. That the pleasure which had attended my work before was gone, that Mr. Porter's conduct, and results generally, had killed the interest I took in such matters, that I had devoted myself more to the subject of ordnance. The fact is I am tired and disgusted.

■ **12 July 1862**
   Brooke to Lizzie, BP

A little recreation would be of service to me now for I am very tired of work. Richmond is indescribably dull and disagreeable. . . . Catesby Jones has been applied for by Genl. Magruder to act as Chief of his Artilery [sic] and of the staff on the trans Mississippi station, Jones thinks he would be of more use there. Our Navy officers—the best of them—will gradually seek service in the Army. I almost wish I had remained with Genl. Lee. But providence regulates those matters and I acted for the best. Dick [Garnett] rooms with me and will I suppose be in town for a week or so. Naval affairs are not progressing at all no[r] will they until some change is made in the Bureaus etc. It annoys me much as I cannot attribute our present condition to the efforts of the enemy. Genl. [Joseph] Johnston I think allowed strategy to run away with him when he moved as he did move and ordered the evacuation of Norfolk. . . . I have some experiments to make in which I take no interest but which Mr. Mallory wishes made. We have no good place for ordnance experiments and therefore they are generally unsatisfactory. . . . I wish I could get hold of my last cruise observations and go to work on them for a change. After the war this work will hardly satisfy me, the other is my proper vocation.

- **15 July 1862**
  Brooke to Lizzie, BP

Today I have been very busy trying to get things so arranged as to permit my getting off next Monday, I got the Secretary to transfer the cotton experiments to Lt Minor as I have already too much to attend to. . . . In military affairs all is quiet. I suppose there will be a considerable lull and in my opinion the Yanks will never do better than they have done. But we shall be better prepared as the days pass. Now we have arms and ammunition and the supply steadily increases for which we can not be too thankful. Our people still hold Vicksburg and will continue to do so. There is nothing like pluck and a little judgment. Rifled cannon are going to Vicksburg, I wish they had some of my 7 Inch Rifles. The authorities here seem fully impressed with the importance of securing our river defence below the city. Mr. Mallory has asked me for my views in relation to seagoing Iron clads, wants them in writing —so there is another piece of work—but fortunately I have felt more like work the past few days.

- **16 July 1862**
  Brooke, Richmond, to Secretary of the Navy Stephen R. Mallory (rough draft), BP

In obedience to your orders of the 15th ins. I submit such views in relation to the construction of iron clad sea going vessels as recent events in connexion with the means at our disposal suggest.

Experiment having shown that with high charges, giving correspondingly high velocities to projectiles, the thickest and strongest plating yet employed when struck at right angles, or nearly so is readily perforated with destructive effect, it is evident that vessels having nearly vertical sides can not be protected from projectiles so fired except by the application of such heavy plating as would render their construction unadvisable.

It becomes necessary then to avail ourselves of the advantages which attend the application of inclined plating by which the force of the projectile is decomposed thereby diminishing in proportion to the diminution of the angle of incidence its effect.

The plan proposed by Capt. Couper Coles R. N. which embraces this principle appears to present more advantages with fewer objectionable features than any which have fallen under my observation. But his plan involves the construction of turrets—frustrums of cones—and as the position occupied by the turrets, on top of the main shield, limits their dimensions it becomes necessary to employ breech loading guns of which the recoil is reduced to a minimum by mechanical contrivances. We have no such guns and I believe their manufacture is confined to the government shops of

England. If then we were to adopt the turret system using muzzle loaders we would dispense with the main shield and place the turret lower as illustrated in the Monitor. In that vessel to further economise space the turret is cylindrical, the objection to the cylindrical form is that in close action it could be readily struck at right angles to its surface and is therefore vulnerable, a single shot penetrating the turret might and probably would silence her battery.

It appears then that a plan which would enable us to bring a greater number of guns to bear upon an enemy to dispense with the turret and be less liable to accident from derangement of machinery—chance shots etc., and which would present no other than inclined surfaces would be preferable to the turret plan.

The plan upon which the Virginia was built presents these characteristic features and with some slight alterations additions etc. what appears a sea going vessel of comparatively light draft could be constructed.

I propose by raising the ports to the height of 6½ feet above the water, and carrying up from the knuckle, at the water line, an iron side, of the thickness usual in iron merchant vessels, to a sufficient height to clear the sea and to support the vessel in rolling, becoming spaces abreast the ports sufficiently wide to permit firing with the gun trained before or abaft the beam, these openings should not spread as in embrasures but should be at right angles to the side to avoid deflecting grape or cannister into the port. When not in action those ports could be readily closed by hinged shutters of light plate iron.

Pilot houses constructed on the same principal [sic] on the main shield and as strong might be placed at each end on top of the shield. Small carronades or howitzers without recoil in each would serve to sweep the decks if boarded by the enemy.

The propeller and rudder should be protected from rams by a spreading shield projecting horizontally from the stern of the vessel the border being iron bound.

The water tight compartment outside of the main shield should be [protected] by water tight bulkheads, being above the water line if perforated the danger could be readily repaired.

The vessel should also be fitted as a ram, and to strengthen her to resist the attacks of other rams it might be advisable to frame a salient angle of heavy timber below the knuckle.

I herewith submit a drawing illustrating these views. It embraces such improvements in form to facilitate putting on the iron as I have heretofore suggested.

■ **17 July 1862**
   Brooke to Lizzie, BP

I am extremely anxious to start [for Lexington] tomorrow and shall try to get off. But there is much uncertainty as to the Routes. . . . Mallory's asking me my opinion about iron clads is very annoying coming just at this time. I have written him a letter and trust it will be sufficient, the longer I delay starting the more difficulties will I have to encounter. I wish your health and strength would permit you to come here for a few days, but of course that is out of the question.

■ **21 July 1862**
   Secretary of the Navy Stephen R. Mallory to Mrs. Stephen R. Mallory, Stephen R. Mallory Letters and Papers, 1846–72, Southern Historical Collection, University of North Carolina at Chapel Hill

I have got the river so strongly protected now that I earnestly desire the whole Yankee fleet to attempt its passage. I went down to inspect it yesterday & Mrs. [Jefferson] Davis accompanied me.

■ **27 July 1862**
   Brooke to Lizzie, BP

I arrived safely in Richmond yesterday evening. Saw the Secretary who is impatient to have the plan of the ship completed to send to England, so I had to work today. . . . I shall work hard to hasten completion of the Richmond and her armament. . . .[17] The trip to Lexington has been of great benefit to me I feel more like work than before. Minor has completed the cotton experiments—proving cotton to be worthless as a defence against heavy guns. . . . I think I will patent that cat-hook which I had patented in Washington just before I left, and out of which I was cheated by the U.S. after taking the money. It is a useful invention.

■ **28 July 1862**
   Brooke to Lizzie, BP

Don't worry about your present situation, Dick [Garnett] and myself will probably be able to arrange it satisfactorily, Uncle William need not suppose that he would be under any obligation to me or Dick either as nothing would be a source of greater pleasure to me than to see him completely situated.

My own opinion is that T— will be the only person really troubled if he should succeed in driving away his own true friends.[18] I have a great deal to do now and am only annoyed by the diversity of the subjects to be considered. However I do not feel that my services are repaid. Mere fighting seems to be the only road to position and even that serves only particular persons.

I wish we had more Lees in the Confederacy. I become restless when I see how things are managed. . . . I paid $20—for the patent today it will be issued in a day or so.

■ **29 July 1862**
   Brooke to Lizzie, Lexington, BP

My plan of ship progresses very well. . . . Now with regard to the subject of change of residence etc. Dick's expenses are very considerable and he has sent all the money he had to spare to C[harlotte] and M[ary] A[nn] but I borrowed from him at his request—the money to pay the bank $350. I paid the bank and left with you 326 or about $300 reserving enough to pay board etc. In other words I have in my hands and yours $350 of Dick's money ready to move on etc. If you change your residence whatever you require for Uncle Williams board you are to take from that money, deducting the amount from the $350. I took it because I needed an advance for you. My pay coming in takes the place of what you expend etc. My $3500 is intact.

Before the 300 is expended Dick will be able to assist further, perhaps you might all move to N.C.—Milton where cousin M. A. is. Still Lexington is certainly a better locality for health in the summer. . . . I do wish I had a house or place to put you in. . . . The weather is too hot to permit me to run about town much although I am very desirous of attending to outside business. . . . I have come down here to look at the Richmond she is progressing now rapidly and will be a very powerful vessel. The outrageous orders of [John] Pope, [David?] Hunter, & Butler will probably draw a proclamation from [Jefferson] Davis. The enemy must be fought with his own weapons. Today Gorgas asked me to get up another R.R. battery but I told him it would be better for the army to do it as I had too much already to attend to, but offered my assistance in the way of advice etc. I must be looking after my guns. A banded & rifled 32 burst at Charleston, not one of my guns, but it had a double charge of powder a shell and a solid shot, enough to burst any gun.[19]

■ **6 August 1862**
   Brooke to Lizzie, BP

Today I have had such a perfect Babel of work that I have done comparatively nothing. The Secretary piles work up in a very indiscriminate manner. . . . We are getting stronger every day and shall soon put the cup to Yankee lips. . . . [Robert B.] Pegram will command in [the] Richmond. He is anxious to have the big gun. I think the gun would be better on Drury's [Drewry's] Bluff. . . . This room is far more agreeable than any other in the house I think I shall keep it if Mrs. Bidgood takes the house. . . . Mrs. B. proposes to have an extensive cleaning operation performed when she takes possession.

[This apparently was the house of Cousin Henry and Cousin Virginia that was to be sold.] . . . There is much chess playing at Mrs. Bidgoods and I begin to fancy the game. Do you understand it? . . . Old George [Minor] and I get on tolerably well together now. . . . You never mentioned hearing of Tat[t]nalls acquittal. The Court of Inquiry must feel badly. The North will be forced to draft to raise men, our govment [*sic*] is about treating deserters very rigorously—shooting them. . . . I wish we had half a dozen Arkansas in the Mississippi, although she is not proof against 11 inch shot.[20]

■ **9 August 1862**
  Brooke to Lizzie, BP

I know that a general impression exists that when the Richmond is completed she will go out. I think not! We ought to construct several like her. One is not enough and successive losses fritter away means. The Yankees will have several before she is completed.

I dont anticipate aid from England. Her policy is encourage the war to weaken both parties. We should always bear this in mind.[21]

■ **11 August 1862**
  Brooke to Lizzie, BP

My big gun is getting on well the first row of bands is on, and we shall soon begin to observe shape in it. I believe its projectile will penetrate any vessel the Yankees have or are building. . . . My $3500 will not be encroached upon if I am economical which I try to be.

■ **13 August 1862**
  Brooke to Lizzie, BP

You must not allow the Yankee howlings to depress you, they are perfectly desperate and every plunge but renders their ruin more complete. The new levies will require a year to fit them for the field and their veterans are whipped veterans so they stand but a poor chance in the South, the more they place hurriedly in the field the worse will be their defeat I think Lee will push them rapidly wherever and whenever he can. I am only afraid they may all go to Washington, that would be their best plan, to take a fresh start next spring. I think we can begin to see our way through now. Lincoln is on his last legs.

■ **16 August 1862**
  Brooke to Lizzie, BP

On Monday Congress meets but I dont know that the prospect is considered very interesting. It will probably do something to increase the Army. Abe thinks we have no more men than are now in the field. We have 50000 stands of arms ready for the new troops, and I fancy our manufactories together with importations and captures will supply all our wants, there is an abundance of powder.

■ **21 August 1862**
Secretary of the Navy Stephen R. Mallory to Mrs. Stephen R. Mallory, Stephen R. Mallory Letters and Papers, 1846–72, Southern Historical Collection, University of North Carolina at Chapel Hill

Our Congress having convened on the 18th is already at work carving out work for all the Departments & giving as much trouble as possible.

My friend Mr. [Charles M.] Conrad (Conradi) has already displayed his venom in moving a resolution in the House to abolish the office of Sec of the Navy & to commit its functions to the Sec. of War. He feels spiteful at the loss of his property in N.O. and chooses to think I could have saved the city. His resolution will show his spleen and venom & that is all.[22]

You must not suffer your mind to dwell on an idea that we are to be "crushed," as you say; but on the contrary you must look at the character of our revolution justly, & you will see that we cannot be "crushed." The very fact that the Lincoln Govt has been forced to draughting men, shows that their people will not fight us without compulsion, and this resort of drafting will render the War more odious & unpopular than ever. . . . To me, my dear wife, the signs of weakness & decay in the U.S. are everywhere evident, and if they can escape a military depotism they will surprise the world.

We can't keep house for less than $15. pr. day. I am paying $15 for a pair of shoes for Jack, $1 pr. doz. for eggs, $20 pr. barrel for flour seventy five cents for sugar, 50 cts. for beef 60 cts. for ham etc.

I am working with unceasing perseverance in getting up iron clad ships and am certain of success. The obstacles in the way would deter most men, but they excite my perseverence.

■ **27 August 1862**
Secretary of the Navy Stephen R. Mallory to President Jefferson Davis, Jefferson Davis Papers, Flowers Collection, Duke University

On the 19th instant Mr. Conrad introduced in the House of Representatives a Resolution instructing the Committee on Naval Affairs to inquire into the expediency of abolishing the office of Secretary of the Navy and of transferring the Navy Department to the War Department.

The fact that Mr. Conrad is Chairman of the Committee on Naval Affairs in the House, and must be therefore presumed to have official relations with this branch of the Government, and to be cognizant of its operations, gives to the resolution consideration to which it would not otherwise be entitled;

and therefore I deem it due to you, sir, to state that, as the Chief of the Department, I challenge and invite the most searching investigation of its conduct, that the triumphant vindication of its course must result from such investigation, and that it is no less due to the Government than to the people and the Department that such investigation should be promptly made.[23]

■ **31 August 1862**

Stephen R. Mallory, Richmond, to Mrs. Stephen R. Mallory, Stephen R. Mallory Letters and Papers, 1846–72, Southern Historical Collection, University of North Carolina at Chapel Hill

So soon as Mr Conrad made his attack in the House, I wrote to three friends in the House, <u>Hilton</u>, <u>Boyce</u>, & [Muscoe] <u>Garnett</u>, telling them that much that was done in my Department, had necessarily to be kept secret; that without this our plans of building, fitting out & purchasing abroad would be defeated; that this very secrecy rendered me liable to misrepresentation which I was unwilling to endure; & that they must demand for me a Committee of Investigation. This was promptly done. The debates are not reported, as only a skeleton of them are taken; and Hilton, Barksdale, Garnett Lyons & others threw down the glove at once & demanded that the House should not listen to vague & idle opinion, but should investigate the condition & conduct of the Navy Dept. Mr. Barksdale of Miss. who introduced the Resolution for this Committee, spent the previous morning with me & worked out the course.

I wrote officially to Luxwell [*sic*] in the Senate demanding that a Committee should be appointed there also. My friends in the Senate, & a large majority of them are,—were unwilling to raise such a committee, but I urged them to do it as the best means of meeting my enemies, confident that my administration of this Department must be triumphantly vindicated. I am perfectly satisfied with both Committees, & glad that [Henry] Foote is at the head of the one in the House.—I have much to be proud of & nothing whatever to regret in my administration. My aims have been large and high. Knowing that the enemy could build one hundred ships to our one, my policy has been to make such ships, so strong and so invulnerable, as would compensate for the inequality of numbers. With the Merimac [*sic*], the Arkansas, the Mississippi, Louisiana etc. I revolutionize the naval warfare of the world, astonished all people by showing what could be done, and the destruction of these vessels, by no fault of mine—just as everybody saw their gigantic power and the consequences thereof, brings upon my head the rage of the ignerant [*sic*] the rabble & the prejudicial, who always constitute the majority of mankind.

I profess to know something of naval affairs, in the largest sense of the word. The condition & history of all the navies of the world are known to me;

my time and study have been turned to the subject, and be my knowledge and ability much or little I have faithfully devoted them to the cause of my Country & fear not the judgment of impartial men, or the verdict of history. —I am determined that this Committee shall demand of Foote & Conrad their charges, of which they are careful to specify none; & that the entire history of the Dept. shall be known & vindicated. Both in House & Senate I challenged I defied the closest scutiny [*sic*], & declared that (to all my friends) rather than not have it, I would make Foote & Conrad the only committee & abide by their report of facts.

Conrad's hostility is personal. Foote is a fool & is crazy besides & hates the administration & the President with an intense hatred. I feel rejoiced at this committee. Nous verons.

You wish me to speak of our prospects politically, & I cheerfully do so, because I regard them as brighter. We are stronger today than we have ever been while our enemy is weaker. As our people have become firmly bound together for this War, those of the North have become discontent[ed] & discord is now predominant in their counsels.

■ **8 September 1862**

Journal of the Congress of the Confederate States, vol. 2, *Senate Documents No. 234*, 58th Congress, 2d Session

In executive session the Senate received the following nominations from President Davis in support of Mallory's letter of recommendation dated September 4, 1862.

Commanders for the War.

Robert B. Pegram of Virginia, lieutenant, Confederate States Navy.
John M. Brooke, of Virginia, lieutenant, Confederate States Navy.

Engineer in Chief

William P. Williamson, of Virginia, chief engineer, Confederate
States Navy [p. 266].

Nominations referred to Committee on Naval Affairs [p. 266].

Journal of the Senate, Sept. 13, 1862.

Mr. Brown, from the Committee on Naval Affairs, to whom were referred (on the 8th instant) the nominations of Robert B. Pegram and John M. Brooke to be Commanders for the War, and William P. Williamson to be engineer in Chief, reported, with the recommendation that said nominations be confirmed.

The Senate proceeded to the consideration of said report; and in concurrence therewith it was

Resolved, That the Senate advise and consent to their appointment, agreeably to the nomination of the President. p. 281.[24]

■ **13 September 1862**

Brooke to the Whitworth Ordnance Company, Manchester, England, BP

You know that in this country we have not such facilities as those which enable our enemies to give form to their conceptions and multiply their means of offence. We regretted exceedingly the loss of those excellent rifles which were onboard the Princess Royal. The Whitworth field gun is held in high favor by our artillerists who appreciate its power and accuracy.

───────────

The results obtained [with the Brooke Gun] are very satisfactory our guns have power but we find some difficulty in procuring material for shells. The results obtained in England with your shell we wish to see illustrated here and to this end some knowledge of the process of manufacture is desirable and from what Capt. Lawson tells me I am led to believe that you will not consider the request to import such information unreasonable. Everything that relates to improvement in ordnance will be gladly received.

The generous sympathy you have shown for our people induces me to enclose for your <u>personal information</u> the accompanying tracing.[25]

■ **17 September 1862**

Secretary of the Navy Stephen R. Mallory to Brooke, BP

You are hereby informed that the President has, by and with the advice and consent of the Senate, appointed you a Commander for the War, in the Navy of the Confederate States, to rank as such from the 13th instant.

You are requested to acknowledge the receipt of this appointment.

■ **20 September 1862**

Brooke to Lizzie, Lexington, BP

A thousand thanks darling for your kind expressions of love and affectionate sympathy in connexion with my promotion. I am more pleased by what you write than even by promotion itself. I told Mr. M[allory] how pleased you were. He was much gratified. I had not before alluded to the subject to him. He did not speak of it to me. . . . Have just shown Genl. Huger a new sabot for rifle projectiles which as far as my projectiles go has succeeded perfectly. He says I am on the right track. I think so. If I succeed, the saving to the Government will be very great indeed.[26]

■ **21 September 1862**

Brooke to Catesby ap R. Jones (copy), BP

I would have written sooner but the fact is I have been annoyed by your not being promoted. I suppose you know that Pegram and myself were promoted on the 13th ins. Neither of us knew of the nominations until they had been made. I supposed there were many and was surprised to learn subsequently that only two had been sent in. Now I sincerely hope that you will be made a commander and then promoted to a Captaincy over me, and I believe that in the very long run your merits will tell. These promotions are "for the war." Today I met [George W.] Harrison who declined shaking hands with me. On asking an explanation he at length informed me to my great surprise that it was in consequence of my having accepted promotion over my seniors, he could not consider me as a friend etc. I regretted the difference of views and although at first inclined to be angry told him that I should not permit his refusal to alter my feelings towards him as I knew he felt what he said. We had some conversation in which he spoke very candidly of the little worth of my services & abilities. I really wish he could be promoted as he seems to think the difficulty consists in not having a chance.

I will let you know if anything turns up worth mentioning. Com [French] Forrest, Arthur Sinclair, Tucker and others are opposed to the introduction of the merit element. Most of them always opposed it. Now they go for the repeal of the law and petition Congress to that effect.

In the main I go for the principle think the abuses that may occur not sufficient to balance the good.[27]

■ **21 September 1862**
Brooke to Catesby ap R. Jones (copy), BP

The long gun is nearly done shall soon try her against iron plating.

Have invented a new sabot which works beautifully as tried in 3 inch parrot gun.

It is all wood a cylinder 3 inches long with conical aperture in which fits the wooden cone b, the explosion drives the cone in splits the sabot takes the grooves and gives rotary motion. A pin, d, keeps all in place before firing. I am about to try it in VII Inch: shell having a ratchet base for the wood

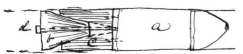

to take in communicating rotation. . . . Gen. Huger is much pleased with it.

There is no news from the Army, all very anxious and impatient. I hope for good results the enemy is active and strong. We got 11000 prisoners 15 to 20 000 small arms 46 field pieces 20 Mountain Howitzers & 1600 fine horses at Harpers Ferry all brought off to Winchester.

Our Army has not yet made sufficient progress to relieve the oppressed Marylanders, Kentucky is all right, Maryland will be in time. Kentucky behaved just so until the Armies got well in. Now she is rising en masse.

I have designed some time since a powerful <u>sea going</u> iron clad, she is building in the right place.

■ **21 September 1862**
  Lizzie, Lexington, to Brooke (to be opened at her death), BP

I will add to this [letter of 30 October 1860] my dear John that you knowing how Pa is situated will always as long as he lives see to his having what is comfortable. If Dick [Garnett] lives he will do all he can & you two can consult together Mary Selden will also help him, but if you ever loved me do see to his comfort in all things I beseech you, & teach Anna like wise.

■ **3 October 1862**
  Catesby ap R. Jones, Saffold, Early County, Georgia, to Brooke, BP

Yours of the 21st was received here yesterday. I congratulate you upon your promotion, I think you deserve it and have so expressed myself both before and since I heard of it.

I have always been in favour of promotion by merit; during the Mexican War I advocated the promotion of Beale, my junior, over me. I rather think that so much opposition is caused by the apprehension that the principle will not be fairly carried out; of course I do not advocate the abuses, but I do not believe that they will counterbalance the many advantages, I should much regret it if the prudent law is repealed.[28]

■ **12 October 1862**
  Richard B. Garnett, commanding Mahone's Brigade, Army of Northern Virginia, Winchester, Virginia, to Commander Brooke, BP

I wish for you to have made for me a grey sack coat warmly lined for winter. I dont care about military buttons if they cannot be easily obtained. Have three large stars, (one large one is in the middle and two small ones on each side) placed on both sides of the collar, which may be a "rolling collar."

We will settle for it when we adjust our accounts. Please send the garment to me by the earliest opportunity.

Our army has recruited considerably in strength and spirit since our return to Va. <u>Invasion won't do</u>. I always thought so.[29]

■ **20 October 1862**
  Catesby ap R. Jones, Saffold, Early County, Georgia, to Commander Brooke, BP

The Chattahoochee progresses very slowly in her equipment, I have been all over the adjacent states; the difficulties and annoyances have been much increased by inattention if not design in Richmond. The secretary must not expect to escape censure when he surrounds himself with such men. . . . The first letter I wrote on arriving here stated the importance of having a surgeon, and I have requested it in every letter I have written to the Secy. but you see with what result. Now this is trifling with men's health and lives, one of our best men I believe would have been now alive if he had been properly attended to. We know that there are plenty of surgeons, and that is the fault of the Department that we have not one. . . . I can get no answer to my application for a crew.

■ **24 October 1862**

John N. Maffit, *Florida*, Mobile Bay, Alabama, to Commander Brooke, BP

On my advent in Mobile—I found officers much convulsed by recent promotions—bitter feeling and irritable sentiment annoyed me sadly. Certainly you come within the <u>second</u> qualification of the law, as I am convinced you would in the <u>first</u>, if opportunity in the field had offered. But the Secty made a serious mistake, when he failed, to first consider, the claims of those, who had won their spurs in battle—and made you, as it were, an isolated promotion. You have earned the consideration of the Govt. and could have recd. it, without existing antagonistic sentiment, if Mr. M. had not neglected to nominate officers who had exhibited marked gallantry in battle with the enemy.

I knew you would not ignore, delicacy and manly pride—to obtain promotion—and I much regret the want of consideration, & liberal action on the part of the Secty of the Navy. Even handed justice should be the prime motive of a secty—failing in this qualification—his nominations are viewed with suspicion—and looked upon as the result of favoritism and personal consideration only—Hence the bitterness in regard to present promotions for comparative titles are freely discussed, and no one gives precedence to [Raphael] Semmes of the Sumpter [Sumter] (who was never under fire) over Tucker (not promoted) and others.

I hate to discuss the subject—though I am entirely free from envy and annoyance. The Govt. can act its pleasure—and I shall not be less happy—for the commendation & approbation of numerous friends, coupled with the proud knowledge of having successfully performed my duty, under trials and difficulties such as no naval officer, ever contended with before—is a satisfaction, comprehensive and cheering—

I've expected nothing from the personal consideration of the Confederate President or his secty—the former despises the Navy and I am no favorite of the latter.[30]

■ **26 October 1862**

Catesby ap R. Jones, Safford, Early County, Georgia, to Brooke, BP

I have just returned from a trip to Tallahassee, where I had gone to see about a crew, had but little success, am promised 15—want 80. I have written to the Department repeatedly, but have not had a word upon the subject, and consequently dont know what to expect.

PS—I have just received 50 men, most of them conscripts who have never seen a vessel. We have no provisions for them, tho we were promised it some time ago.

5

Developments in Ordnance

26 October 1862

Brooke journal, BP

On the [blank] inst. one of the 6.4 Inch Rifles designed by me, such as the Merrimac had onboard in addition to the 7 Inch Rifles of similar pattern, was fired with wrought iron bolt shot at a target composed of 3 layers of 8X2 inch plates bolted to oak 17 inches thick. The experiments were very satisfactory, With 8lbs. [of powder] a bolt of 85 [pounds] broke through two plates, cracked the 3rd and also broke the timber. With 12lb. charge penetrated all three, glanced slightly upward, and passed through the wood, but partially, in the wake of a preceding shot. The bars or plates were 8 ft long, the course next the wood vertical, the two outer courses horizontal. The bolts were designed by me and were cupped at the base. The cupping causes the base of the bolt to take the grooves of the rifle perfectly. Both shot were <u>set</u> up considerably by the shock, but that fired with 12lb charge <u>least</u>. I observed that the gases were cut off most effectually in the grooves, the space opposite the lands being powder marked. A shot with triangular point was also fired but as I anticipated did not penetrate well. It was steel pointed, but the steel was of inferior quality. A Mr. Hopson of Texas first proposed that form. He came first to try a shot which he supposed would go point first from a smooth bore.

I reasoned with him but he persisted in asking for a trial. The trial was made from a smooth bore and was unsuccessful, the target was missed, the projectile tumbled etc. Mr. H. then tried it from a 3in Rifle; it penetrated 2 inch iron going point first of course as the sabot—"driver"—gave it rotary motion. The edge of the steel point was not injured which led me to propose trying it on one of the cupped shot. I would have tried Hopson's shot with tapering rear end driver, but the target was too much broken up.

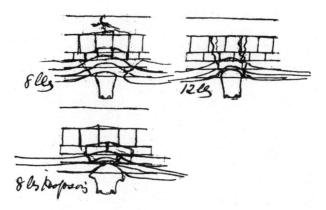

12lbs is a heavy charge for the gun of 9000lbs. I propose putting 18 inches more banding over that already on the gun. Less than ⅙ the weight of projectile is too little to give high velocity.

I am also getting up design of the same gun increased at muzzle from 11 to 12.5 inches. I am extremely anxious to perfect our Rifles; the only difficulty consists in want of proper facilities. Yesterday I was interrupted, getting up plans and specifications of an Iron clad ship for the Secretary similar to that furnished by me to Capt. Lawson, the lines and detail by Constructor W[illiam] A. Graves.[1] From what I see in the papers the English have not done much more in penetrating iron than we have here. As long ago as May I prepared drawings of the treble banded 7In Rifle to bear a charge of 20 to 30lbs of powder.

I have designed in all:

7In Rifle, single banded, 15000lbs. weight
6.4In Rifle, single banded 9000
One 7 Inch Treble banded trunnion fitted, forged on band and
     holding breech strap, 19000lbs.
One solid shot smooth bore 8in gun about 12000
One Double banded 7In with brass trunnions, 15000 lbs.
One double banded 6.4, weight about 12000
The new bronze sabot of my design seems to act well and is
     considered much superior to the Tennessee Sabot.

- ■ **28 October 1862**
  Brooke journal, BP

Yesterday and the day before I was employed in revising specifications of an iron clad ship to be constructed in England. The same that were sent by Capt Lawson some time ago. Roof or shield like that of Merrimac but vertical sides of the thickness usual in iron vessels, with ports cut in both shield and sides. A few days ago, Mr. [Charles A.] McEvoy proposed a new arrangement to retain plunger of percussion fuze in place until fired, to avoid the delay which now attends adjusting the fuze, screwing it in after removing safety pin. The plunger was turned off at base leaving a projection to pass through the diaphragm. On this projection was screwed a piece, 1oz of lead, which was to drop off on firing, releasing the plunger. One was fired, the plunger & lead together were too much for the diaphragm which drew from the case; the shock of the plunger on striking bottom of cavity of shell was very great, upsetting the plunger considerably. This experiment indicates that the present diaphragm is too weak to stand with certainty the shock of the plunger alone. I have therefore increased its thickness to 4/10 of an inch, it was 25/100 before.

a lead
b plunger

The lead was to act
as in the Alger Safety
fuze.

I had first thought of putting screw thread on the projection at base of plunger, on the supposition that the rotary motion of the projectile would cause it to unscrew, but as the projectile traverses 40 feet in making one revolution I was afraid that in close action the plunger might not detach itself quickly enough.

Lt. [David] McCorkle now at Atlanta proposes substituting the spun [?] wafer for the cap, putting the tube through the plunger. Experiment would determine the practicability of making this application. We must carefully avoid any arrangement which might produce explosion of the shell in the gun. We have tried what I term the "ratchet sabot," in 7In shells and solid cast iron bolts; it takes the grooves perfectly. Shall send some of the shells for trial at Chapin's [Chaffin's] Bluff where Capt. T[homas] J[efferson] Page is in charge.[2]

Mr Fred Volck has nearly completed drawing of the 6.4In Rifle with two sets of bands and enlarged chase. This evening gave orders at the Tredegar to put three additional bands 6X2 inches on the 6.4In Rifles of 9,000lbs weight, commencing 2 inches before the rear of present rear band and extending 18 inches over the other bands which extend 30 inches. The gun will be increased in weight from 9000 to [blank]lbs.

Today Col. [William P.?] Miles of S.C. was at my office. He desired some information on the subject of the advantage to be derived from the use of high charges. Wished to know if the 10 inch Army Columbiad would bear 20lbs. I told him that if the guns would bear it the charge would be the best against iron clads. Showed him my letter to Lt [Alexander] Warley on the subject of high charges for Rifle guns, explained results of experiments with our rifles.[3] The Tredegar now has a supply of Clover Dale Iron, the only iron well adapted to the manufacture of guns of heavy calibre.[4] Lt [Hunter] Davidson also called today at my office. Asked my opinion as to the probable effects of large charges in torpedoes for the bed of the James, 2000lbs. of powder. I thought it well to plant such. He stated that when the magazine of the Missouri steam frigate exploded in the harbor of Gibraltar, 3500lbs. of powder, several small vessels 150 to 200 yds from her were capsized, that two sentinels were thrown from the walls onshore and killed.[5] Today consulted Mr. Heinrich. as to the mode of soldering platinum to copper. He will solder some to the bouching of Treble banded 7 Inch rifle now nearly completed at the Tredegar.

■ **30 October 1862**
Brooke journal, BP

Went to the Tredegar this morning. Mr. Delaney [Matthew Delany] told me the vent of the Treble banded gun would be bored soon, commencing this evening. The bouche is of hammered copper from the bloom—it is quite malleable. Mr. [Stephen R.] Mallory has directed Comdr [Frederick] Chatard who is ordnance officer of Drury's [Drewry's] Bluff to experiment in firing projectiles from a rifled 32 pdr under water. Mr. Conrad, Chairman of the Naval Committee, was at Capt. [George] Minor's office today. He asked me some questions in relation to a proposition of a Mr Angeman to construct self-propelling torpedoes. I had reported on it. There are rumors in town of interference with affairs on this continent by the great powers. We have now a tolerable supply of good gun iron coming in from the furnaces "Cloverdale" and "Grace." Have furnished drawings to Tredegar for the new 6.4In Rifle. Have sent drawings of the Ratchet sabot to several stations.[6]

■ **1 November 1862**
Brooke journal, BP

Yesterday with Mr. Volck visited the Richmond and the yard opposite Rocketts.[7] The R. had steam up and I was informed that 45 revolutions with 28lbs of steam only were obtained. 3 of the 7In Rifles are onboard and I hope soon to see the Treble banded gun onboard. It will be her bow gun, the vent is being bored now. Mr. Graves vessel, to be iron clad, is pretty well advanced, frames up clamps in etc. A few stern frames yet to go up. She will be a strong and fine vessel. Mr. Mallory is desirous of having some experiments made in firing guns under water. [He] has ordered Comdr Chatard to make some. Told me to think of some way of doing it with facility. He, the Secretary, thought the gun might be lowered between two vessels, gun boats, but I apprehend damage to one of them as the projectile might glance. It is impossible to say what course it would take, particularly if conical. Today Mr. McEvoy made experiments at Chapin's [Chaffin's] Bluff battery. A fuse-time-to be ignited in the gun by percussion was tried. The shell exploded in the gun and the muzzle of the piece, One of the old 32pdrs of 63 cwt, rifled and banded, lost 6 inches of its muzzle by the operation. The shock probably dislocated the fuse. I was afraid it would do so. The fault may be easily remedied. Of 3, 8 inch incendiary shells, only one appeared to explode, shock of discharge evidently disrupting powder chamber attached to fuse case. Two fuses, McEvoys conical plunger-concussion fuses, were tried. Shells—32pd Rifle—6.4 bore entered bank showed [?] no sign. I am convinced that the percussion fuses heretofore used in the Confederate Service are not sufficiently strong in rear of the plunger—that the pin or diaphragm is knocked out by the plunger of which the inertia is very great. I am anxious to have the experiments necessary to determine this fact made.

I visited the [Richmond] Naval Ordnance Works of which Robt. Minor is Superintendent, everything well regulated. Work of the best character executed there.[8] Saw model of a boat I proposed long ago, the organization of a boat brigade, 8 boats with weapons etc. Jon. T. Wood Lt. has just destroyed a fine clipper of 1100 tons, the Allegheny. We have her chronometer and barometer at the office. He burned her in the Chesapeake.

■ **3 November 1862**
Brooke journal, BP

Today carried Bouche—copper—to Heinrich to have platinum plate soldered on. I suspect we shall have to resort to some other method of securing it. Also made some computations for graduation of sight bars for rifles 7 and 6.4 Inch. Allowed 7ft for height of gun above water. Computed elevation required to strike point aimed at instead of to strike water line with gun levelled. Got order to Capt of Gunboat Hampton to afford Mr. McEvoy facilities in testing fuse cases—percussion.[9] Recd letter from Capt Page, Comdg. battery at Chafins [Chaffin's] Bluff. He coincides with me in opinion as to the cause of premature explosion of his shell in the gun at Chafins [Chaffin's]. Lt [William H.] Murdaugh visited my office; he is ordered to assist Comdr. [Archibald] Fairfax who is to get up a Government Foundry. Saw John Taylor Wood. Proposed that he should take charge of the boat brigade, if I can get it up, proposed before to Davidson. Wood likes the idea. Will see what I can do towards it.

We expect a strong effort on the part of the Yanks this fall. Guns are being made with tolerable rapidity. Beauregard wants two of my 7 Inch Rifles for defense of Charleston. We hope soon to have some blooms from Shenandoah to be turned as bolts solid. I trust that we may get them. Target is being prepared for the Treble banded 7 Inch gun, rifle. Warley writes from Charleston that he prefers the 10in Columbiad to the 7 Inch rifle on account of its higher initial velocity.[10]

■ **5 November 1862**
  Brooke journal, BP

This afternoon Herbert Bryant called to see Lizzie and myself. He's adjutant of the 17th. Regt. Va., was wounded at Sharpsburg and paroled, [and] was permitted to reside with his mother in Washington. He bought 3 pairs of shoes as a present from Mary Bryant to Anna who was delighted with them.[11]

Am now employed perfecting system of sighting guns, 7In and 6.4 Rifles. The Strap—breech—of heavy Treble banded rifle was keyed up today. It fitted admirably. Heinrich is at work on the bouche. We hope to have her completed by Monday evening. A temporary carriage and target are being prepared at the Tredegar. I am extremely impatient for the trial of our percussion fuses by Mr. McEvoy; there is some delay in getting a gun boat. Everything now depends on getting heavy guns rapidly. There is no news.

■ **6 November 1862**
  Brooke journal, BP

Today a sudden change in the weather, cool and cloudy. Heinrich soldered the platinum to copper bouche with gold alloy 18 carats fine. The small model, scale ⅛, of 10 Inch double banded smooth bore is finished. Showed the Secretary a model of a boat 30ft. long with plan by Wm. Davidson. Boat builder now quarterman at Rockett's [sic]. Secretary orders one built. This boat is one of 8 I proposed to have constructed and mounted on wagons to operate against the Yankees on Chesapeake and Potomac. I found today that the sights for 6.4 and 7 Inch Rifles were not correctly placed, they should be 49 inches apart. Recd. a letter from Catesby Jones.

■ **10 November 1862**
  Brooke journal, BP

A fine day. The bouche has been placed in the treble banded gun and in a day or two I hope to test the gun on an iron target. Today sent for Mr. Davis, boat builder. The Secretary directed him to commence one boat to be employed on wagon. Captain [Samuel] Barron has been ordered to the command of the James River flotilla.[12] He left request at my office to be furnished with drawings of guns onboard Richmond, character of projectiles etc. Rob't. Minor is sick. I hope he will soon be out again. Asked Capt. Minor to have bolts hurried up for guns.

There is a report by Central cars that the enemy have taken Fredericksburg, that [James] Longstreet has been pushed back from Cullpepper [sic] to Gordonsville. I put very little confidence in these reports. By delay we have probably lost some important machinery at Fredericksburg.[13]

■ **18 November 1862**
Brooke journal, BP

This morning the Secretary was too unwell to come to his office but sent word to me that he would wait no longer for the target in course of construction at the Tredegar, but to get the gun—7In Treble banded off to the Richmond as soon as possible. I therefore proposed to try it across the river at the Tredegar to test the breech strap trunnion bands etc. Went down to the Tredegar and Lt. [Alexander M.] DeBree having already placed a target on the opposite side or rather at the foot of the hill on Belle Isle we fired three bolts at it.[14] The distance by Lt. DeBree's calculations is 750 yards. To the eye it appears less. The first shot was one of my cast iron ratchet saboted bolts, charge 17lbs.; the sight bar was set at 750 yds. The bolt passed above the target and penetrated the bank, good line shot. The bar was then placed at 600 yard mark, charge 20lbs. The bolt passed above the target, also a line shot, [and] buried itself in the bank. The sight was then set at 600 yd again and a third bolt, Tennessee sabot, fired, Mr DeBree aiming at lower edge of target. The shot struck near the point aimed at, a little to the right. Of the Tennessee Sabot my opinion was confirmed; it does not give good range. But if Mr. DeBree's distance is correct, the gun overshot the graduations in yards: 150 yds with 20lbs and nearly the same with 17lbs. The recoil was easy, about 2 feet, chassis inclined 3 ½°. Not a finished chassis, but a rough one for temporary use. The wrought iron work of the gun was not affected perceptibly by the firings. The ranges by which the sight bar was graduated were those obtained by English 6.4 In Rifles and by our rifles at Norfolk, 6.4 and 7 Inch also, but these last were not strictly applicable as the experiments were made at 8°, but the English gave a curve corresponding. I suppose that with the ordinary charge of 12lbs the range would be about right. We must endeavor to obtain some ranges soon.

I was one of a Board to fix rank and uniform of the new grades, Capt. Barron presdt. We met this morning, but he excused me to attend to the gun firing. This evening I called on Mr. Mallory and reported results. Capt. Pegram, Col [Thomas S.] Rhett and others were present at the firing.[15] All very much pleased. I think the initial velocity must have been very high. It is possible that the grain wedges slipped a little and this caused the gun to shoot somewhat high. Still I am inclined to believe that the range of the bolt with these high charges is greater than we had supposed it would be. The other day we tested our percussion fuses to determine their strength. The discs,$^{25}\!/_{100}$ of an inch, stood perfectly, McEvoys percussion & time fuse—ignited by percussion in the gun bids fair to succeed perfectly. The large gun will probably be got onboard tomorrow.

■ **26 November 1862**
   Brooke journal, BP

The gun was safely placed onboard the Richmond, all pleased with it. The deck was not properly constructed by Mr Porter to receive a pivot gun, and we consequently have trouble in fitting the carriage. The deck is too high amidships. Last Sunday night it occurred to me that the wear of vents in rifled guns might be retarded by putting a steel bouche clean through, permitting the end to project a short distance into the chamber to prevent the draw of flame & gas along the sides of the chamber or bore. I shall apply the principle if it does not interfere with sponging etc. Probably 4/10 of an inch would be sufficient.

The secretary has ordered two more guns of the same pattern as the treble banded VII inch.

■ **4 December 1862**
   Secretary of the Navy Stephen R. Mallory to Brooke, BP

The following recommendation of the Board of Officers who inspected the defences at Drewry's Bluff is submitted to your attention.

"Sight bars—The guns are sighted, but we recommend that the range at different elevations and depressions be ascertained by adjustment [?] and the bars marked accordingly."

Proceed to Drewry's Bluff and report to Captain Lee for the duty of adjusting the sights of the guns in the best possible manner without delay.[16]

■ **7 December 1862**
   Brooke journal, BP

Yesterday I went to Drury's [Drewry's] Bluff and reported to Capt. Lee as having been ordered by the Secretary to adjust the gun sights etc. Capt. Clark of the Engineers walked over the works with me. The Navy guns are generally sighted, have bars graduated to degrees but no yards marked upon them. Three of four 10In Columbiads, Army guns, are not sighted. Capt. Lee will direct Lt [James] Waddell to report to me. He is Ordnance officer of the Bluff.[17] Nearly all the officers there are under the impression that some considerable allowance must be made for the height of the Bluff, 89ft., even in using <u>tangent</u> or <u>bar</u> sights which give simply angle of axis of bore with direct line to the object. I am now having made a Quadrant with spirit levels using the arc and vernier of a sea quadrant. It will give elevation by bore to within three or four marks. I may also attach to the muzzle bar a vertical bar with mirror [?] to determine dispart of gun. Some rough measurements have been made at Drurys [Drewry's Bluff] by which distances of piles in the river were ascertained. I propose to try each gun.

Day before yesterday a second long gun to be treble banded was cast. I must test the metal etc.

■ **9 December 1862**
Brooke journal, BP

Today went to Drewry's Bluff with Waddell, met Major Frank Smith. Inspected the guns. We fired 4 shots from the 8In Solid Shot gun Army Columbiad. A barrel was placed at 916 yds dist., as measured by Major Smith. The first two shot were fired level, height of gun above water 85ft., shot both fell short. Then by tangent [quad]rant 2°, fell short. 4th shot by Gunners Quadrant, 1°, struck near barrel. Major Smith will measure the distance of points struck.[18]

The Gunners Quadrant, very rough, measured distance between sights = 117.75 inches, inclination of bar to bore-axis-57°. I find that the bar was erroneously graduated, 1° being marked at 2 inches it ought to have been 2.42 In I am inclined to believe that the powder was weak. Major Smith is to remeasure the distances, and in a day or two I shall have proper instruments for determination of elevations, will then fire the 8 inch and other guns.

1863

■ **12 January 1863**
Brig. Gen. Richard B. Garnett, camp near Greene's Station, to Commander Brooke, Richmond, BP

I recd. your letter of the 8th Inst. today and hasten to reply to it. You had better continue to send the monthly remittance to Pa. and let me know occasionally how our accounts stand, as it may serve as a check on my expenses, though I spend little except for the necessaries of life. I can not send you the $100 00/100 for the "sague" until the end of the month, as all my ready money is advanced for marketing. I cant get them to appoint me a single staff officer at Richmond, and some of my mess mates have no means of paying their mess bills, and therefore have to live on credit. I being the endorser I wish I could get some one to stir them up at the War Dept.

I am very sorry to learn that Lizzie is suffering from her cough again. I recd. a letter from the old gentleman a few days since, and am glad he is once more about.

I too, am very busy. . . .

It is some what gratifying to learn that "Billy" has "hauled up" again, I would write to him if I thought it would do a particle of good, but I have had too much sad experience in such cases to hope that any good can come of advice from friends or relatives.

■ **6 February 1863**
  Brooke journal, BP

The want of mechanics and the consequent slow progress in preparing guns, instruments etc. is discouraging.

The instruments I devised for experimental purposes are but just completed although ordered long ago—Gunnery Quadrant and plane table arrangement. I propose now in a few days to try and determine the ranges of our rifles, etc.

Recently I have determined the density and tensile strength of some of the iron of our guns. The metal is better than I thought. A clumsy fellow broke the glass jar or vase used with the hydrometer and no other can be procured. I have however purchased a large earthen ware water cooler which will answer the purpose tolerably well and may be able to repair the other. The Tredegar turns out guns so very slowly that I lose patience.

I am extremely anxious to have double banded rifles, 7-In—and 6.4In We have now three of the latter at Drewry's Bluff. I have recently endeavored to stimulate the forging of wrought iron bolts. The Army has ordered a large number which interferes with the making of ours. I have distributed a number of blooms among the shops and hope to have some good solid ones soon.

With these projectiles and double banded rifles we need not fear the enemy's iron clads. I have furnished designs for shrapnel shells for the rifles. McEvoys time fuze attachment will be supplied as I proposed. A few days ago Anton Schonborn came in from the West where he had been serving as Engineer under Genl [Albert] Pike—got him appointed instrument maker for the Navy.[19] He will have his work room at the Ordnance works. Heard recently of the death of my old ship mate Lt. Hen K. Stevens a noble fellow who was killed at Bayou Tesche. Capt. [Duncan N.] Ingraham has driven off the Blockading fleet at Charleston but they have returned. It is supposed that the enemy will soon attack that place.[20]

■ **14 February 1863**
  Brooke journal, BP

This evening by direction of the Secty. the following officers met him at the Dept. to consider the feasibility of boarding the enemys iron clads at Charleston should they succeed in passing the forts and obstructions: Comms. Forrest, Barron, Lee, Comdr. Pegram and Arthur Sinclair, Lts Minor & Waddel[l] I was of the number. The Secretary said that it was proposed to use the common steamers of Charleston for the purpose, putting some troops as well as sailors onboard. The Com: Forrest, said that in his opinion the only way to manage would be to take a kedge and hawser and attach the kedge to one, then the people on shore could clap on and haul the vessel in.

Capt Barron said that the boarding was feasible and should be attempted, that he would board all the iron clads simultaneously, even when underway. Sinclair said the difficulty would be that one iron clad could sweep our men from the others. Pegram & Minor thought the plan of boarding not promising enough to warrent [sic] the attempt. I thought preparations should be made and the attack if circumstances should justify it, that I considered it extremely difficult to board if the enemy kept underway. Lee thought the attempt should be made although he did not believe it would succeed. Waddel[l] did not think the prospect of success good but volunteered to go. The Secretary having summed up the opinions of the officers above mentioned dismissed them.

Yesterday Mr. Strange fired a shell under water from the experimental gun. It developed the fact that projectiles may be thrown well under water and I think an effective gun may be made. On Monday I shall probably make some experiments with it.

The jar for water used to determine sp.gr. of iron has been repaired and I shall now be able to go on with experiments on iron for cannon. Lt. [Catesby] Jones has been ordered to Selma to Superintend the ordnance works there. Am having an incendiary shell—carcass—drawn for Rifles.

- **16 February 1863**
  Brooke journal, BP

Longstreets Corps is moving towards Richmond as Hookers Army withdraws from the Rappahannock. An attack upon Charleston is considered iminent [sic]. Major Norris of the Signal Corps loaned me a copy of Dahlgrens report on Ordnance, iron clads etc. which I am having copied. It contains little of interest except that he has increased the charge of his X1-in guns to 30lbs, the charges of the 1X-in to 13½ lbs. This we knew could be done by former proofs of those guns, although I consider 30lbs a trying charge for the unstrengthened X1-in gun.

Today I determined sp.gr. of twelve samples gun metal at the Tredegar. I have much trouble in making these experiments—as the jar is broken—mended—and distilled or rain water is difficult to get.

I hope to tabulate all my experiments, or rather their results, in a few days. I consider it of the first importance to establish a system of experiment to determine the character of our gun metal.

I[n] a day or two the long gun onboard the Richmond will be fired at a target, 8-inch iron, near Drurys [Drewry's] Bluff. Mr. Strange will probably be ready with his gun tomorrow. I think we shall find it difficult to apply the principle to submarine guns on a large scale, but it can be done. I propose a 6.4In caliber. The difficulty will be in excluding water. Three vessels, steamers, have just arrived in Charleston with valuable cargoes, ordnance stores etc. Steamers.

The Tredegar works has not had for some time wood of which to make patterns for casting guns I designed long ago.

■ **19 February 1863**
Brooke journal, BP

Yesterday the Secretary referred a letter addressed to the President by Mr. Strange to me. It contained a report on his experiment of the 13th ins. Today I wrote a request to Col. [Jeremy] Gilmer for two boats to be used by Mr. Strange in supporting his gun during experiments to be made in deep water. Designed a shell of bloom iron to penetrate plating! Furnished tracing to Capt. Minor. It will be made at Charlotte of the  blooms used in making bolts. Mr. Talonelle introduced to me at my office [blank] professor of Natural philosophy of [blank]. I had some pleasant conversation with him on various subjects, particularly ordnance & chronometers. Showed him diagrams etc. Wrote several reports on inventions. One to deluge ships with inflammable liquid to be subsequently fired. Another on torpedoes to be attracted by iron clads—magnetic—impracticable both. Lts. [William A.] Webb, Waddel[l] and others are ordered to Charleston.[21] Com Arthur Sinclair is ordered to command the Atlanta ironclad at Savannah. I believe that Catesby Jones will not be ordered to Selma as he has started to join [John B.] Magruder.[22] Troops from Lee's Army passed through today. In the afternoon visited the Tredegar. One of the long treble banded guns is having the band of 2nd tier turned off.

■ **25 February 1963**
Brooke journal, BP

This morning there was some fog but it cleared off and we had a delightful day. About 10am the Secretary, Postmaster Genl Mr. Keys, the Messers. [Asa and Nelson] Tift,[23] Capt Lawson and myself went onboard the Beaufort and down to the Richmond to try the treble banded 7In Com: Barron was onboard. A target had been put up about [blank] yds from the vessel at the foot of the Bluff. It was composed of four layers of 2X8 inch iron bolted on 22 inches of wood firmly backed with clay so that it formed as it were part of the bluff. Yesterday the range was obtained with cast iron shot by a canvass [sic] target through which three shot were put. One took off the head of a red bird. The first shot fired today was of wrought iron with Tennessee sabot weighing 140lbs. charge 25lbs. It struck lower edge of the bulls eye, passed though the outer plating, broke the two next layers of plates so that the pieces could be taken out, and broke also the fourth so that the wood could be seen in the crack; but we must wait until the target is taken down to see full effect. The gun did not recoil to a taut breeching.

The 3rd shot was one of my cupped wrought iron bolts, 120lbs., charge 10lbs. It struck on the edge of an outer plate—half nearly—cut a piece clearly out, went through the two next layers and remained imbedded in the plating, its head being in the 4th layer and nearly through. The rim of the cup had preserved the form of the bore—rifling—perfectly, not torn or chipped in the slightest degree.

The 2nd shot was a similar bolt, charge 25lbs. Passed through the target. All appeared satisfied with this exhibit of the power of the gun. If the target had not been backed by clay it would I think have been destroyed. The Richmond then got underway and we made a pleasant little trip up the river. She moved at the rate of 3 ½ or 4 knots, turning very easily. We left about 4 P.M. in the Beaufort. I regret that the 2nd shot missed, as I think it would have penetrated to a greater depth than the others did.

■ **26 February 1863**
Brooke journal, BP

A disagreeable rainy day, the snow melting renders the streets wet and muddy. This morning gave evidence before the Committee of investigation now employed in overhauling Navy Dept. Among other things recently submitted to me for examination is a plan of annoying the enemy with an inflamable [*sic*] fluid, which burns readily on water. A Frenchman named Pierre [blank] has the secret. After two little experiments, one in the presence of the Secretary, [?] P- has been set to work.

Mr. Strange applies for some compensation for his labor, etc. I think the platinum bouche of the treble banded 7-In rifle will protect the vent tolerably. Shall try to obtain more platinum.

Mr. [John F.?] Tanner of the Tredegar says he will cast a double banded 7In this week. My experiments on iron have been completely interrupted lately.

■ **27 February 1863**
Brooke journal, BP

A damp disagreeable day. This afternoon met Mr. Mallory and took a walk with him. Talked of guns etc. I said that I thought an 8in rifle on the plan of the Richmond's 7in would be a good gun [but] would give it about 2 inches more diameter. Think I will make a drawing of it. There is no news.

■ **16 March 1863**

French Forrest, Chief of Office of Orders and Detail, for Secretary of the Navy Stephen R. Mallory, Richmond, to Brooke, BP

Proceed to Drewry's Bluff and report to Commander R. B. Pegram for duty, in preparing a code of Signals for the Navy.

Reported March 24th 1863

R. B. Pegram
Comdr.

■ **25 March 1863**

Brooke journal, BP

Today visited the Richmond as one of a board to arrange code of signals. Dined onboard. A few days ago Mr Mallory informed me that Capt Minor would be ordered to Selma to superintend erection of foundry etc. and that I would be placed in charge of the office. Have sent design of double banded X1-in gun to the Tredegar to have flasks etc. prepared. Recd. today a letter from Catesby Jones at Charlotte where he has command. Saw today report of experiments with torpedo at Charleston. I think the enemy will find it difficult to take that city.[24]

■ **28 March 1863**

Brooke journal, BP

I mentioned a day or two ago to Mr. [Thomas A.] Jackson, Naval Engineer, my intention of using slow and quick powder in the same cartridge to reduce initial strain and yet preserve velocity of the shot. Capt. Minor proposes to turn the office over to me on Monday next, the 30th.

■ **30 March 1863**

Secretary of the Navy Stephen R. Mallory to Brooke, BP

You will report to Commander Geo Minor and relieve him from the charge of the office of Ordnance etc.

Reported March 31st /63

George Minor Comdr
in charge

1 April 1863

Brooke journal, BP

Yesterday called to see Capt. Minor who was confined to his bed with rheumatism. Relieved him of charge of the office of Ord. & Hydrog.

Mr. McEvoy broke the hydrometer vase accidentally through a [?] defect in the hydrometer. May now use an earthen ware vessel. Will order glass from abroad. This evening went to the Tredegar to hurry up guns. One of the 7in rifles single banded will be ready on Saturday.

We expect to hear hourly of an attack on Charleston or Savannah.

■ **8 April 1863**

General Orders issued from Naval Commandant's Office, Mobile, Alabama, Franklin Buchanan Letter Book 1862–63, Southern Historical Collection, University of North Carolina at Chapel Hill

Commanders of vessels and Batteries under my command, in which Navy Guns are mounted, will make the following reports quarterly, through me, to the Office of Ordnance and Hydrography.

The number of times each gun is fired, with the weight and kind of projectile, and charge of powder, stating also the number of each gun and other distinguishing marks upon it. In the first report to be forwarded on the first of July next, state as far as can be ascertained the number of times each gun has been fired previous to the receipt of this order, giving the charge of powder, weight of gun and kind of projectile, if possible.

As the information is deemed important, and is required for special purposes, the report will imbrace [sic] all important information on the subject.

■ **8 April 1863**

Brooke journal, BP

Yesterday the enemy attacked forts Moultrie & Sumter. Were repelled. Today started 1-7in rifle Single banded to Charleston. Suggested it being used in defense of city proper. Secretary approved. Sent also 425 bolts, cast & wrought. Tomorrow shall send a double banded 6.4in rifle with 100 bolts & 50 shells to same place; this gun is double banded. Capt. Minor is still sick.

Yesterday visited Tredegar and hurried up guns. They are now out of gun metal. There is no immediate demand for guns for boats.

■ **11 April 1863**

Brooke journal, BP

Yesterday Col. [Josiah] Gorgas showed me a telegram from Genl. Beauregard in relation to damages to forts Sumter & Moultrie in which he says, "Brooke's rifle guns are invaluable, they sunk the Keokuk," and requested Gorgas to send more if they could be obtained. I told him that two had gone on, one 7in, one 6.4 double banded. It affords me great pleasure to know that my labors have produced good fruit.

This result verifies my opinion that it was fortunate the Merrimac was not supplied with bolts on her first engagement with the Monitor as in that case our destruction of the Monitor would have enlightened our Yankee enemies. As it was they accepted the Monitor as a standard, hence the Charleston fleet of Monitors instead of better vessels. We have taught them again, and I trust we are so well advanced as to defy their attempts to follow. We have about 50 of my rifles in service.

■ 14 April 1863
Brooke journal, BP

Fine pleasant day. This morning went with Mr. Mallory and Mr. Orr of S.C., Butler King, Mr. Watts and Mr. Maxwell of Florida to Drewry's Bluff to practise with treble banded rifle at iron plated target—the one fired at with same gun before on the 25th Feb. Went first onboard the Richmond, looked at her, then landed and visited the batteries on the Bluff. Col. Gorgas and Major [Isaac] St. John were with us. Met Frank Smith and his wife, a very nice little woman, took a look at the double banded rifles in iron battery. Visited Franks quarters; he gave me his observations for height of bluff etc. Went onboard Richmond. Crew were exercised at Genl. Quarters, then fired at target, distant 260 yards. I wished to try cast iron bolts, ratchet sabot; first shot 128lb bolt, 16lbs. powder, struck in hole made on the 25th Feb. Supposing it had missed the target, fired another, same charge, aiming little to left of bulls eye. Struck, shot broken into small fragments, plates much indented, all four cracked but not displaced. Fired 128lb shot, cast iron, with 20lbs powder. Struck higher up on target, broke all four plates and

cracked timber, then fired one of my reamed cup bolts, wrought iron, 20lbs powder. It struck on uninjured part of target, broke through and passed into the wood without the slightest deflection. The base of shot was just 18 inches from face of target. This was fully equal to anything I could have anticipated.

The copper bouche yielded and the priming wire could not be used. I went to Tredegar on my return to town and directed that Mr. Hercus and an assistant should go in the morning on board and take out the bouche which must be changed. I regret the copper would not stand. The party were all much pleased with the trip and with the gun. The bolt of my own was good. The firing surpassed that of the other day.

■ 16 April 1863
Brooke journal, BP

The bouche of the Treble banded 7-in was removed with difficulty—the inner orifice was closed, copper yielding. A steel bouche is being made, a spare one also. Mr. Delany proposes dispensing with the lower screw thread and using a washer above. I propose leaving the bouche projecting above the surface of the gun square to be taken out at pleasure. The lower part will be groined in.

■ **20 April 1863**
  Catesby ap R. Jones, Charlotte, North Carolina, to Brooke, BP

I am glad that Genl. Beauregard has mentioned your gun, it will tend to convince those who are not judges, and also those who have no opinion of their own, of its merits, and may also silence those who would not see, of which class I am sorry to say there were not a few. What I thought of them is known by the preference I gave them in the battery of the Virginia. By the bye I understand Fairfax has never forgiven me for that preference, you recollect that I substituted 1Xin guns for the six guns of his own that he had selected for the battery of the Virginia. There can be no doubt that your gun is the best in the Confederacy.

———————

Your X1in will be a powerful gun—and I think would smash the ironclads at close quarters. Why not band all guns? . . .

Soft iron is very important for us, the work now is very unsatisfactory. I should like to have 100 tons of the Alabama Iron or some other soft iron, and a few tons of it as soon as possible. I have heard nothing of the iron from Salisbury, and do not expect much from it. Capt. Pinckney was here yesterday, he says we could get soft iron from the Graham furnace, Wytheville, Wythe Co. Va. . . . Capt. P. says the iron can be sent by canal to Richmond—and thinks there would be no trouble in obtaining 100 tons—but as I said before there is pressing want of it for present use. It is all important that the men should have constant and steady employment, their work is better and they do more.

■ **21 April 1863**
  Statement of Lt. Col. Joseph A. Yates, Artillery, Headquarters, Fourth Military District, Georgetown, S.C. (copy), BP

Answers to questions proposed to me. 1st I consider the Brooke gun decidedly the most efficient gun in use for operating against Iron-clad vessels, owing principally to the fact that the projectile is wrought iron. I think it superior to the 10 or 15 inch Columbiad for operating against such vessels. Against wooden vessels, no doubt, the heavy smooth bore guns are very destructive; the idea has occurred to me that if round shot of a greater diameter than the armor to be operated upon is thick, be used, that they will penetrate.

2d I think the flat headed bolt or cylinder has a decided advantage over the conical ball, when used against Iron-clads for the following reasons—The flat headed half of it strikes the object—directly on its head—acts as a punch, for as a general rule if you desire to punch iron, you should not used [*sic*] a pointed instrument, but one whose end will be as wide as the iron to be perforated is thick, for example: to punch a plate one inch thick use an instrument with a head one inch in diameter. (This information I derived from an old Iron Smith of intelligence and experience.) Again, if you get an angular fire, (which is most frequently the case) the bolt striking on its edge or angle, formed by its sides and head, will not be deflected, but will I think, cut in with great effect, making an irregular ragged hole not easily repaired. I would here however remark, that the shot used in the Brooke gun and known as the Brooke projectile, is not a perfect cylinder, but terminates in the frustrum of a cone, but this very short. The conical ball I am of opinion is not the proper projectile against iron-vessels, for if the ball does not strike upon the point or apex (which experience teaches us is more frequently the case) it will be deflected from its course the shot lost. Against wooden vessels I think, they may be used with effect. . . . Against sand and brick work I would use almost any other projectile in preference to the flat headed bolt. . . .

In conclusion I am impressed with the opinion that Iron-Clads are most formidable vessels if used as means of defence for harbors etc, but do not think they will answer for offensive operations against Forts. The deepest penetration of the 15-inch shot or shell in the wall of Fort Sumter was 33 inches except when it struck the face of the embrasure, where its crushing effect was great.

- **27 April 1863**
    Brooke journal, BP

On Saturday the 25th, went to Drewry's Bluff with Govs. Brown of Mississippi, Henry of Tenn. and several ladies. Visited the Richmond, the long gun had just been rebouched. Fired one cast iron shot, 12lbs charge, at the target. Struck point aimed at. The bouche will I think answer, there is a spare one.

It may be easily removed and replaced. Today an impression was brought up. The bouche is even with surface of chamber, except on forward side where it projects very little on the slope. No wear yet visible. Conversed with Miss Phillips on the way up. Genl. [William H.] Whiting at Wilmington has applied for the Raleigh's battery until she shall be ready to receive it. Will prob[ably]—send two 6.4-in rifles to him this week. Obtained several ounces of platinum from the North through Major Norris of Signal Corps.

■ **30 April 1863**

An act to authorize the appointment of a chief constructor in the navy, *Register of the Navy of the Confederate States to January, 1864*

President authorized to appoint by, and with the advice and consent of the Senate, one Chief Constructor in the Navy, whose compensation shall be three thousand dollars per annum, and who shall perform such duties as may be directed by the Secretary of the Navy [p. 78].[25]

■ **May [1863]**

Adm. Franklin Buchanan to Brooke, chief of ordnance and hydrography, Franklin Buchanan Letter Book, 1862–63, Southern Historical Collection, University of North Carolina at Chapel Hill,

Your letter of the 21st ulti has been received. I have been informed by the Ordnance Officer of the Army here that he can accomodate us by stowing in their magazine 16,000 pounds of powder. I hope the Battery for the "Tennessee" will be ready in the course of a month or six weeks, she will be ready about that time, she will carry 10 heavy guns. Please inform me what the Battery is to be and order the carriages.

■ **23 May 1863**

Col. Alfred Rhett, Headquarters, First Regiment, South Carolina Artillery, Fort Sumter, South Carolina, to Lt. N. H. Van Zandt, naval ordnance officer, Charleston, South Carolina (copy), BP

I have the honor to inform you, that in the engagement of the 7th April, two Brooke Guns, one of the Navy pattern, the other the Army Gun were used in Fort Sumpter [Sumter].

Charge in each gun was 13 pounds of powder (9 large grained, 4–ordinary cannon powder). Projectile—the wrought Iron Brooke bolt-weight, a little less than 120 pounds. Both guns were mounted on the 10 in: Col. wooden carriage.

Forty two shots were fired from one and forty four from the other. Thirteen pounds is the highest charge the recoil of the Gun will admit with safety upon these carriages.

The effect of these was decidedly greater upon the Iron Clads than any other we had, as seen with good glasses during the engagement and by observation on the wreck of the Keokuk.—

Six 42Pdrs. rifled and banded were used. Charge—7 pounds—Weight of square headed cast iron bolt—ninety-odd pounds.

■ 2 June 1863

Catesby ap R. Jones, Selma, Alabama, to Brooke, BP

I wrote you a long letter yesterday immediately after assuming command, giving you some idea of matters as they presented themselves to me, and I am sorry to say they do not improve on acquaintance—you may judge how the establishment has been conducted from the rolling mill, the excavation for the foundation for rollers is nearly completed, to my amazement I find that the stone for the foundation has not yet been ordered, it will have to be quarried and I send a special agent to morrow to attend to it. I order a certain roof to be completed and find the timber is not yet ordered. . . . Capt. Minor said there was a first rate man we could get for master blacksmith, we have no one here that will answer. . . . We have but one lathe that can be made to answer for turning of guns, can we get a suitable lathe? . . . Capt. [Ebenezer] Farrand is doing mischief: he has a small shop where a few men employed in punching and preparing iron for gun boats, which you are aware does not require much mechanical skill, yet he pays a dollar more than either the army or navy, creating dissatisfaction among our men. [Charles C.] Simmes [Simms] remonstrated with him, but without effect, and S[imms] reports that some of his best men have left him to day. Cannot Capt. F be directed to conform to the usual rates? I am waiting for the instructions—Semmes [Simms] is of great assistance to me. We are in great want of pattern makers and machinists, if everything else were ready, we could not turn out much work.[26]

■ ca. 5 June 1863

Brooke journal, BP

On the night of [blank] about 2 a.m. the Crenshaw Woolen factory took fire and was destroyed. It was situated within the Tredegar enclosure and the fire spreading consumed the pattern shop, blacksmiths shop, boring mill, and molding sheds. The old foundry was damaged but the new one escaped. The machine shop was entirely destroyed.[27] The two treble banded 7-in. rifles in process of construction were in the latter but fortunately were not much heated as but little burning wood fell upon them. As soon as practicable water was thrown in their vicinity but not upon them. The bands of one opened a little at the joints, about $1/32$ part of an inch or $1/30$; the other was scarcely affected. Unfortunately patterns of 7-in and double banded X-In. were burned, the latter was but just finished and would have been placed in the foundry the next day.

The patterns are now being made chiefly at our own shop under Minor's supervision. He is also getting up a rifling machine. The Tredegar is being rebuilt and I am satisfied that in the end the fire will prove to have been a benefit to the Government, particularly if the war continues several years, as the works will be enlarged and a stimulus has been applied to the proprietors and employees. Since the fire, two 6.4-in rifles double banded have been cast. They are still in the pit. This evening I saw Genl. [Joseph] Anderson at the works and proposed to him that as his works could not bore and finish guns as rapidly as they were cast, it would be well for Sampson & Pae to set up a boring mill and assist. He agreed to this and sent for his superintendent, Mr. Campbell, who will see Mesrs. Sampson & Pae. But the General seems disposed to remove the difficulty by increasing his boring mill and adding to his power to finish. The prospects now are that we shall rapidly furnish guns as soon as a little more preparation is made. My idea is to make guns as rapidly as possible [and] to employ every means to that end. My office is getting on very well [and] I hope soon to have all that we require in the way of munitions of war and of the best quality. Lizzie and Anna went up to Lexington, leaving Richmond on the 1st ins. I recd. a letter from her today from Lynchburg. There is great anxiety to hear of Johnson's [Joseph E. Johnston] movements against Grant who is besieging Vicksburg.

■ 6 June 1863
Catesby ap R. Jones, Selma, Alabama, to Brooke, BP

I cannot find out that <u>any work of any kind was done for the Navy</u> whilst it was <u>in the hands of the Army</u>. It is hard however that the workmen should remain so long unpaid, and as it makes them discontented, I think it would be well if we paid them, tho I have told them that I had nothing to do with what occurred prior to the 1st of June. We are now doing a good deal of work for the army. . . .

We are in urgent need of steel for tools. I sent a mem. of sizes we want now, can you send us a supply of assorted sizes. What is to be the official name of these works—they are something more than naval ordnance works. We can do nothing with the gun pit till we have the cement. We want stone masons and cutters, none are to be had here. . . . I should like to have two or three of them. . . .

Where can be get machinists?—our force should be doubled. . . .

I have so much to do at the works that I don't know where to begin.

■ 11 June 1863
Catesby ap R. Jones, Selma, Alabama, to Brooke, BP

The more I learn of this establishment the more I am amazed at the manner it was conducted and I may say constructed. I hope you will see that the Civil Engineer for us is a competent and skilful person, if he is not, I would rather be without one. The Civil Engineer and Steam Engineer are both much wanted now. . . .

The men have asked for an increase of wages to put them on an equality with those employed by Capt. Farrand.

■ **20 June 1863**

Lizzie Brooke, Lexington, to Anna M. Brooke (to be opened at Lizzie's death), BP

You are older now than you were when I wrote my first letter to you in case I died so I will add some things which you can now understand, that is about a step mother. Yr mother never wishes you to think a step mother c'ld love you like y'r own own Mother but if it pleased God to take yr own Mother away & place another one in her stead, you ought always to be obedient gentle & submissive to her. In that way you would make her love you & yr Father would be pleased yr own Mother in Heaven would be pleased because you would follow the Bible honor y'r "Father & Mother" she would not have you forget y'r own dear Mother who loves you so much. Yet 'twould not be forgetting her but remembering what she taught you from the Bible to obey all who are over you to love y'r Father & follow all that is good Pray to God, obey all who are over you & you will meet yr Mother in Heaven is her sincere prayer for her own devotedly loved child—as you render obedience to God & yr Father you will always please me—Let yr Bible be y'r guide & pray always.

■ **22 June 1863**

Catesby ap R. Jones, Selma, Alabama, to Brooke, BP

My letter to the Secretary will have informed you that I had to raise the pay of our men, of course the army must follow. I hope Capt. Farrand will be directed not to raise wages without consulting before he does it, its too late to consult after. Col. [George W.] Rains informed me that the Governor of Georgia had raised the pay to six dollars in the workshops of that state. . . . The books and instruments Mr Jackson refers to could be transfered [*sic*] to the works, where he could have access to them, we need books very much. . . .

From what I hear the loss of the Chattahoochee and the conduct afterwards should be inquired into.

■ **25 June 1863**

Catesby ap R. Jones, Selma, Alabama, to Brooke, BP

With reference to details, Gen. Rains informed me there would be no difficulty if application were made to Gen. [Samuel] Cooper, not to the Secry. of War. I would advise that you see Gen. C– yourself.[28]

If you can arrange about the M. Master and Commisary [*sic*], I wish you would. Why could not they be directed to comply with my requisitions as they do with those of the Army. A separate [*sic*] account would be kept for the Navy. Such matters are very troublesome and annoying and what is worse, prevent my attending to more important duties. If you know any good mechanics in the Army I wish you would have them detailed.

■ **29 June 1863**
Catesby ap R. Jones, Selma, Alabama, to Brooke, BP

Yours of the 23r was received this morning—We are making reamers faced with steel. I will send you a list of machinery as soon as made.

A Paymaster is very important to us. I am now convinced we lost in one bill last week several hundred dollars which we would not have done had there been a Paymaster attending to the Foundry. He leaves to morrow for Mobile to make payments, why could not one of the numerous Paymasters there make these payments on the order of Capt. Farrand. I have no objection to Paym Dhiel, it is only that his necessary absence embarrases [*sic*] us. I understand Farrand intends applying for Simms to assist him in his duties. I wish you would see that he is not detached, as it would be impossible for me to attend properly to the duty. If necessary (tho—I do not wish it) we could have charge of all that Farrand has here, preparing the plates for the Tennessee and overlook [oversee?] the contractors who are building the gun boat, under the supervision of Capt. F. One great advantage would be that there would be one naval establishment here, now there are two separate [*sic*] organizations.

■ **30 June 1863**
Brooke journal, BP

Vicksburg still besieged. Johnston very quiet. He is said to have about 40,000 men. I fear that unless he speedily moves, Vicksburg will fall. This evening we hear by Petersburg that Federal papers brought in flag of truce boat state our army to leave occupied Harrisburg, the capital of Pennsylvania, and York. The city of Richmond is ready to meet any attempt of the enemy to divert Lee's attention. There are some 15 or 20,000 Yankees reported in this vicinity. On the 23d a daughter was added to my family. All well when last heard from.[29] A few days ago Capt. Webb attacked two [?] monitors in Warsaw sound, lost his ship by getting aground. She was entirely too weak to contend with the enemy, only 4 inches of iron and four rifles two 6.4's & two VII—in single banded. The XV-in shell of the enemy crushed in her shield at the point struck.[30] The weather has been very damp and disagreeable for the past week.

■ **8 July 1863**

Brooke journal, BP

Today Richmond has suffered quite a revulsion: first we have news of glorious victories by Lee. Now it said that he falls back heavily pressed by the enemy to Hagerstown from Gettysburg where tremendous battles were fought, that the Potomac is unfordable, that his pontoon bridge has been destroyed, etc. Then it is reported that Vicksburg has fallen. The Secretary of War thinks our affairs in disastrous condition. Well, I d'ont. Lee was necessarily obliged to fall back and I suppose he anticipated it. It is not to be supposed that his Army could permanently occupy Pennsylvania. We have nothing official from Lee's Army.[31]

■ **11 July 1863**

Diary of Matthew F. Maury, 27 April–29 December 1863, Matthew F. Maury Papers, LC

Brooke–Jno. M.–Pichon's type and account of Fr. guns–rifles & smooth bores. [Maury had just recently returned from Paris and apparently told Brooke what he had learned about French ordnance.]

■ **22 July 1863**

Brooke journal, BP

We have had an unusual quantity of rain this month but today the weather has been remarkably fine. I have recently had a barometer repaired and hung up in my room. It is now high and I hope will continue so. Lee's Army fell back from Gettysburg slowly and in good order with large captures, the enemy too severely beaten to follow. Lee has recrossed the Potomac, saving everything. But the glory of the campaign can not compensate the family of Genl. Richard Garnett who fell in the assault by Picketts Division on the fortified heights held by the enemy at Gettysburg.[32] That assault has few parallels. Vicksburg has surrendered, and Genl. Johnson [Johnston] falling back has a fine opportunity for the exercise of his peculiar talent. Charleston is sorely pressed. [John A.] Dahlgren of ordnance fame commands the forces afloat, and with his Coast Survey Charts and the aid of a few angles and his tables of ranges, shells fort Wagner on Morris Island while the inland forces endeavor to approach, and make frequent assaults with great loss. We are deficient in guns and there is a want of knowledge and skill on the part of our artillerists to respond to this long range firing. A double banded 7-in [rifle] started from here Monday week is there now, but the gun boats could not leave their positions to exchange a rifled 42 pdr for it. The gun would have been sent long ago but the employees of the works were called off to the environs. It was delayed and then car could not procured. Two double banded 6.4-in rifles left on Sunday evening. I advised the

Secretary to send them six weeks ago. The pattern of X-in double banded smooth bore is ready with exception of pattern of breech. The new foundry is in operation. I am hurrying it up as rapidly as possible, am anxious to get the X & X1-inch double banded guns finished. Mr. Elliot Lacey is now employed determining gravity of iron etc., DeBree being sick.[33] I fear Mr. Volcks services will soon be lost to us as he wishes to return to Europe, having lost his mother. With the exception of the fabrication of cannon the ordnance Dept. is doing well. The Tredegar boring mill is not working well. But I trust it soon will be. Our Selma foundry hangs fire, being a joint affair with the Army. The gun pit is a failure so far. Charlotte and Atlanta are doing well. I must be getting out some solid shot for X & X1-in smooth bores.

- **30 July 1863**
  Deed of Col. William Garnett, BP

Know all men, by these presents, that I William Garnett, of the town of Lexington, in the county of Rockbridge, do hereby, give to my Grand-daughter, Anna Maria Brooke, my woman Nancy Todd, (who was her nurse), for, and in consideration, of the love and affection I bear her; and for the further consideration, of one Dollar to me in hand paid, before the signing and sealing of these presents, the receipt whereof, is hereby acknowledged, and I do hereby warrant and defend the title of the said Nancy Todd, to my Grand-daughter aforesaid, against the claim or claims, of all persons whatsoever. In testimony whereof, I have signed my name, and affixed my seal, this 30th day of July 1863.
  Admitted to record before C. Chapin, County Clerk on July 30, 1863.

- **31 July 1863**
  Capt. John C. Mitchell, Commanding Artillery, Fort Johnson, James Island, South Carolina, to Capt. W. F. Nance, Acting Adjutant General First Military District, Headquarters, Charleston, South Carolina (copy), BP

Burst at Battery Simpkins, James Island, S.C. on July 26, 1863 a 6.4 inch Brooke double banded rifle gun loaded with 12 lbs. of powder and bolts. It had been fired 56 times. One cannoneer was killed and three were wounded.
  [Mitchell states:] "I was myself present when this gun was first fired from my Battery. I then directed that the cartridge should be always particularly well rammed down, because the bag was shaped like those of the Dahlgren guns, & did not properly fit the bottom of the bore; also that each ball, before being placed in the muzzle, should be carefully wiped off & greased. Every time I was at Battery during the day I myself saw that these directions were properly complied with; and, after a careful investigation since made, I have every reason to believe that they were in no case neglected."

Mitchell's explanation is "that the amount of metal in the breech was not enough, considered relatively to the strength of the bands & the large charge of powder (12 lbs.)—and that the upper band ought to have extended back as far as the lower one."

Brooke stated the accident was caused by the cartridge being well rammed down as directed by Mitchell. "This was precisely what ought not to have been done, for the cartridge was designed to leave air space. It was in contact when pushed home to the bottom of vent."

■ **31 July 1863**
   Brooke journal, BP

Today fired the 2nd treble banded VII-in gun, at Tredegar. First, 17 lb. charge, cast bolt ratchet sabot 120lbs. 2nd, 20lbs powder and 120lbs bolt as before. The powder was Nos. 8 & 9, half of each. Separate large grain at bottom of cartridges. The gun shot beautifully, the report extraordinarily loud. Shall send the gun and carriage to Charleston for Iron Clad Charleston. Had some correspondence with Genl. [Joseph] Anderson of Tredegar in relation to casting guns in longitudinal flasks. The Army burst one of my guns, a 6.4 of 9000lbs with 2nd tier of bands applied at Charleston: 60 rounds, 8° elevation, 12lb charges, enough to burst it. One half the breech came out, one band blew off interior after one, the fracture as I had predicted from castings at the Tredegar. Two double banded VII-inch rifles sent for Palmetto State & Chicora could not be taken on board. Two 6.4 double banded never sent to Charleston will with exception of one double banded VII-in be mounted on the Charleston.

■ **3 August 1863**
   Brooke, Office of Ordnance and Hydrography, Richmond, to Gen. Pierre G.
   T. Beauregard, commanding at Charleston, South Carolina (copy), BP

As the Navy Rifles are being used by the Army to some extent, I desire to call your attention to several points, which have an important bearing upon the character of the results to be obtained.

The treble banded and other heavy Navy Rifles were designed to be used against Iron-Clads at effective ranges which are attained at lower elevations than the ports alluded to in your telegram admit of. The long range of the rifle is inseparable from the power of penetration, but the results of distant firing are generally so meagre, that this feature was considered valuable only as enabling the Artillerist to throw an occasional shell at some distant object, perhaps a wooden vessel. The contest between ships are generally decided by few shot. It is not possible with the materials at our disposal to make rifles capable of enduring many rounds with such charges as are required to penetrate armour. For this reason it is anticipated, that the higher charges will only be employed when the prospect of hitting is good and the effect would be decisive. The superior power of penetration which is given by high charges compares more favorably with that of inferior charges as the distance of the object decreases. If then these guns are to be used for siege purposes or continued firing at long ranges, it will not be expedient to use such charges as are employed on board ship, as was the case with a 6.4-inch rifle, which burst recently in a land battery at Charleston.

This gun, I am informed, burst at the 60th round, charge 12 lb. elevation 8°; this, the powder being good, would give a range of about 3,400 yds; this same gun at an elevation of about 9½° would have obtained the same range with a charge of 8lbs, and would in all probability have stood many more rounds, although weak. Twelve pounds is the maximum charge for long ranges with shell, that is in ports which admit of but limited elevation. The range in that case is increased at the expense of strains greater than would result from the increased elevation and smaller charges, could such elevation be obtained, but it was never contemplated to so fire with high charges more than a few rounds. With low charges, their endurance will be augmented, but the whole strength of the gun is required to support the charges upon which we rely to disable an iron-clad opponent. A moment's reflection enables us to appreciate the enormous strain, to which a rifle without windage, its projectile three times as heavy as a round shot is subjected, when fired with a charge nearly one-half greater, than is considered safe in a smooth bore of the same calibre.

If then they be used as was the 6.4-inch alluded to, or even with lower charges at similar elevations, it is not to be expected, that they will be found efficient, should occasion arise for their employment for the purpose for which they were designed. The treble-banded gun with a wrought iron bolt and 20 lbs charge will penetrate a turret eight or nine inches thick, at four or five hundred yards, perhaps at greater distances. In such case, one might reasonably anticipate disabling the vessel.

The treble banded gun although vastly stronger than the other rifles is proportionally strained by the very high charges which it is proposed to use at the decisive moment, when the distance warrants accuracy and penetration, viz: 20 lbs with wrought iron ball of 120lbs. It is not possible with our limited means of experiment to say what number of rounds with such charges may be fired; we only know, that the probability is largely in favor of disabling the enemy, if engaged as proposed, before the gun yields. In this matter we have no choice. We take the risk or decline the combat. The enemy labors under the same disadvantages. A XV inch smooth bore gun burst recently on board the iron clad "Lehigh," the Blakely gun and other Rifles at Vicksburg have failed in continued firing with high charge—Nor does it appear that the guns of Armstrong, Whitworth and others with all the means at the command of their constructors have done more than prove that under favorable conditions, rifles have sufficient endurance to permit the disabling of iron clads of which the armament is arranged as on board the Monitor. To diminish the excessive strain to which guns are subjected, before the inertia of the projectile is overcome, and yet not lose velocity, the Naval Ord. Officers have been instructed to use two sizes of powder in the cartridges of rifles, the large grain at the bottom, the small next to the projectile, not mixed as has been proposed. I do not know that this plan of division has been adopted in the Army, but as I mentioned it some months ago to Col. Gorgas, who approved the idea it is possible. Lt. Van Zandt, Naval Ord. Officer at Charleston will be instructed to prepare such cartridges for the treble banded gun, which I trust may have at least one fair shot at a Monitor.

Some time ago I sent you by one of your aides a diagram calculated to facilitate the pointing of guns, which I trust safely reached its destination.

In addition to the ammunition usually supplied there will be with this gun a few shrapnel with the necessary fuzes from 1 to 15 sec'ds, and McEvoys "Igniter" a table of ranges, time of flight etc. will be furnished with them.

Being the first of the kind, it would afford me much pleasure to have their action carefully observed. I have been induced to offer these remarks by the consideration, that your time must necessarily be occupied by important matters and that you would be pleased to receive such observations as my attention to this particular subject might enable me to make.

On August 1st Beauregard had telegraphed asking what disposition to make of a treble banded and other navy rifles.

■ **4 August 1863**
Lt. Robert D. Minor, superintendent, Naval Ordnance Works, Richmond, Virginia, to Brooke, BP

The VII inch treble banded Brooke rifle, of 20,950 lbs. no. 33 was proved and inspected on the 31st ultimo at the proving ground near the Tredegar Works.

The gun was mounted on an Army carriage and chassis, at a distance of rather more than a hundred yards from the target, which was an old one constructed of eighteen (18) inches of oak, with twelve (12) feet of earth backing.

The first charge was with seventeen (17) pounds of Navy powder, Nos, 8 & 9, and a cast iron bolt of 120½ lbs. weight with ratchet sabot. The target was penetrated at an uninjured part, the bolt coming out, through twelve (12) feet of earth, and showing that it had taken the rifle motion well. The gun was uninjured. The next charge was with twenty (20) pounds of Navy powder, Nos. 8 & 9, and a projectile similar in all respects to the one used at the first discharge. The target was penetrated at an injured part, the bolt coming out point first through twenty (20) feet of earth. The gun was uninjured, bands, straps, and trunnions all being in good order and condition.

The gun was subsequently marked according to the established regulations, and forwarded in charge of a special agent to Charleston South Carolina, to be placed on board the U.S. Steamer "Charleston."

■ **10 August 1863**
   Brooke, Richmond, to Lizzie, Lexington, BP

Yours of the 17th ins was recd. this morning. That is the most unchangeable baby I ever heard of. "Always about the same." I hope Charlotte arrived safely. We have no news, the heat intense 94° in this room shady side too. . . .

I feel much enervated by this heat—used up—am tired of work, office, and guns. Bothered with communications etc. I wish I could go to some quiet place to rest with you a little while and recover some elasticity of spirit. . . . By the way I now keep Toup's Mary waiting at meals always in time. . . . Toups & his Pa got off on Whigs & democrats today. I do hope you have less heat in Lexington. Cool dry weather would cure the baby entirely I think. You dont know what a heap of work I do. If you could see the office letter book you might form an idea I will show it you one of these days. . . . Kiss Lou & Hanna. [Lizzie seems always to have gone to Lexington when a baby was expected and stayed for some time after its arrival.]

■ **10 August 1863**
   Diary of General Josiah Gorgas, 58–59

The President seems determined to respect the opinions of no one; and has, I fear, little appreciation of services rendered, unless the party enjoys his good opinion. He seems to be an indifferent judge of men, and is guided more by prejudice than by sound discriminating judgment. I have been surprised to hear his condemnation of men and measures—in the field and in the Cabinet—yet apparently without any idea that it was for him to correct them. He sneers continually at Mr. Mallory and his navy, and is at no pains to conceal his opinions before that secretary. Yet he never controls him in any respect; nor will he yield to the opinion of the country which has long since pointed to a change in that branch of service.

■ **14 August 1863**
   George W. Gift, CSS *Gaines*, Grants Pass, Mobile Bay, to Miss Ellen Augusta Shackleford, Ellen Shackleford Gift Collection, Southern Historical Collection, University of North Carolina at Chapel Hill

With your letter came several others. One from Commander Brooke, (who makes the rifle guns) in answer to a note I addressed to him relative to the bursting of two of his guns at Vicksburg. He explained the cause from the facts furnished by me and ended his letter by making a request to hear from me again upon any subject. I answered by giving him a minute and detailed description of the submarine boat that we sent to Charleston, argued the feasibility of the invention and predicted success. I also wrote him about a subject that I will not mention, inasmuch as it is a "scheme," and I am not fortunate in getting my views adopted now-a-days, so if I am disappointed Brooke and I alone shall know it.[34]

■ 3 September 1863
Diary of General Josiah Gorgas, 60

The shelling at Charleston still goes on, with no marked effect. After an examination of the present condition of Fort Sumter, engineers have decided that the Fort can be held, and it is still held. The probability is that the monitors will make their first attempt to run by during the night. We are throwing projectiles at the rate of about twenty-five tons per day; one thousand rounds. The large imported gun [Blakely] 12 ¾ inches is probably now in position. The ball or bolt weighs 670 pounds; the gun 22 tons; English.

■ 4 September 1863
Catesby ap R. Jones, Selma, Alabama, to Brooke, BP

The progress of the works has been as unsatisfactory to me as it has been to him [Secretary of the Navy Mallory]—and I have requested him to have me relieved if the force is not increased[.] I might be reconciled to our slow progress if I did not know that it could and should be different, and I would not regard the troubles and annoyances in conducting the works if there were any results. I would prefer active duty and hope some one will be sent here who will be more content than I am to move at a snails pace.

I have been disappointed with [George] Peacock, he had never cast a gun before coming here, has had no experience with air furnaces, and knows nothing about the treatment of metal, nor is he a judge of it whilst in person—of course this increases my troubles, he has made many failures, so that I have not yet been able to test the metal in small guns. The two VIIin promise well, but there are a thousand things to be done before we can be in full operation. I have not been able to test more than one a week—sometimes the furnaces, sometimes the castings, yesterday the reservoir gave way and the metal did not by several feet fill the mould. . . . I know very well that you assist us as much as possible.

■ **7 September 1863**

N. H. Van Zandt, Charleston, South Carolina, to Brooke, BP

By yesterday's mail I sent you a drawing of the big Blakely Rifle, and as soon as the Working drawing, giving dimensions, is completed that will be sent also. If you can get off from your duties for a few days I would advise you to come and examine this monster gun which throws a bolt weighing 655 pounds. I am in the receipt of your last letter dated from, I forget where, informing me of the illness of one of your children.

■ **11 September 1863**

James H. Rochelle, CS Receiving Ship *Indian Chief*, Charleston, South Carolina, to Brooke, BP

The monster English gun burst this morning at the fourth discharge, the breech cracked in three places, the other one will doubtless do the same and the reason is evident—at one point there is only <u>six inches</u> of metal between the cartridge and the outer surface of the breech, now put thirty six pounds of powder in a gun with six inches of metal behind and a mass of iron weighing six hundred and fifty five pounds before it, ignite the charge and which will start the first, the six inches or the six hundred and fifty five pounds? Any one can answer the question.

■ **12 September 1863**

A. Frederick Volck, St. Georges, Bermuda, to Brooke, BP

I have always looked up to you as my truest friend I had south of the Potomac, and was not deceived. I fear though, that you greatly overrated my work, or my capability of performing that particular branch. What I did do under your direction was done with pleasure, and can look back with satisfaction at the hours spent in your office. I wish I cl'd. have done better than I did. After leaving Richmond and having safely arrived at Wilmington, I had to lay over 2 whole weeks in that horrible place. But we finally got away on the 5th inst, and laid at anchor off Ft Fisher until Saturday the 6th. Weighed anchor at 11½ p.m. and ran out past blockaders and by a glarring [*sic*] moon light. We cleared the coast in safety and had a most delightful trip during the whole time we were on board. . . . We made Bermuda lighthouse on the evening of the 8th. . . .

Our party consisted of Comdr Barron Lieut. [William] Whittle, Prof [Albert T.] Bledsoe and myself. . . . On Wednesday next we all leave direct for Liverpool, in the screw propeller Florida. My cotton has all arrived, and specie is plentyfull [*sic*].

- **13 September 1863**

  Diary of General Josiah Gorgas, 62

I am pained to hear of the bursting, on trial, of one of the two 600 pounder rifle Blakely guns just received from abroad. In fact the bursting is a sort of national calamity so much was expected of these guns. A triple banded rifle of the Brooke pattern, has also burst. It is more than difficult to make any of them endure anything like smooth bores.

- **ca. 14 September 1863**

  Comdr. John M. Brooke, chief of naval ordnance, to Secretary of the Navy Stephen R. Mallory (rough draft), BP

On inspection of a drawing of the Blakely Rifle burst at Charleston I am of opinion that the chamber was intended to be used as an air chamber to diminish the pressure in accordance with Manat's law pressures of gas are inversely as the volume. . . .

I therefore recommend that the remaining gun be so fired placing the cartridge wholly in front of the chamber and using No 11 navy powder.

Gorgas: What is the meaning of this?

Referred by the President to Col. Gorgas, endorsed by him as follows Capt Brookes suggestion is pertinent.[35]

- **14 September 1863**

  Brooke to Lt. N. H. Van Zandt, naval ordnance officer, Charleston, South Carolina (copy), BP

Your very interesting letter in regard to the large Blakely rifle, with enclosed drawing, has been received.

Upon examination of the drawing I am of opinion that the chamber was not intended to receive powder, but to serve as a gas chamber, the powder-cartridge—being placed at its mouth; as I have consequently suggested, that the gun be so fired, using N 11 Navy powder. I am aware of the popular opinion, that the existence of a space unoccupied by powder or other material in the rear of a projectile endangers the gun. This opinion is based upon the observed fact that guns frequently burst when the projectile is not home, which is attributed to a sudden resistance opposed to the expansion of larger volumes of gas than would have been formed had no space existed; but this is opposed to experiments made with powder in shells and other vessels, and we may attribute the bursting of guns, in the case alluded to, chiefly to the fact, that the great strain which occurs in starting the shot is thrown upon a part of the gun which is not so strong as that part immediately around the charge when in its proper place. The pressure of gases is inversely as their volumes.

Now the effect of the gas chamber of the Blakely gun would be, supposing its capacity equal to the space occupied by the cartridge, (bore between mouth of chamber and rear of projectile) about one half of what it would be if there were no gas chamber, the breech in that case being solid. On the other hand when the chamber is filled with powder we have the full strain due not only to the charge but to the additional quantity of powder used. If my supposition should prove correct, the remaining gun now at Wilmington may render good service.

It might be supposed that the gas chamber would involve great loss of propulsive power, but this cannot be, for the capacity of the gas chamber is very small as compared with the capacity of the whole bore into which the gas expands as the projectile moves. The strain which attends starting the shot, from a state of rest, is diminished, but not the propulsive power which acts continually in the bore, that, is not materially diminished.

I am the more convinced of the correctness of my supposition from the fact, that I have been considering the principle alluded to, without reference to the Blakely gun.

I have to thank you for the efforts you have made to furnish accurate information to this Office, and trust that the advantages to be derived from such labor will be illustrated by satisfactory results in this case.

■ **15 September 1863**
Catesby ap R. Jones, Selma, Alabama, to Brooke, BP

Our foundry is capable of turning out more work than will be required for Naval purposes and it will always give me pleasure to cast for the Army whenever we can. And as it is to the interest of the Army that we should have a large force of Moulders, it has occurred to me that they might assist in procuring them or at all events might inform you where they are to be had and have them detailed for these works. I have asked the Secry. to relieve me. . . . I would prefer active duty. . . . I hope to be authorized to built [*sic*] houses for the men, I had intended to deduct the rent from their pay. The officers should have quarters. Will not the Secry. allow the mechanics to be furnished with medicines as before; they actually refuse to purchase medicines for themselves, they say they cannot afford it; it certainly is a great tax. I understand a Doctor is ordered but unless he can give them medicine he will only be of half the service he might be. I am not satisfied with the iron, I hope it will improve now that we have control of it. One furnace is in operation, & the rolling mill ought to be shortly, the other furnace should be completed as soon as possible. The rolling mill is small, it cannot roll plates for gun boats, only manufactured iron.

What about a Blacksmith?—the boring of guns is delayed for want of tools.—What of the Master Blacksmith?—we want one badly.

■ **16 September 1863**

Acting Master Charles A. McEvoy, Richmond, to Brooke, BP

I beg leave to submit the following report of a trial of Bormann fuzes made on the 15th inst in compliance with your order.

The fuzes—eight in number—were made at the C. S. Naval Laboratory, Richmond, inserted in shell and fired from a 12 pdr Boat Howitzer.

Charge of powder used 1. lb.

The first four fuzes were cut at 3 seconds, two of which exploded in 3 seconds—one at 4 and the other at 4½, after leaving the gun.

The remaining four were cut—3 at 4, and the other at 5 seconds, all of which exploded in proper time.

The results might be considered very satisfactory from the fact that all the shells exploded, with the exception of 2, in proper time, and none failed to explode at some time, but in no instance prematurely. Yet I think it would be advisable to give them a further trial before making a large number of them.

■ **18 September 1863**

N. H. Van Zandt, Charleston, South Carolina, to Brooke, BP

I have <u>heard</u>, & I now believe it quite probable, that the Treble Banded Rifle was fired with 20 lbs of Rifle Powder.

Genl Ripley told Comm. Ingraham that he had no powder but large grained & that he used no other. His statement & this cartridge do not agree. . . .

It is provoking to have your guns damned by ignorant ordn officers who know not how to use them & I get vexed & my temper gets the better of my prudence.

As I stated today at the Hotel there is not a man in Charleston except myself,—not even Capt Ingraham,—who knows how your gun is constructed—but they all say the gun is strengthened with bands & the thickness of the base not increased. I rather astonished them today when I told them that the base in the thinnest part was two inches thicker than through the bands & that measured through the cascable it was fourteen (14) inches thicker—Am I not right? I refer especially to the double banded VII inch Rifle.

The drawing of the Blakely sent to you, & which I learned from your telegram was recd.—gave you all the information it was at that time possible to obtain nor do I expect that the exploring will add to my knowledge,—but I shall examine & see. I am glad you recd the tracing (?) & that you were glad to get it, for it cost me a great deal of time as well as personal annoyance. The Army are as jealous as they are ignorant of ordn subjects. I am trying to have an order given to burst open the cracked "Blakely" so as to "see into it" but I have little hopes of success.

Your suggestion, or opinion, with regard to the "Gas Chamber" has quite upset all their preconceived notions & I must confess that I made the most of it for the navy.

■ **20 September 1863**
   Col. Josiah Gorgas, chief of ordnance, to Gen. Pierre G. T. Beauregard, commanding, Charleston, South Carolina (extract copy), BP

The suggestions as to the probable uses of the <u>air space</u> or gas Chamber are due in the first place to Comd Brooke; and that the construction of the gun is founded on the date furnished by the experiments of Capt. [Thomas] Rodman is, from hypothesis; the views of Capt. Blakely being wholly unknown.

■ **26 September 1863**
   Franklin Buchanan, Naval Commandant's Office, Mobile, Alabama, to Brooke (unofficial), BP

When shall I have the guns for the Tennessee? she is ready to receive them. What is to be her armament? she can carry very heavy guns. Mr. McCorkle has informed me that he has recd. orders to make carriages for 7in rifles for her. The "Nashville" and "Tennessee" are progressing very well, particularly the latter, but for the delay in getting the iron from Selma her armour would nearly be completed, her hull, and I hope her Engine, will be completed before I receive her guns, the Genls. will not obey orders, when they receive them, to send me men, not one can I get from them. Both the "Nashville" and the "Tennessee" are fine vessels, superior to the old "Virginia," the "Nashville" has been ready for her <u>iron</u> for nearly a month, but not a <u>pound</u> have the contractors for her, my impression is they <u>were intended</u> to provide it, but took it for granted the Government would iron her, and this I think <u>now</u> will have to be done. The difficulty in getting transportation from Selma and other places on the rivers has delayed the work very much, the rascally blockade-running has deprived us of many of the best freight boats, nearly all have been captured, either going out or returning, lately a very valuable one has been captured with a full cargo for the Government. Write to me and give me the Navy news, what is Mr. Mallory doing with the Provisional Navy bill? I hope they will send me two first rate Captains for "Nashville" & "Tennessee" and give me Johnston or Bob Minor for my Fleet Captain. I want <u>working men</u> who can assist me, men who think more of their <u>duties</u> than of <u>any</u> <u>thing</u> <u>else</u>. I am attending to all kinds of duty, if I did not, we should be "astern of the lighter" in our preparations here.

Give my regards to Mr. Mallory, De Bree [*sic*], [Edward] Tidball, Mitchell, Col. [Richard?] Beale and all other friends.

[Braxton] Braggs victory is a glorious one as far as it goes, I hope to hear of a <u>final</u> defeat of [William] Rosecrans "ere long."[36]

■ **26 September 1863**
Catesby ap R. Jones, Selma, Alabama, to Brooke, BP

I am more troubled than ever from sickness & want of results. We have made many failures, not altogether [George] Peacock's fault, as we have very indifferent workmen. As I wrote this morning not a man from the Army yet.

We have not yet bored a gun, tho have several in the mill—We are reaming one of them.[37]

■ **30 September 1863**
Col. George W. Rains, Commanding Government Works, Augusta, Georgia, to Lt. Col. Joseph A. Yates, First South Carolina Artillery, Charleston, South Carolina (copy), BP

I have just received a telegram from Genl. Beauregard saying that the remaining large Blakely gun by direction of Col. Gorgas will be subjected to trial under my direction, but that if I cannot come down to attend to the matter, he will turn it over to you and major [William S.] Bassinger [Basinger], as the other members of the Board. I have replied to the Telegram saying that I cannot spare the time at this period to return to Charleston, neither is it necessary, since you gentlemen can fully attend to the matter as well as myself.

You will perceive by the report that I recommend that a powder be manufactured expressly for this gun, having grains of one inch in diameter. I would suggest on the trial that, the charges commence at 30 lbs of this large grain powder, which I will send you, and gradually increase to 50 lbs. or 55 lbs; the latter weight of charge not to be used however if a sufficient velocity be obtained with the smaller weight. . . . . He suggests starting with 30 lbs. powder and a shell projectile at the horizontal, then at 2°, 5°, 10°, 25°. The test to be repeated with 35 lbs., etc. at each firing the gun would be carefully observed. When the shell had been fired the same process should be repeated for bolts, except the range should not be raised beyond 10°. The range should be accurately observed by some means such as a line of floats put at set distances.

■ **2 October 1863**

Lt. N. H. Van Zandt, naval ordnance officer, Charleston, South Carolina, to Brooke (telegram, Southern Telegraph Company), BP

Blakely Gun fired as you suggested with reference to gas chamber charge fifty five pounds. No. Eleven Navy powder & one shell, success perfect will write. . . .

Endorsed: Respty returned by direction of the President to the Navy Deptmt

Burton H. Harrison
Private Secty
Oct:5.63

■ **5 October 1863**

Lt. N. H. Van Zandt, naval ordnance officer, Charleston, South Carolina, to Brooke, Richmond, BP

Yesterday the Big Blakely 12.75 Rifle was fired six times as follows:

1st charge 30 lbs. Army Columbiad	1 shell
2nd charge 35 lbs. Army Columbiad	1 shell
3rd charge 40 lbs. No. 11 Navy	1 shell
4th charge 45 lbs. No. 11 Navy	1 shell
5th charge 50 lbs. No. 11 Navy	1 shell
6th charge 55 lbs. No. 11 Navy	1 shell

Ricochet one mile with 50 lbs. Elevation 2°. Fired from R. R. Flat upon which it was lashed.

Gun examined after every fire no strain discovered.

The charge was placed between the "Gas Chamber" & base of shell. Shell warbled very much—but did not tumble—Projectiles did not fit—Great trouble in loading with shell in consequence of shell not fitting—Your suggestion is quite "a feather in your cap"—accept my congratulations.

The Columbiad powder is mixed,—containing all the sizes from No. 11 Navy to fine Mortar.

■ **7 October 1863**

Catesby ap R. Jones, Selma, Alabama, to Brooke, BP

Yours of the 2nd is just received. I am glad you have made the change in the gun. I think it will increase the endurance. I should prefer the chamber to have been advanced rather more. Send the drawing as soon as you can that we may conform to the change.

A rumour here prevails, more direct than usual from Richmond, that Simms and I are to be ordered abroad and that Capt. Minor is to come here. Please let me know what foundation there is for it. Of course we could not be better pleased, and the orders cannot come too soon for us. We would like to know if there is any probability of it and if not of Minors coming.[38]

■ **21 October 1863**
   Adm. Franklin Buchanan to Secretary of the Navy Stephen R. Mallory, Franklin Buchanan Letter Book, 1862–63, Southern Historical Collection, University of North Carolina at Chapel Hill

The "Tennessee" is progressing fast and will soon be ready for her guns. As there are none prepared for her, I respectfully suggest taking the guns from the two Floating Batteries built here. These four heavy guns with the 7 in. Brookes, which I loaned some time since to the Army until it was required, will give her a good Battery, and as she will carry only six guns, one more probably could be sent from Richmond, if not, I can procure from the Army a 32 pounder.

I have all the ammunition and equipment for the guns I speak of and as other guns are cast they could be sent here to be placed in the iron-clad batteries.

The four guns in the Floating Batteries are, one (1) 9 in. Dahlgren, one (1) 7 in. Brooke rife, two (2) 6.4 Brooke rifles double banded.

■ **23 November 1863**
   Acting Master Charles A. McEvoy, Richmond, Virginia, to Brooke, BP

In compliance with your order I proceeded on the 21st inst to the C.S. Steamer Richmond lying in James River, off Drewry's Bluff, for the purpose of firing four shots from one of her VIIin guns.

The object of the experiment was to test a new sabot constructed from a drawing dated Oct 29th 1863.

The projectiles fired were unloaded shells, having their fuze apertures stopped with wood. A target five feet square was erected on the bank of the river at an estimated distance of 860 yds from the ship.

The charge used was 12 lbs of No 8 powder.

The gun in every instance was aimed by Capt. R. B. Pegram of the "Richmond."

The first shot hit the bank at the right edge of the target, and on a line with the bull's eye.

Two pieces of the sabot were noticed to fly from this shot and fall in the water about 300 yds from the ship.

The second shot hit the target near the center almost entirely demolishing it. No pieces were seen to fly from this shot.

A piece of the demolished target was found, about 2 feet wide by 5 feet in length and put up as a target.

The third shot struck the target and buried it in the bank. Two pieces of the sabot were seen to fly from this sabot and strike the water about 400 yds from the ship.

The fourth shot was fired into the bank at the site of the last target. No pieces were seen to fly from this shot.

After the firing three of the shot, with their sabots entirely gone, were recovered from the bank, also two pieces of sabots.

As regards rotation and the direct flight of the projectile, the sabot seems to be all that can be desired.

■ **24 November 1863**

Brooke to Lt. Col. A[lfred] L. Rives, in charge of Engineer Bureau, Richmond, BP

It is extremely desirable that an experimental battery should be erected at some convenient point on James River commanding a tolerable range, for the purpose of ascertaining correctly the ranges etc. of Naval guns. It is probable that a suitable site could be found in the vicinity of Chapins [Chaffin's] Bluff—the guns, one rifle and one smooth bore, to be mounted about nine feet above the water—Although such a position would not be favorable in case of attack by the enemy's vessels, the guns might render some service if protected by suitable works.

Will you do me the favor to cause an examination of the locality to be made by an Officer of Engineers, and if a suitable site be found, render such aid as may be necessary in establishing the battery?

2nd End. by Col. W. H. Stevens, Engineers, dated Nov. 29, 1863, states: "My force is so depleted by Expiration of impressment that I cannot now furnish the labor necessary. As soon as the new impressment if filled I shall take pleasure in assisting Comdr. Brooke."

■ **25 November 1863**

Brooke, chief of ordnance and hydrography, to Secretary of the Navy Stephen R. Mallory, *Official Records, Navy*, 2d series, II p. 547–52, [Report is on operations since January 1863 under Comdr. George Minor's direction]

Ordnance workshops have been established at Charlotte, N.C., Atlanta, Ga., Selma, Ala., and at Richmond, and in addition, private shops were employed in the manufacture (in most instances under the supervision of naval officers) of ordnance, gun carriages, projectiles, etc.

[Brooke wanted all major items and most minor items pertaining to armament of vessels to be produced by naval establishments in order to ensure "uniformity of construction and excellence of workmanship."]

In consequence of the judicious distribution of these establishments all within convenient distance of each other and of points to be supplied, the mineral and other resources of different sections of the country are equally drawn upon, and transportation is divided among the various railroads.

To obtain increased security . . . the various establishments have been, so far as practicable and consistent with economy rendered independent of each other. . . .

Under the command of Commander Page the works at Charlotte have been improved by the addition of machinery manufactured there, adapted to the construction of marine engines and other heavy work.

[The Charlotte] laboratory continues in successful operation, although some difficulty is experienced in procuring certain materials.

The Ordnance works at Atlanta, under the superintendence of Lieutenant D. P. McCorkle, have been actively engaged in the manufacture of projectiles and various articles of equipment required for the vessels at Mobile and other points. A large number of projectiles have been supplied the Army of the West from these shops.

The Ordnance works at Richmond, organized and put in operation by Lieutenant R. D. Minor and of which he was in command until the 1st October 1863 when he was relieved by Lieutenant A. [M.] de Bree [sic], have rendered important service. Heavy guns were rifled and handed them. . . . A large number of gun carriages, projectiles, and ordnance stores of all kinds have been made.

At Charleston, gun carriages, projectiles, etc. have been manufactured under the supervision of Lieutenant Van Zandt, and this office is indebted to his exertions for much information of importance, relating to observed effects of service upon guns of comparatively novel patterns. [The demand for guns was so great that the Ordnance Officer did not have time to conduct experiments.]

The cannon foundry and rolling mill in process of construction at Selma, of which joint purchase was made by the Army and Navy . . . has been wholly transferred to the Navy. Under the superintendence of Commander Catesby ap R. Jones, assisted by lieutenant Simms, very considerable progress has been made toward the completion of these works. . . .

But to reap the full benefit of the labor thus far expended in obtaining this important object it is essential that the force now employed be increased. Skilled labor can only be obtained by detailing mechanics from the Army. . . .

The deficiency of heavy ordnance has been severely felt during this war. The timely addition of a sufficient number of heavy guns would render our ports invulnerable to the attacks of the enemy's fleets, whether ironclad or not. I therefore earnestly urge the adoption of measures which shall be more effective than those now employed in increasing the force at Selma.

The powder works at Columbia, S.C., under the superintendence of Mr. P. B. [T. Baudery] Garesché have been conducted with singular skill and with commensurate results.

Heretofore all heavy guns have been made at the Tredegar Works in this City, and until recently the Army also was entirely dependent on that establishment for guns suitable for coast defense. In consequence of the difficulty of procuring iron during the past winter and the occurrence of a destructive fire just as the iron was obtained in the spring, the manufacture of guns was so far suspended that during an interval of five months none was made. But these works are again in operation, and with the facilities afforded by the application of additional power the completion of a new foundry and boring mill, the number of guns produced in an equal interval will be double what it was before the fire, and they will be generally of greater power and caliber.

[Until he relieved Minor, DeBree served as assistant inspector of ordnance at Tredegar.]

A record has been kept of the character of metal in individual guns as determined by tests of tensile strength and density and the appearance of fracture. The samples are carefully preserved for purposes of comparison. In perfecting and applying this system I have been assisted by Lieutenant DeBree and Mr. Elliott Lacey. Mr. Lacey now performs the duties of inspector and renders valuable assistance in making such computations and mathematical investigations as are required in connection with the operations of this office.

The establishment of the Mining and Niter Bureau has proved eminently advantageous to the Naval Ordnance Department, facilitating its operation by providing supplies of coal, iron, and niter to an extent not anticipated [under Colonel St. John]. The steamer Patrick Henry without attention diminishing her efficiency as a vessel of war, has been fitted up as a school-ship for midshipmen, of whom 52 are now on board receiving instruction in the various branches of education essential to a naval officer. The organization has been perfected by Lieutenant W. H. Parker, and it is now only necessary to complete the number of officers contemplated in the plan of organization to ensure the most satisfactory results.[39] Measures have been taken to provide printed ordnance instructions for the Navy. They are much needed, indeed indispensable to the maintenance of a uniform system of instruction in all that relates to the preparation of ships for battle, and the proper handling of their guns. [Owing to the advance in prices Brooke recommended that the government supply navy employees with necessaries at lower than market rates and also low-cost housing near naval ordnance works for the employees at a moderate rent.]

■ 30 November 1863

Catesby ap R. Jones, Selma, Alabama, to Brooke, BP

As I expected there is a call for guns before we have one ready—and after my interview with the President I cannot but believe that we might have had the men that would have enabled us to have answered the call before this. It does not appear to be considered that unlike works that have been established we have to make the machinery before we can commence the work that is wanted. I must say that I think it very strange that after all my applications we have had not more than a very few mechanics added to our force through the Secretary, and that he should now expect to have the guns just as he wanted them. It would appear that my letters on those subjects made no impression on him, and as they are not heeded I would be justified in believing as far as the results show that it was a matter of little importance. The fact is I am tired of this duty, and wish I had any other, even if I could have men I would prefer something else more in the regular line I dont object to hard work, but I do object to work when the proper means are not afforded me and where more is expected than is possible. I wanted to get the bands last June, so that I might have had them ready for the guns—and also hoped to have lathes to turn them. I shall now take all the lathes for the bands, and stop the work in the rolling mill. . . . Our Blacksmiths are not accustomed to such heavy work, which will increase the delays. This like everything else has had to be learnt. The present delay is independent of the failures in the Foundry, and is occasioned by the small number of mechanics, to all of whom the present work is novel. . . . I am now working night and day.

■ 8 December 1863

R.ichard L. Page, commanding and ordnance officer, Charlotte, to Brooke, *Official* Records, Navy, 2d series, p. 566

We have no leather on hand for fuze washers, and have not had since we come here.

We make what we use out of scraps of leather (upper is the best) by drawing it through a shaver or splitting knife used by harness workers.

■ 19 December 1863

Partial Report of Board of Officers assembled by special orders no. 278, Headquarters, Department of South Carolina, Georgia, and Florida (copy), BP

Board called to determine and report upon the proper weights of projectiles and charges of Powder for the various Calibers of Heavy Artillery used in the defence of Charleston and also the greatest angles of elevation which should be allowed in Service.

The Board met pursuant to the above orders in the City of Augusta. . . .

In writing upon the subject of the proper weight of Projectiles and charges for Artillery it may be observed that conclusions based upon Mathematical calculations have been avoided. The number of elements entering into such analysis is so great and variable, that to embrace all the conditions into a satisfactory equation would be impracticable and without which the results would only lead to error. Among the elements referred to, may be enumerated the varying tenacities, elasticities, densities, ductilities and compositions of the different metals and alloys of which Artillery is made. . . .

From the foregoing it will be readily admitted that in a matter so entirely practical as the Service of Artillery which involves the safety of those who are employed in its use as well as its efficiency against the enemy, Conclusions based on existing facts and experiments should only be relied upon. For the Smooth bore artillery sufficient data has been accumulated to determine satisfactorily the general ratio of weight of a ball and corresponding charge of powder, and the same may be said with some limitation in relation to the projectiles and charges for the Smaller Calibers of Rifle guns; but for the heavier Rifle pieces, a sufficient number of facts derived from experience has not as yet been attainable to certainly determine either the weight or form of projectile or weight of charge. Hence it is proposed to approximately determine these points and leave their ultimate solution to a future time when more experimental data may have been collected. In the numerous experiments made in England and in the United States with Rifle Guns, the old customs of refering [sic] the charges of powder to the weight of Projectiles, as have been the custom with smooth bore artillery, has been continued, but singular enough the proper weights of the projectile itself, seems generally to have had no settled determination, except in a few cases. This want of a system of Rifled Artillery, has been the source of much confusion and loss, but was the necessary result of isolated experiments in a new field of Arty. Rifled guns may be satisfactorily arranged into three classes. The first embracing all those having a less caliber than the 24 Pdr and which have been made expressly for such purpose of the best materials, and hence having relatively the greatest degree of strength. The Second referring to all calibers between the 8 inch Gun and 24 Pdr the latter included, this class may be divided into the banded and unbanded, and is mainly composed at this time of all smooth bore guns Rifled and generaly [sic] single banded. The third class will include the 8 inch and all calibers above; this class like the preceeding [sic] one, in Our Services; is mainly comprised of guns originally made as smooth bores, or on smooth bore patterns, and having single or double bands. As the projectile is the agent that does all the work its form, dimensions and weight should be first determined and then the proper charge of powder to project it with safety and accuracy be ascertained and adapted.

The principal advantages of the Rifled Projectile and its accuracy, capacity as a shell and sustaining power, the latter giving it great range, hence the proper form, and dimensions, to ensure those qualities is the problem to be served. The elongated projectile presenting less surface to the powerful resistance of the air than the ball of the same dimentions [*sic*] has been universally adopted for all rifle Cannon, its superiority being abundantly proven in all experiments for distances exceeding 500 or 800 yards where great resistance is experienced, and long and accurate range essential. The pointed extremity experiment as well as theory has satisfactorily determined to have the advantage over the spherical forms for accuracy and extent of range: and as these two qualities are essential to the skill it may be assumed that this kind of projectile should have the elongated form with a more or less pointed forwarded [*sic*] extremity. The form of the rear end of the shell is generally governed by the necessity of having a ring or sauser [*sic*] of expanding metal attached to it to fill the bore and grooves and hence has a more or less flat surface. Numerous experiments in England determine that the projectile should not exceed 2½ to 3 calibers in extreme length seven in exceptional cases, thus the Armstrong projectile is from 2¼ to 2½ calibers and the Blakely from 1¼ to 2 calibers in length, the larger the gun the shorter the projectile. In cases of the Whitworth Gun on account of its small hexagonal bore allowing a great twist and having considerable velocity, the solid projectile is 3 calibers and the shell nearly 4 calibers in length. The Parrott shells vary from 2½ to 3 calibers, and the most approved of our service vary from 2 to 2½ calibers in length. It is believed that the Parrott shell of 3 calibers is too long for its rotary velocity, rendering it liable to turn over in its flight, particularly in long ranges; at the same time it is desirable to attain as long a shell as is consistent with accuracy on account of its increased sustaining power and capacity of charge.

In order to establish a system of ratio of weights of projectiles and calibers, it is proposed to refer to the weights of the ball which nearest belongs to the particular caliber. This is assumed as sufficiently near for the purpose that a

3 inch caliber corresponds to a ball of 3 lb.
3½ inch caliber corresponds to a ball of 6 lb.
4 inch caliber corresponds to a ball of 9 lb.
4½ inch caliber corresponds to a ball of 12 lb.
5 inch caliber corresponds to a ball of 18 lb.
5½ inch caliber corresponds to a ball of 24 lb.

6 inch caliber corresponds to a ball of 32 lb.

7 inch caliber corresponds to a ball of 42 lbs.

The ratio of charges of Powder to projectiles in England, in the United States and in this country has been about 1/8 for the smaller and medium guns. In the Whitworth guns and Armstrong Guns of smaller caliber the ratio is 1/6 in the former 1/7 in the latter for the small pieces and 1/7 and 1/8 respectively for their larger calibers of 80 and 100 pounders, in the Parrott gun the charge of powder is about 1/10 for all calibers.

Bands add greatly to the strength of a gun if it has a sufficient strength of Breech, when they are properly put on, but it is plain if they are placed in a position with too little or no compressing strain on the Gun they add but little or no effective strength; and if they have been put on with too great a strain, they may burst asunder by their own contractions. Hence skill & experience are required for such work, and as such cannot always be obtained at this period, due allowance must be made in estimating the additional strength of the Gun. As each load is generally about One third (⅓) of the thickness of the metal of gun, and as wrought iron is about twice the strength of cast iron, it may necessarily be inferred that each load in the general case confers not less than One Third additional strength to the gun.

As regards the expediency of use, high Angles of elevation for heavy Artillery except for Mortars, the utility of practice may well be doubted in many cases, for it is evident that no certainty of the projectile attaining any limited object, as a single Ship, can be anticipated by firing a 10 inch Columbiad at 25° elevation, and throwing a shell over two and a third miles, nevertheless at Camps of the Enemy, Forts, Fleets, etc. such practice might be beneficial particularly in winter weather.

In relation to the proper form for bolts for Rifled Guns, it may be observed that a projectile with spherical or conical extremity cannot be made to penetrate water at the low angles required to strike a vessels bottom below the water line, but that a flat-headed Bolt has penetrated 30 feet of water at a slight angle, and still retained great penetrating power. In striking inclined surfaces of iron plating it is also more probable that the sharp edge of the bolt will take hold than if it had the spherical or conical termination which might cause it to glance off. Experience has shown this to be the case—the principal advantages of a long projectile having a given caliber are its superior maintaining power and increased capacity; for a Bolt, which it is assumed will only be employed at short ranges, neither of these are applicable, hence for a given weight its length is of but little moment. . . .[40]

Board members: Col. George W. Rains
                        Maj. John G. Barnwell
                        Maj. Wm. S. Basinger

■ 21 December 1863

Lt. John R. Hamilton, Liverpool, England, to Brooke, BP

Since I last had the pleasure of writing I have visited the Elswick Ordnance Works at New-Castle on Tine, where Sir William Armstrong makes his guns. I was very graciously received and carried without reserve through the various departments, in which I saw cannon at every stage of construction. I have never seen such a complete works, surpassing in extent anything in Washington in former days and everything has been combined to facilitate and perfect the art of gun making, that machinery and skill can achieve.

In addition to what are commonly known as Armstrong guns, there seems to be a prejudice against all such breech loaders both in the English Army and Navy, although there are officers in both services who speak favorably of them. Yet I think it is clearly the opinion of all, that unfortunately no system of breech-loading now known is adapted to the heavy ordnance required at the present time. The 12 pounder and 42 pounder has worked well, and even some of the larger guns, but it [is] evident to me from what facts I have been able to obtain, that except on an iron-clad turret, that there are no circumstances under which a muzzle-loading gun is not to be preferred to a breech-loader. These latter require careful and perfectly instructed men, great attention to the brech [sic] screws and protection from weather. All of these defects however I believe centre in the vent piece. Except at this one point no guns have surpassed Sir William Armstrong, in that first and most essential quality endurance. Whatever his opponents and enemies may say, not one of his guns has ever burst into fragments, and one of them a 12 pr. has been fired 3,263 rounds and is perfectly good now, and some six guns of the same calibre stood an average of 2000 rounds without injury, I have read carefully through . . . the Evidence given before the Ordnance select committee; and I think, that the summing up of this evidence is conclusive in proving the extraordinary enduranse [sic], of the Armstrong gun of all calibres, in spite of the defect in the breech pins. I think also, that it is clearly proven, that cast iron guns are not to be depended upon, as rifle pieces firing heavy charges. Blakely himself who has had a good deal to do with cast iron guns when called on to produce a piece of great endurance always had recourse to hammered steel, if he can get it. . . . It is still more significant that the Yankees have just given Mr. [Sir Henry] Beisimer [Bessemer] £10,000 for his patent to manufacture his puddled steel in the United States, and you will soon hear of Parrot guns with steel cones, doing better work, than has yet been got out of cast iron by the Yankees. There are many other manufacturers of steel who enjoy just as high a reputation as Mr. Bersemer [Bessemer] and if we had the same facilities of transmitting the material as our enemy possesses I have no doubt that Richmond would produce as good guns as Washington will. I cannot of course at this distance form any estimate of your ability to carry on work at this time, but if you should deem it essential I am very sure, that I could obtain for you very accurate information upon all that relates to the manufacture of steel for heavy ordnance, and could further employ a skilled workman to go out to superintend any works that you might think of starting for the purpose. . . .

Although Sir William Armstrong now uses a steel core for his gun, he still builds up his guns with wrought iron forgings and coiled bars of wrought iron. The Elswick Ordnance Company, object to cast steel hoops because of their brittleness, and to welded plates as not having sufficient strength to give the necessary compression. . . . Thanks to your efforts we have obtained very efficient cast iron guns, but as I have no reliable information of the endurance I have taken the liberty [to] write you the result of the experience extending over several years on this side, and to tell you the Yankee arrangement made with Mr. Bessimer [Bessemer], as I suggested in my former letter steel hoops can be sent over if required. The prinicpal [*sic*] which Capt Pelliser of the English Army is endeavoring to introduce . . . is simply to line as it were the old cast iron guns now in service with wrought iron. . . . the wrought iron core is screwed in at the breech. . . . The Blakely guns sent to Charleston were constructed somewhat on this prinicpal [*sic*] as were some of Capt B's earlier guns. He thought it too expensive at that time for general manufacture. The Captain is now of opinion that the proper mode of constructing a gun is to commence with a core of steel, and to build up the gun with steel hoops of increasing hardness. This is no doubt a good plan if exactly the right kind of material can be obtained, but so far as I am able to judge from all that I have seen and read, I would rather for the present rely on the accuracy and endurance of an Armstrong muzzle-loading gun with the shunt rifling than any other that I know of. The 600 pounder of 22 tons is undoubtedly the greatest achievement in artillery on this side of the water at least . . . and that in the contest with iron plates, that artillery has won the battle. . . . The shot is a steel one and has screwed into it ten bronze studs at or near the bore. . . . It is not a flat-headed shot. . . . I do not know that this form is as good as the flat headed shot, but it is about the only form that Sir William could make and not interfere with the former's patent. [Hamilton then explains in detail the rifling system of the Armstrong Gun. Armstrong used a hammered steel core, made possible by developments in steel manufacture, upon which coils of wrought iron were shrunk.]

Of the manufacture of the Whitworth gun I can tell you very little. . . . What I know of it I have only been able to gather from Magazines and newspapers. I send you enclosed a drawing of one of his guns. I procured a letter of introduction to Messers Whitworth but although they very kindly offered to show me their guns, and works for manufacturing machinery, they declined showing me the shop in which the guns are made, or in the course of construction which was the only thing I wanted to see. Mr. Whitworth enjoys the reputation of being one of the best machinists in England and does beautiful work. I believe the prejudice against his cannon is confined entirely by many to his system of hexagonal rifling. In small arms I think from all I can learn and read that he is ahead of the world. . . . I have yet to learn however of the adoption of his [ordnance] system by any foreign government. . . .

Capt. Blakely I learn has entered into large contracts with the Russians for guns; I am not aware that he has yet established any works so extensive and complete as those of Sir William Armstrong at Elswick or Mr Whitworth at Manchester. The guns sent to Charleston were made in this town, and I know that he gives out a great deal of his work.

I have been endeavoring ever since my arrival in Europe to gather the very best information on the subject of guns; and I have reached the conclusion from all that I have seen, read, and heard, that I prefer the muzzle-loading gun as made by Sir William Armstrong to any other manufactured in all Europe.

[James D.] Bulloch is in Paris. . . . The amount of work and bother that he has to get through with in twenty-four hours would kill most any other man. I have heard rumors over here of efforts being made by several very ancient, although not very profound salts about Richmond to susplant [*sic*] him. If it is in your power, crush any such conspiracy at once. To be deprived of his services here would be fatal at this time as happy as he would be to get to sea.[41]

■ 24 December 1863

David P. McCorkle, Naval Ordnance Works, Atlanta, Georgia, to Brooke, BP

I wish to gracious you would have shoulder straps abolished in the Navy. Our men hollow [*sic*] yankee at us. Why not have an anchor on the collar, backed by stars, for instance a Lieutenant with one commander with two; Captain with three & so on.

■ **ca. 31 December 1863**
Brooke to Lt. John R. Hamilton, England (rough draft), BP

Your letters of Dec. 21st and [blank] fortunately escaped the blockade and I have read them with great pleasure. The a[ccom]panying extracts from the Times are interesting and give a very good idea of what Monster guns can do.

The information contained in your letters is importa[nt] for although many of the facts stated had been gleaned from Ordnance reports and discussions of Engineers etc. published in England incidentally reaching the confederacy the more general and comprehensive statements which you give enable us to form a more correct and definite id[ea] of the present condition of Ordnance abroad than w[ould] otherwise have been the case, and to estimate with more precision the value of that which we now hav[e].

In the beginning of the war, prior to the evacuat[ion] of Norfolk efforts were made to establish at the Navy Yard a gun factory, the machine[ry] for making coils was nearly completed and it is probable that had not the place been evacuated we would by [now] have had guns much like those of Armstrong. As it was however we were driven by necessity to considering the best means of making such material as we possessed stand the strain to which under the most favorable circumstances it would be subjected. We were the first to construct heavy rifles and to employ high cha[rges].

It would afford me pleasure to give you a detailed account of our ordnance work but a moderate degree of reticence where ones paper[s] may fall into the hands of the enemy is advisable a[s] was illustrated in the case of the Merrimac Virginia and Monitor. The enemy believed that our guns had exhibited their full power in that action, they accepted the Monitor as a standard of strength and much to my satisfaction, although it was uncomfortable to see the guns under a cloud, [and] went wild building their wonderful ships. They believe even now the contest in which the Atlanta was captured she being hard and fast aground demonstrated the efficiency of the Monitors for Naval combats. Not a shot from the Atlanta struck, she fell into their hands by one of those accidents which frequently [occur].

6

Personal Sorrow and
Continued Activity in Ordnance

1864

■ **11 January 1864**

Brooke to Commodore Samuel Barron, England, *Official Records, Navy*, 2d series, p. 572

A supply of standard works embracing all branches of art and manufactures connected with the construction of guns, projectiles, fuses, powder, timberworks, mining, etc. is much needed. Asked that [William H.] Murdaugh or some other officer be detailed to gather information on changes in ironclads and ordnance being made in England and France.

■ **14 January 1864**

Col. Alfred Rhett, Headquarters, Fifth Military District, Department of South Carolina, Georgia, and Florida, Charleston, South Carolina, to Commander D. W. [Duncan N.] Ingraham, BP

I have the honor to state that the 7 inch Rifle (Brooke Gun) . . . whilst in my command at Fort Sumter was fired upwards of 557 times.

This gun has fired 437 shells, weighing 97 pounds, mostly at about 16° elevation, only once or twice as high as 23°. The charge mostly used was 10 pounds, some shots were fired with 8 pounds.

The range obtained with a charge of 10 lbs and 23° elevation could not be accurately ascertained. It was somewhere about 7600 yards. With 20½° elevation and at 10 lbs. it threw a number of shells . . . (about 6600 yards).

This statement, I regret, is not as full & accurate as it ought to be, from the fact, that a fire was kept up day & night, with little intermission, and the different reliefs for many days, & from the fact, that most of our papers were destroyed during the bombardment.

This gun may have been fired a few times not reported, but it may be relied on, that it has fired 557 times— 120 bolts & 437 shells.

These guns being completely untried, I gave them my personal supervision, and was present on the parapet during nearly all the firing from them.

■ **22 January 186[4]**

Lt. John R. Hamilton, 10 Rumfort Place, Liverpool, England, to Brooke, BP

I send you herewith some wood cuts of the 600 pounder Armstrong gun, and of the effect produced upon a target representing the Warrior's side,— distance 1000 yds. I also send you a newspaper slip, with a detailed account of some experiments with spherical steel shot, to which I would particularly call your attention. Steel projectiles of all kind[s] can be manufactured in this country, and all the recent experiments show that steel is the metal best suited for the purposes of penetrating and destroying armour plates. . . . it is now the general opinion that wrought iron cannot be carried on a ship of sufficient thickness to keep out the new shot and shell, and it [is] supposed that the plates will have to be made of steel, which promises double the resisting power. In a former letter I wrote you about steel hoops for banding guns. . . .

I am in hopes of being able to get Messrs Fraser, Trenholm & Co. to send out some of the steel spherical shot, on their own account. Fired from seven & eight inch guns made by you with 20 & 25 lbs of powder, the inferior armour of the Monitors could never resist them.

I will probably have to remain in Europe for some months longer, and I sincerely trust that if I can serve you in any way here, that you will not hesitate to call on me. In the mere matter of books and reports on Ordnance I might help you. The French literature is particularly rich on the subject. . . . I think of going over to Paris simply to see what can be picked up about ordnance in France, and to get hold of the many excellent books published there.

■ **26 January 1864**

Diary of Matthew F. Maury, 1 January–31 August 1864, Matthew F. Maury Papers, LC

had my hair cut for 3d̲ Rec'd letter from Dabney [Maury]—Sep 28—and from Brook[e]—Oct. Wrote to Blakely for Brooke's information & sent his message to Murdaugh.

■ 28 January 1864

Captain Alexander T. Blakely, Royal Artillery, 34 Montpelier Street, London, BP

I have received your note of yesterday containing Capt. Brooke's enquiry about my big cannon. These 13-inch guns were commenced early in 1862 when steel could not be had in the masses it can now. They were intended to defend a harbour against ironclad ships & I calculated, & I think correctly, that with a charge of about 50 or 60 pounds of powder even the cast-iron shells could be projected through 4-inch iron—certainly this 650 pound shot could.

Very great strength was not necessary for so small a comparative charge provided the full force of the powder were prevented from acting on the gun at the instant of ignition. This was one of my reasons for planning the air-chamber, although the same purpose might have been answered by not ramming the powder home, a method of relieving cast-iron guns and of securing

great uniformity of range, which I venture to recommend. Of course great care must be taken always to ram down the cartridge to exactly the same point & more powder may be used than could be safely if rammed home. The effect on the gun between the cartridge & shot is less than if the cartridge is simply elongated. I did not think a simple cast-iron gun hooped would be strong enough, so I had these last guns made on a plan which I cannot help thinking would be useful to your nation, namely of two concentric tubes both of cast-iron—the inner one of Lowmoor iron and quite a plain tube without any moulding whatever and only 5 inches thick. Such a tube can be made of perfect soundness in every part.

Over it I fitted another shorter tube with trunnions

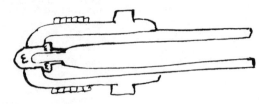

The outer tube I made of stronger & less stretching cast-iron. . . . The longitudinal strain I divided proportionely [*sic*] between the two tubes by making the surface ABCD (see Fig. 1) of the inner tube acted on backwards by the powder present a surface of about 70 round inches to the front, while the bronze gas chamber EEE (Fig. 2) only showed a frontage of 100 round inches all the pressure in which it communicated to the outer tube. I attribute the breaking of the breech in firing more to the absence of pressure on the surface ABCD of the inner tube than to the excess of pressure on the gas chamber, which by mistake they filled with powder. There is a vast difference between pressing with a couple of thousand tons on one of two objects lightly attached to another to which no pressure is applied & pressing both in the same direction exactly in proportion to their weight. In the one case they must be separated. In the other there would be absolutely no tendency to separate. Of course I do not mean that in a gun of 20 tons weight & fixed by its trunnions such an absence of strain can even be approached, but I do think nearly all tendency of the gas chamber to leave the inner iron tube would have been obviated by placing the charge where it could have acted during the first instant on the inner iron tube. Had the breech then blown out the inner iron tube should have broke also & part gone to the rear.

I did not quite wish the cartridge placed as Capt Brooke imagines, namely quite in front of the chamber. My reason was that I feared the gas might penetrate between the bronze chamber and the iron & so act on a large surface.

To prevent this I desired the powder to be placed in a long limp thin cartridge, part of which should enter the chamber; or else as a pear-shaped cartridge. Capt Brooke's experiment with the 2nd gun which has been fired with perfect success with 55 lbs powder in front of the chamber proves that he was right & I was wrong.

Pray thank him for the interest he takes in my weapon. . . .

P.S. By the way if you have an opportunity caution your officer not to overload my guns. On the Florida they constantly fired 20 pounds powder from my 6 inch gun out of cast-iron hooped with steel.

■ **ca. January 1864**
  Report on bursting of treble banded seven-inch gun at Sullivan's Island by
  Col. George W. Rains (copy), BP

[This gun] is a cast iron gun banded with wrought iron about two-thirds of its length, with a second band from the trunnion to the breech and partly encircling the latter; over the charge is still a third band which with the stout wrought iron strap from trunnion to trunnion passing round the extremity of the breech, completes the exterior of the gun. The bore is seven inches in diameter and rifled with seven grooves and terminated at the bottom in a form resembling somewhat the Gomer chamber. . . . the gun had been subjected altogether to thirty-three discharges, twenty-one of which were with 20 lb charges and wrought iron bolts weighing each 118 lbs at an average elevation of 3½ degrees. This weight of powder amounting to nearly one sixth of the projectile is regarded as a heavy charge for a large rifle gun, and the fact of its being repeatedly fired with such charges is evidence of its strength of construction.

The principle of banding cast iron guns, when properly executed, has been demonstrated from the experience gained during the present war, to be a true one and highly advantageous where it can be applied. In the case of a gun triple banded over that portion having the greatest strain, if the bands have been skillfully put on, the relative strength of the metal employed is more closely approximated, for the bands being so put on, the first on the guns shall be in a state of compression, the second neutral, and the third in a state of extension, fulfills the theoretical demands for an equal strain on each at the moment of ignition of the charge, which with a single band would be impracticable. Hence a triple banded gun, strengthened by a breech strap to the trunnions as is the case with the gun under consideration, if properly constructed, combines great strength with comparative lightness.

From all the circumstances of the case the Board are of the following opinion:

First That the triple banded gun has shown itself of great strength.

Second That 20 lbs of powder and the gun being fired at an elevation with a wrought iron ball, weighing 118 lbs must be considered a heavy charge and only to be sustained by a careful manufacture of the gun in all its parts.

Third That notwithstanding the maximum charge the gun would have continued to sustain the strain had not the exterior bands at the breech been ruptured at the 21st round of heavy charges.

Fourth That the firing of the gun with 13 lbs of powder at an elevation of 8° after cracking of the exterior bands sustaining the breech, caused the rupture of the gun at its lowest portion.

[Brooke's endorsement]: This gun after being banded was heated—the bands—to a red heat by the burning of the building at which it was placed at the Tredegar foundry. [This must be an allusion to the Tredegar fire mentioned earlier.]

■ **28 January 1864**

Catesby ap R. Jones, Selma, Alabama, to Miss Ellen Augusta Shackelford, Gift Collection, Southern Historical Collection, University of North Carolina at Chapel Hill

I am much indebted to you for your kind note informing me of the movements of Mr. Gift[.]

Having advocated the expedition [probably the cruise of the blockade runner R. E. Lee to Halifax] from its inception I was much interested, and had great hopes of important results. As the originator of the expedition, Mr. [George W.] Gift is doubtless much chagrined at its failure, tho he is not responsible for it. I hear he has arrived in the Confederacy, if so, we may soon expect a detailed account from him. [Was this the scheme concerning which Gift wrote to Brooke?]

Since I left the Chattahoochee I have been constantly and arduously occupied, and for my labors here, am now being repaid in the shape of heavy guns which we are now sending into service. The smallest gun that we cast is larger than any you saw on board the Gunboat [*Chattahoochee*]. Tho the service is important I much prefer to be more active, and from a letter received to day am encouraged to hope that I may command the ironclad Tennessee, now at Mobile, the Admiral having applied for me.[1]

■ **28 January 1864**

Lt. N. H. Van Zandt, Naval Ordnance Office, Charleston, South Carolina, to Brooke, BP

By the way the two VI[40] Brooke Rifles on James Island have been fired quite 1000 times each—they have been rechecked twice & require a third bouching. I shall endeavor to visit the battery before I leave Charleston but as the Yankees command the harbor & fire at everything on the water it is most difficult to communicate with the batteries. I shall try it by land.

The treble Banded Brooke on Sullivan's Island has become a great Pet with the troops on that Island. They say they "can hit a Barrell at the distance of a mile every pop." The VII inch "defective" Brooke Rifle,—it came from Savannah I believe,—is also a great favorite. Its accuracy is equal to the Treble Banded. [It was "defective" because Brooke was dissatisfied with the apparent character of the metal.]

I am satisfied that your Rifles, VII inch, if fired at 35° elevation will give a range of 4½ miles with 12 pounds or 14 pounds of powder.

■ **29 January 1864**

Diary of Matthew F. Maury, Matthew F. Maury Papers, LC

Communications to the Times & Standard denouncing as a "Yankee trick" the report that is going the rounds of the press as report of Sec. Navy—Law

& Law with a list of Brooke's books—660 vols—what discount upon trade prices will you furnish them for?

■ **February 1864**

William N. Brooke, Richmond, to Col. William Garnett (copy), BP

As you have several times expressed a desire in letters to Lizzie to have some account of John's progress, and as his time is so fully occupied as to make it almost impossible for him to write at any length, I resolved to try myself, with a little assistance from him, to give you such information on the subject as would be likely to prove interesting.

I shall repeat, what you, no doubt, already know, but about which there is a good deal of confusion in the minds of many people, when I say, John does not so much lay claim to the discovery of any unknown principle in the science of gunnery or rather ordnance, or to the invention of an entirely new gun, as to the merit of having recognized, in the very beginning of the war and in advance of our enemies and the Europeans, the superiority and practicability of <u>heavy rifled guns</u>—and of having produced, with the inferior materials and limited means at command, guns fully equal in effective power to any that we know of in the world, long before the Yankees had any such guns in the service—The "Merrimac" was armed with rifles similar to that which sunk the "Keokuk," while the Monitor had only large smooth bores, and it was only owing to our want of wrought iron bolts at that time that she did not meet with the same fate that the Keokuk afterwards met [at] Charleston.

The intrinsic excellence of his guns he considers to consist in their great strength resulting from their weight and form. This [his] shot differs from those in use among the Yankees and Europeans more than his guns, and he considers it as being more in the nature of an <u>invention</u> than the gun, and as having quite as much to do with the result.

I believe I sent you some time since a paper, which I hope you received, containing extracts from the reports made to the Federal Government by the Yankee Naval Officers in command of the Iron-Clad fleet which attacked Charleston, in which all give the most ample and satisfactory testimony to the terrible efficiency of our Ordnance and admit without reserve the decisive character of their failure and the hopelessness of any further attempt with their present means.

———

The turrets of every one of the monitors was so damaged as to either refuse to revolve or to work with great difficulty. There can be no doubt we adopted the best form of armour for vessels of harbor defence in the "Merrimac."

Commander [Archibald] Fairfax of the "Nantucket" says: "The effect of their fire upon the Keokuk, together with that of their heavy rifle shot upon the Monitors, is sufficient proof that any one vessel could not have withstood the concentrated fire of the enemy's batteries."

I must say that I am disappointed beyond measure at this experiment of Monitors overcoming strong forts.—It was a fair trial.

All the Yankee Captains agree that the attack was a complete failure.

It should be observed however that the entire result on this occasion can by no means be attributed to the rifle alone. The heavy smooth bores no doubt did the iron-clads great damage, breaking and indenting their plates and giving the turrets such shocks as to disarrange and cause them to become jammed. But where penetration was effected, which is the great desideration, the rifle did it. It is known . . . that the terrific shot of which Capt [Percival] Drayton [*Passaic*] speaks was from the Brooke rifle, and that rifle penetrated and probably contributed more than any other gun to the destruction of the "Keokuk." . . .

The correspondent of the "London Times" in a late letter from the Confederacy on American Ordnance says, that there can be no doubt that the two great successes of the war in Ordnance are the Parrott and Brooke Rifles, and that he does not feel at liberty to mention the exact results obtained by the Brooke rifle, but they are such as would in his opinion astonish Europe.

You are aware that rifle guns, owing to the great strain upon them (which is I believe estimated at 4 to 5 times as much as the strain upon smooth bores) are much inferior in endurance to smooth-bores—and that the life of a rifle is generally very much shorter than that of the smooth bore. A smooth-bore which would stand 3000 or 4000 discharges would be considered a most excellent gun; its life would be long enough to accomplish all the work that would be likely to be required of it. Recent official reports and unofficial accounts as to the endurance of the Brooke rifle have not only been highly satisfactory, but have far exceeded reasonable expectations.

I may say here that whenever John makes a gun he preserves specimens of the core of the gun which are carefully labelled with a number corresponding to the number of the gun and with the density and tensile strength of the metal carefully determined by machines for the purpose. A record is thus kept here which reveals at a glance the character of any gun wherever it may be.

Lieut. Col. [Joseph] Yates, a very intelligent Ordn[an]ce Officer, who had commanded the Brooke rifles on Sumter in the attack of the Iron Clad fleet on that port, and sank the Yank iron-clad Keokuk, recently visited Richmond. He is enthusiastic in his praise of the Brooke Rifle. . . .

It is true that several of the Brooke Rifles have burst after a comparatively low number of fires, but in every instance where an intelligent account of the circumstances attending the disaster could be obtained, it has been clearly traced to extraordinary causes which would have burst any gun, or to a reckless ignorance and carelessness in the management.

To give you two instances. A short time since, some shells of peculiar construction were brought to John with the request that he would have them tried in one of his guns. He declined doing so on the ground that the shells in question would probably burst the gun owing to defective principles in their construction which he pointed out, explaining the defects and foretelling the manner in which the shells would act and the manner in which they would be found to be broken after discharge. Subsequently and without his knowledge some of the shells were fired from one of his guns at Chapin's [Chaffin's] Bluff under the direction of the Army and the Gun burst. The shells were recovered and found to be broken precisely in the manner predicted.

Another case was that of the 7 inch treble banded Brooke sent to Charleston with special instructions. It had been heated red hot in the fire at Tredegar which made it dangerous. It burst and a hoard of army officers reported it burst because of excessive charges.

Harm is done by the papers reporting immediately every time a gun bursts. The uninformed public jumps to the conclusion the cause is in the gun and tends to condemn them all. The official report which shows the cause is given to only a few and the public continues to labor under a false view. If the reports were made public in the papers much harm would be eliminated and officers and men would keep the confidence in their weapons it is so essential to have.

The science of Ordnance has had a prodiginous [sic] development in this war, so much so that guns of such weight and power as were hardly thought at the commencement are now in common use. The enemy owing to the great advantages they have over us in the abundance, variety and quality of material, and in facilities for manufacturing, have as was to be expected, surpassed us in some respects in which we were in advance in the beginning of the war. We led the way as to heavy rifles, but they have produced and now use rifles throwing a much greater weight of metal than ours. The question therefore naturally suggests itself whether our Ordnance is still adequate to contend against their progressive improvement. I think it is. We only want guns of sufficient power to penetrate their iron clads. We have done that and we think that the power of our rifles has not even been fully developed, and that the 7 inch treble banded Brooke rifle, if it has a fair trial will penetrate any iron clad they may bring against us. John thinks the Yankees have overdone the matter, they have increased the size of their guns until they have become unwieldy, greatly reducing their rapidity & accuracy of fire. A fact of which they themselves seem to have become conscious for they are withdrawing some of their heavy guns and substituting lighter ones. John however intends making some guns a little heavier than heretofore. He is making some powerful smooth bores and an VIII inch rifle. He has made up to the present time about 75 guns of different patterns, and the rate of production is increasing so rapidly that he expects to be able to furnish all that may be necessary. Those he has already made are scattered all over the Confederacy on this side of the Mississippi—principally on ship board. The Army has a few.

■ **February 1864**
William N. Brooke, Richmond, to Col. William Garnett (copy), BP

You already know John's connection with the Blakely Gun at Charleston—that he first suggested the probable use of the "Gas Chamber" as he termed it, and the success attending the use of it is suggested by him—that his solution was accepted by Col. [Josiah] Gorgas, Genl Beauregard and others without reservation as explaining the legitimate purpose of this Chamber, but that he expressed at that time strong doubt as to Blakely's having intended so to use it—a doubt which others would not listen to so plain was it they said, that he must have so intended.

It is important in this connection to know that the discovery seems simply to have been the natural conclusion to which a line of investigation he was already pursuing might have led; for the [he] was then considering the advantage of leaving a space behind the Cartridge in the Chamber. This accounts for the apparent ease with which he recognized the application of the gas chamber when all others were at fault. He was thus helped to the end of the journey by the unintentional unconscious assistance of another.

As regards the value of the discovery, John has no doubt that it will have an important bearing in the manufacture of very heavy guns. Sir Wm. Armstrong's celebrated 600 pdr, although producing a wonderful effect, was, according to one account severely strained upon trial. Considering therefore the excellence of material & unlimited means of execution at Armstrong's command, it would seem that the limit of material strength has been reached and hence the importance of any discovery which will enable us to relieve the strain upon the material without diminishing the propulsive force required to drive the enormous shot from the monster guns of the present day.

■ **1 February 1864**
Capt. Charles C. Pinckney, army ordnance officer, Charleston, South Carolina, to Lt. N. H. Van Zandt, naval ordnance officer, Charleston, South Carolina, BP

It has occurred to me that, in the absence of any official record of the firing from the Brooke Guns used by the Army in the defence of Charleston, an approximate statement of the number of shots fired from them, might be of interest to the Ordnance Dept. of the Navy. This, I think, can be arrived at with sufficient accuracy. I purpose to attempt this in reference to the two Guns that have been most used, viz the two VI[40], which have been all along at Fort Johnson.

You are aware that I have been for a long time the Ordnance Officer here. I received these Guns when turned over to the Army, and all ammunition used by them passed thro' my hands. I have examined my books and made up a total of projectiles issued which I know to have been fired from these Guns—principally shell & Bolts from Richmond—but also including many 32 pdr. Rifle shot & shell of various shapes & patterns which you may remember were sometimes used.

From this, and from frequent conference with Capt [John] Mitchell, with Capt Hill & Lt. Mazzïk respectively Ordnance Officers of the port, and others, I am convinced that these two Gun[s] have been fired near two thousand times, in the proportion probably of about 1100 or 1200 for one and seven (700) or eight (800) for the other. This may be an understatement but is certainly not too great.

You are aware that the former of these guns has been twice bushed and that the vent is now two or three sizes, but the accuracy of its fire seems undiminished. The precision with which they planted their shot or burst their shell in the enemys works day after day & night after night is notorious to all who have watched the defence of Morris Island and Fort Sumter.

The seven inch VII in Gun on Sullivan's Island which came here under the title of "defective" is admitted by all to be the best shooting Gun on the Island.

It gives me great pleasure to bear testimony to the excellence of these guns for I am convinced that the impression which at first prevailed was unfounded—Indeed fuller experience has dissipated this idea—and I think there would now be a general concurrence in Capt Mitchell's view—"that the Brooke Rifle is without any sort of exception the best Gun we have."

■ **3 February 1864**
Matthew F. Maury, England, to Brooke, BP

The books shall be attended to immediately. You speak of funds over here, but do not tell me where they are. I however will try not to let you want the necessary things your requisition calls for.

Your message about the printing has been delivered to Murdaugh. He is in Paris. Your enquiries have been referred to Blakely—Behold his reply. [Given in separate communication]

The forged report of the secretary of the Navy has been doing us incalculable prejudice and much real harm in England & the continent. It has internal evidence of a counterfeit, still seeing (?) and others here much more posted up and more entitled to speak for the Sec. than I am, and who kept silent, I should have hesitated had it not been for a letter happily recd about two days ago from Bob Minor at Bermuda giving an account of what he had been about. That thanks to Bob—tell him—left me in no doubt as to the true character of the other.

■ **3 February 1864**
  Diary of Matthew F. Maury, 1 January–31 August 1864, Matthew F. Maury Papers, LC

[Colin J.] McRae—Do you know anything about any funds for Bur. of Ord & Hyd? I have an order for about £250 or £300 worth of Books—will you pay bills for those approved & certified by me? Answer right away.[2]

■ **3 February 1864**
  Diary of Matthew F. Maury, 1 January–31 August 1864, Matthew F. Maury Papers, LC

Sec. Navy—His Report a Yankee trick—copy—Brooke—Blakely's letter—Books if I can get the money will be delivered in Bermuda to Walker at London prices.

■ **11 February 1864**
  Diary of Matthew F. Maury, Matthew F. Maury Papers, LC

Letter from [James D.] Bulloch: He has funds for the books for Brooke.[3]

■ **15 February 1864**
  Lt. Col. J. A. de Lagnel and Maj. R. C. Taylor, Board of Officers, Chaffin's Bluff, Virginia, to Adjutant and Inspector General's Office, Richmond (copy), BP

Burst at Chaffin's Bluff, Virginia, on [20 January 1864] a 6.4 inch single banded Brooke rifle gun loaded with 6 lbs. of powder and an experimental shell of 62 lbs. weight. The gun was mounted on a ship carriage requiring a crew of 16 men. . . . The elevation was 1° 30. The gun had been fired in all about 20 times. The gun was carefully loaded under the supervision of Major Taylor.

[The Board felt that the character of the gun] forbids the supposition that the gun burst because of faults inherent in it. The cause must be found elsewhere;—and the Board are of opinion, after an examination of the projectile recovered . . . that the accident is due to the projectile used; the strain being intensified by the quick action of the comparatively small grain powder.

[The shells were obtained from Army Ordnance. The report was called for by the secretary of the navy in orders to Brooke.] In an endorsement on another copy of the Board's report, Brooke wrote: "I had declined permitting these projectiles to be fired from Navy guns, regarding them as liable to wedge in the bore from the driving in of the base. The wrought iron sabot causing the base which is weakened to form a conical wedge."

■ **15 February 1864**
Memorandum of conversation, Brooke with Lt. George W. Gift, BP

The conversation concerned the bursting of two rifled guns at Vicksburg, concerning which Gift had written Brooke on July 30, 1863, from the C.S.S. Gaines at Mobile. Gift had gained his information indirectly through officers who had been at Vicksburg. Gift reported the guns (7 inch) had fired 200 to 300 times with 12 lbs. powder and usually bolts, as shells were short.

20 February 1864
Brooke journal, BP

Today a board of which I was a member concluded its examination and report upon a vessel or rather its shield now on the stocks at Rocketts built or building by Mr. [John] Porter. The members were Comdr. Mitchell, Chf. Engr. Williamson, Col. J. T. Wood, Mr. Porter & myself. I suggested the following alterations of his plan: to substitute a belt of timber for stanchions in the hollow sponson, to take away a planking of pine between the rafters and inner oak lining and to add on equal thickness to the fore and aft planking outside the rafters. These suggestions were adopted. Other changes were an addition of one more inch of iron under the sponsons and to mount four guns instead of two as proposed by Mr. P.

We were all directed to report upon the best plan of shield or casemate in our opinion. It was determined to postpone the consideration, as Col Wood and Comdr Mitchell were not prepared to give an opinion. Before separating I suggested we should urge the importance of increasing to the greatest extent practicable the strength of shields to be hereafter made. I exhibited to the board drawings of my plan for a sea going vessel and will suggest the building of one in the Confederacy. I recd today from Lt. Hamilton a letter accompanied by cutting from newspapers with illustration etc. of firing by Armstrong with his 600pdr gun.

Hamilton says that in his opinion Blakely did not intend to employ the chamber in his 600pdr as an air or gas chamber, that he believes the idea originated with me. I shall make inquiry into the matter.

Some time ago the Army burst my treble banded gun on Sullivans [sic] Island by the use of excessive charges. A Board reported it as a gun of great strength. It had been heated red hot by the burning of a building at the

Tredegar. Another one has been put in its place. Two 6.4-inch guns have been fired on James Island, about 1500 rounds each.

Our Navy now has the Selma Foundry, [Catesby] Jones in charge. He has sent to [Franklin] Buchanan some six or seven double banded VII-in rifles. [David] Farragut has just attacked Grants Pass. The Yankees have published effect of shot on the Monitors off Charleston the wrought iron bolts penetrated 11-inches of one inch plating. [T. Boudery] Gareschè is making powder.[4] Our dense powder is too slow.

■ 7 March 1864

Lt. Col. J. M. Williams, Mobile, Alabama, to Catesby ap R. Jones, Selma, Alabama, BP

Burst at Fort Powell [Mobile?] on February 29, 1864, a VII inch Brooke Gun loaded with 12 pounds of powder and a shell of 130 lbs. The elevation was 8°. Seven shells bursted in the Gun. The Shells were made at Selma. The last shell burst in the Gun.

The bursting of the Gun was attributed to the premature explosion of shells, but upon more careful Examination of the fracture I believe that the cause was a defect in the gun itself.

[Jones reported to Brooke on this gun from the Naval Gun Foundry at Selma.] He stated: "The only defect we were aware that it had, was an enlargement of the bore commencing about ten inches from the muzzle.

Doubtless the gun would not have broken but for the defective shell. But the question will arise whether the gun should not have been strong enough to have withstood the additional strain caused by the breaking of the shell. I think it should have been.

What one usually called premature explosions of the shell in the gun generally proceed either from defects in the shell or from the inferior quality of iron of which the shell is made, which is broken by the shock.

The shell first made at Norfolk were made of bad material which would account for their breaking in the gun." [Jones's letter was dated 1 April 1864.]

■ 14 March 1864

James D. Bulloch, Liverpool, to Secretary of the Navy Stephen R. Mallory, *Official Records, Navy,* 2d series, p. 607–8

He hoped to get off a steamer by April 5. On it would be a quantity of cast steel, zinc, and block tin ordered by Commander Brooke for his bureau.

- **18 March 1864**

  Diary of Matthew F. Maury, Matthew F. Maury Papers, 1 January–31 August 1864, LC

Brooke—Books have been shipped to Major Walker in 3 boxes . . . Major Walker—Books shipped freight paid Str. Harkaway 16th ins.

- **21 March 1864**

  Lt. Col. Joseph A. Yates, Commanding Artillery, Fort Johnson, South Carolina, to Brooke, BP

Your letter of the 15th Feby came duly to hand, and should have been answered before, but for the difficulty of obtaining certain information in reference to the 6.4 guns, they having been under the command of several officers at different times during the siege, and even now I can only give you an approximation to the number of shots fired from them.

Gun No. 39, date 1863, weight 10,668 has been fired between 1700 & 1800 times, and subjected to the severest test, viz, on one occasion this gun was sent to Charleston to be bushed. The officer in charge very carelessly dismounted the gun with a charge in. Upon its being drawn at the work shops, and examined, it was found to be rifle, instead of cannon powder. The cylinders were filled in Charleston and sent down for use, and there is no way of ascertaining how many were used of that character of powder before this discovery was made.

The projectiles used vary in kind, some of your bolts, other bolts made here with brass sabot, and shell with brass sabot, the average elevation used about 7½ degrees, charge 7 lbs. In short, taking all the circumstances combined, added to the fact of the gun having been at first in the hands of inexperienced artillerists, it is my opinion that this gun gave evidence of great endurance.

I regret however to inform you that a few days ago while firing upon the enemy she burst at the muzzle, breaking off about fifteen (15) inches. It is impossible to account for this singular accident, as the shell was distinctly seen to leave the gun, and fell but little short of its destination. Upon close examination I notice that the grooves are somewhat worn just where the fracture occurred.

It is reasonable to suppose that this gun should burst, after such long use. I have been expecting it some time, but had lately come to the conclusion that she never would, as up to the day of bursting she shot with great accuracy. I would add that she has been bushed twice. Her bursting is much regretted by the officers in charge of the Battery, they looking upon her as a sort of pet gun.

I have recommended that the muzzle be cut off and a thin band be put on so as to cover a small longitudinal crack. I believe she can yet do good service.

Gun No. 42, calibre 6.4. weight 10,665 date 1863, has been subjected to the same test, but has not been fired more than 700 times. She is now in position and perfectly good.

I will now answer your question in detail.

1st I think a seven inch rifle gun can be fired with good aim in action quite as often as a 10 in smooth bore Columbiad: the difference of time necessary in loading a rifle gun is gained in elevating her, as the process of elevating a 10 in Columbiad is very slow.

2nd The accuracy of fire of 7in rifle, compared favorably with that of 10 in gun. Once the angle of deflection is ascertained she can be fired with great accuracy. The account given of this gun by the Army correspondent of the Charleston Courier of the engagement of the 7th April is with the enemys Iron Clad Keokuk, in which the firing of this particular gun was noticed.

3rd The effect of the shot from the 7 in rifle gun against the enemys Iron Clads was most satisfactory. In no instance was it noticed when the shot struck that they glanced or were broken. In taking the gun out of the sunken Keokuk, it was observed that a wrought iron ball from the 7 in gun had buried itself to its base in her turret, others had passed entirely through. One entered the port breaking off the top spire on the right side of gun, another entering and striking the gun on left of the chase, hereby disabling her, which was noticed during the action.

I have no doubt that 10 in round shot added greatly in the destruction of this vessel, and injury of the others, but a large majority were broken to atoms against their iron armor, without apparent effect upon them.

In regard to the influence of distance, in this respect I regret I have no means of ascertaining or judging, but there is no doubt in my mind as to the advantage over the smooth bore.

4th My answer to your first will answer this question viz, if properly served it is a gun of great endurance. The smooth bore Columbiad (Army pattern) used in the same battery with your 6.4 rifle are much worn, having lodgements throughout the bore. One of them burst after having been fired about 800 times, another of the same gun burst in the engagement on the 7th April at Fort Sumter. I must here remark however that one of your 6.4 rifles burst at the same time with the Columbiad, at Battery Simkins. As I was then stationed on Morris Island, Battery Wagner, I have no knowledge of the bursting of this gun.

With regard to the statement of Captain [John] Downes, to the effect that a shot broke through 11 plates of his turret, I am not in possession of any facts to enable me to determine what kind of shot it was. Taking for granted the plates were one inch thick, making in all 11 inches I am disposed to think it must have been a rifle bolt, as from observation and my little experience I do not believe 10 in cast iron shot would penetrate 11 inches of wrought iron, but would have broken to pieces.

I would with pleasure give you an account of the engagement with the enemy's iron clads, but the detailed account of the war correspondent of the Daily Courier was obtained from reliable officers who observed the engagement, and were very generally correct. . . .

I am glad to hear you are getting on well with the guns you are now constructing, and I believe the 11 in guns you are making, with wrought iron spherical shot will prove most formidable gun against Iron Clads. At any rate I would be happy to have an opportunity of trying some of them.

P.S. We now keep accurate accounts of shots fired at this Post, which it has been almost impossible to do heretofore.

■ 24 March 1864

Col. Josiah Gorgas, chief of army ordnance, to Brooke, BP

I have received your communication of the 19 cont'g tracing of plan for "adjustment of sights by mirror." The conception seems to be simple and practical, and I hope you will follow up the matter and devise some instrument which can be used in the field to verify the sights.

■ 27 March 1864

George W. Gift, Richmond, Virginia, to Ellen Augusta Shackelford, Ellen Shackelford Gift Collection, Southern Historical Collection, University of North Carolina at Chapel Hill

Commander Brooke has been talking for the past half hour—I am writing in the Office of Orders & Detail—upon several interesting subjects in his interesting way and has succeeded in diverting my attention from my duty. I have had an interview with Mr. Mallory and am satisfied that I will have his support in all I may undertake. I called, by appointment, upon Mr. [Christopher] Memminger, Sec. of Treasury, on yesterday and he proposed to build half a dozen blockade runners adapted for Apalachicola and seemed delighted with the idea of finding a point from which the blockade can be run with so much ease and certainty. He will do everything to forward my plans.

■ 1 April 1864

Capt. B. E. Dickson, Second South Carolina Artillery, and Capt. A. C. Gaillard, First South Carolina Artillery (board of two officers), Fort Johnson, James Island, South Carolina, to Headquarters, Artillery Forces, Fort Johnson, South Carolina, BP

Burst at Battery Simkins, James Island, S.C. on March 19, 1864 a 6.4 inch Brooke rifle gun loaded with 6 lbs. of powder and a 65 lb rifle shell. The elevation was 7½°. The gun had been fired about 1700 times [endorsement by Lt. Col. Joseph A. Yates, Commanding Artillery Fort Johnson.]

The officer in charge said the gun was "in every respect properly loaded." However, he had not for some time used any oil or grease because of the total want of lubricating materials. Board ventured to give no cause for the bursting of the gun. [No comment by Brooke.]

■ **8 April 1864**
Diary of General Josiah Gorgas

It is three years ago today since I took charge of the Ordnance Department of the Confederate States, at Montgomery—three years of constant work and application. I have succeeded beyond my utmost hopes and expectations. From being the worst supplied of the bureaus of the War Department it is now the best. Large arsenals have been organized at Richmond, Fayetteville, Augusta, Charleston, Columbus, Macon, Atlanta and Selma, and smaller ones at Danville, Lynchburg and Montgomery, besides other establishments. A superb powder mill has been built at Augusta, the credit of which is due to Col. G. W. Rains. Lead smelting works were established by me at Petersburg, and turned over to the Nitre and Mining Bureau, when that Bureau was at my request separated from mine. A cannon foundry established at Macon for heavy guns, and bronze foundries at Macon, Columbus, Ga., and at Augusta; a foundry for shot and shell at Salisbury, N.C.; a large shop for leather work at Clarksville, Va.; besides the armories here and at Fayetteville. A manufactory of carbines has been built [end p. 90] up here; a rifle factory at Ashville (transferred to Columbia, S.C.); a new and very large armory at Macon, including a pistol factory, built up under contract here and sent to Atlanta, and thence transferred under purchase to Macon; a second pistol factory at Columbus, Ga.; all of these have required incessant toil and attention, but have borne such fruit as relieves the country from fear of want in these respects. Where three years ago we were not making a gun, a pistol nor a sabre, no shot nor shell (except at the Tredegar Works)—a pound of powder—we now make all these in quantities to meet the demands of our large armies. In looking over all this I feel my three years of labor have not been passed in vain. [p. 91]

■ **11 April 1864**
Secretary of the Navy Stephen R. Mallory to James D. Bulloch, *Official Records, Navy,* 2d series, p. 623

Experts whose services Brooke desired to procure: steel mill superintendent, three assistants, three skilled in casting heavy cannon, three first class molders, three first class pattern makers, eleven first class machinists.

■ **18 April 1864**

Capt. R.ichard L. Page, Fort Morgan, Mobile, Alabama, to Brooke, BP

Your letter with the mirror sight came duly to hand and I shall try to make it useful at my guns.

I have also recd. from Charlotte 500 percussion Primers which are very useful and certain with the hammer which is fitted to all your guns . . . in my command.

You would indeed be surprised to find how defective and almost entirely useless I have found my ammunition to be at the Batteries under my command.

While engaged in overhauling it, I was much gratified by the arrival of Col. [Stapelton] Crutchfield, with orders from the Ord. Dept. to perform thoroughly just what I was doing. I have found him (Col. C) a most valuable help to me in bringing to sight defects that might have been attended with most disastrous consequences if attacked before these evils could be discovered.

Nearly all the cartridges for Rifles & Smooth bore guns, have been condemned on account of quality of powder—also a large number of cartridge bags of improper shape—being generally too large—nearly all the cartridges of the 7 in Brooke Gun are put up in 42 pdr. Bags. entirely of a different shape from those preserved for the Gun.

The shell I have for the 7 in. rifle Gun are not bushed, which is a great error, as I find it almost impossible to screw up the Fuses. The rust cannot be gotten out of the threads of the screw, I have a large number of hand grenades but not a single fuze plug.

The Friction primers are good for nothing—almost all of them failed under trial. Those made at Richmond 1864 are very superior—indeed perfectly reliable. Our mode at Charlotte of making these primers are doubtless defective, they should be pushed and not drawn through a die as we are or were compelled to do.

My guns are not sighted nor have I anyone to do it for me. I cannot understand in a <u>fixed</u> battery why this should have been neglected. . . .

An experimental Battery of heavy as well as field Artillery would be of great value to the army, for proper instruction of artillerists, two of which should be permanently stationed at each Gun in all the fortifications. When the troops are ordered away as is frequently the case, these <u>two</u> well instructed artillerists would remain to teach the new men and to see the Guns properly served. I could not believe until now, that a regiment called heavy Artillerists, would be as ignorant as I find them. I am strengthening the Fort all I can—securing magazines, building traverses etc. I am also constructing a fine water Battery, which will do more execution than all the Guns in the Fort.

I am perfectly satisfied that the enemy can pass our Guns day or night.

No Obstructions can be placed in the channel after a careful investigation of the bottom, depth of water, strong winds & tides. But I told you before that Mobile cannot be taken by water on account of the shallowness of the water, strong obstructions near the city under the guns of forts were placed for the defence of the passage to the city.

The land defences are also very strong.

I have no inspecting instruments of any kind for shot, shell or cartridges.

■ **30 April 1864**

Brooke, chief of ordnance and hydrography, to Secretary of the Navy Stephen R. Mallory, *Official Records, Navy,* 2d series, p. 641–42—covers period since 27 November 1863

Calls Selma Naval Foundry most important and says: . . . in the casting of heavy guns, rifles of 7 and 6.4 inch caliber, has been commenced and, although the want of skilled labor has proved a serious drawback, Commander Jones has succeeded by suspending all other work and concentrating his force upon the manufacture of guns, in furnishing eight or nine for the defense of Mobile. These guns are double banded and are known to be effective against ironclads of the monitor class. Four of them have been placed in battery on shore, the others are on board the ironclads.

The ordnance works at Atlanta, Charlotte, and Richmond have been improved by the addition of new tools and machinery, and are in condition to supply the wants of the service, provided the requisite number of mechanics for whose details application has been made can be secured.

Until the operation of casting guns was commenced at Selma, the Navy was entirely dependent upon the Tredegar Foundry for heavy guns, but until recently, owing to various causes—want of iron and accidents to machinery—the production was totally inadequate to supply the ironclads already in commission. In order to facilitate the work, arrangements were made at the Naval Ordnance Works to aid in banding guns cast and bored at the Tredegar, but the want of a sufficient number of mechanics, blacksmiths particularly, has not rendered fully available the facilities offered, by the possession of the requisite machinery.

There are in the Southern States more than a sufficient number of mechanics to work these establishments to their full capacity and to supply all the heavy ordnance required to arm the ironclads and other vessels completed and building, and to furnish guns for the defense of our ports against which the ironclads of the enemy can not stand. But these men have been swept into the Army en masse and their services can only be obtained by special and individual detail. Months are generally occupied in the process, and so rarely are applications granted that the services of no more than one in ten are secured. Constant efforts is being made to supply the deficiency of labor but with slight results.

Great inconvenience from merely detailing mechanics from army for navy work instead of transferring them to Navy Dept.

Navy Dept. needed 200 mechanics and had names and addresses of more than 100 serving in the field with the army.

12 May 1864

James W. Cooke, CS *Albemarle*, Plymouth, North Carolina, to Brooke, BP

We yesterday succeeded in raising one of the Southfields Guns it is a Dalgren [*sic*] 9 inch. . . .

I expect today to raise the 100 Pr rifle; if so I shall mount it until your gun arrives. Our great difficulty is the want of transportation, I sent a Steamer up on the 24th Ultimo & she broke her propeller & has not yet had it repaired or a new one furnished. . . . The commodore then left in the "Fora" [?] and she ran into the blockade and has sunk in 20 ft water so that she is out of sight and I fear will be lost. The Cotton Plant, and the Egypt a steamer that I brought down from Aligator river are the only steamers we now have in use.

I think that I prefer your Gun to all others during our last engagement with the enemy on the 5th the smoke was so dense that I was unable to see the effect of the shot, I have since been informed that we sank one of their largest steamers & cripled [*sic*] two others; but they have succeeded in getting them up & taking them round to Newbern. We were struck 44 times and twice in one place, but I considered our most serious injury was the shooting away of the chase of the after gun, apart from the loss of the Tender which was a very fine boat and well fitted up.[5]

■ 16 May 1864

Comdr. J. W. Cooke, CS *Albemarle*, Plymouth, North Carolina, to Brooke, BP

I have succeeded in raising two 9 inch Dahlgren [sic] Guns and one 100 pr Parrott do from the Southfield and hope to succeed in getting the others. The Parrott Gun I mounted to day on the river fort and I wish to know what I shall do with the 9 in Dahlgrens [sic], as I have no projectiles for them.

I am very anxious to receive the Gun to supply the place of the Stern Gun I think your Gun is superior to all others, and had I have had two broadside Guns I think that I should have succeeded in sinking the whole Yankee fleet. We were struck 44 times and tha[t] too at short musket shot range; they also endeavor to run us down and when that failed, endeavore[d] to surround us with a seine, bu[t] fortunately the lines parted in payin[g] it out. Have you sent a Torpedo?

14 June 1864

Notation on envelope states hour of Lizzie's death, BP

For Lt. John M. Brooke to be read when I am dead.

Lizzie died at 4:45 a.m., Tuesday, June 14, 1864. She had been in declining health for several years and died of consumption. She had written letters of instructions to be opened at her death on:

August 11, 1860
October 30, 1860
September 21, 1862
June 20, 1863

15 June 1864

Records of Shockhoe Cemetery, Richmond, Virginia

On this day Lizzie Brooke was interred at the age of 37.

■ **20 June 1864**

Secretary of the Navy Stephen R. Mallory to Comdr. James D. Bulloch, *Official Records, Navy*, 2d series, p. 675

Ship the steel, tin, and zinc ordered by Commander Brooke and saved from, the <u>Matilda</u> as early as practicable. We are much in want of those articles in our shops for manufacturing purposes.

■ **23 June 1864**

Lt. Col. Joseph A. Yates, First South Carolina Regular Artillery, Headquarters, Fort Johnson, South Carolina, to Brooke, BP

Sometime since I received your kind letter enclosing diagram showing practical method for arranging sights to guns which is quite ingenious, as well [as] very serviceable, and of course correct. . . .

In my last letter giving some account of the use of your Guns, I mentioned that the 6.4 gun that had been fired so often had the day previous to my writing burst at the muzzle, breaking off about 15 inches, much to my regret, but I determined to give her a more thorough test—and sent her to the city and had her cut off and banded at the muzzle, leaving two horizontal cracks extending back towards the breech about eight (8) inches, which cracks are now entirely covered by band. She was again mounted and has been fired about one hundred and twenty two (122) time[s] without any apparent injury and with the same wonderful accuracy, distance 2,800 yards—being the distance of the enemies Batteries from her Chamber. She still maintains her reputation as the best gun of her size in the district, in which opinion I fully concur. Knowing that no Officer feels a deeper interest in our branch of service than yourself, and that you are anxious to know all that is going on, so as to assist you in further advancement of its service, for which you have already done so much, I enclose the Report of a Board of Officers assembled for that purpose.

■ **4 July 1864**
Brooke, Office of Ordnance and Hydrography, to Flag Officer William W. Hunter, Commanding Naval Forces Afloat, Savannah, Georgia, William W. Hunter Papers, Flowers Collection, Duke University

To secure uniformity and accuracy in reports of the number of fires from each gun in service, the accompanying blank forms have been prepared. You will please cause them to be distributed to the Commanding Officers of the vessels under your command, to be filled up and forwarded to this Office with the usual quarterly returns.

■ **28 July 1864**
Catesby ap R. Jones, Selma, Alabama, to Brooke, BP

I must have more aid in conducting these works. We have 200 negroes to clothe and feed in addition to feeding the mechanics, and this occupies much of my time and troubles me very much, tho the Paymaster should attend to it. I asked to have Mr. Fournier appointed a paymaster, but since then, Mr. Ickes formerly, a merchant of this place, and who has acted as our Agent, has informed me that he would accept the appointment. He would then relieve me of all anxiety on account of supplies, and I wish you would ask for his appointment and urge it as it would make us more efficient, besides in other modes being beneficial. Our present Paymaster has no experience, and does but little more than pay bills—he would do very well on board ship. . . . This matter is more important than you may suppose and I hope you will arrange it.

I have six guns waiting bands, have not blacksmiths to forge them. The double banded ten inch is a very fine gun and will I think do credit.

■ **3 August 1864**
Matthew F. Maury, Bermuda (?), to Brooke, BP

Ill [sic] attend to the gun cotton with much pleasure. Murdaugh I think is in Scotland at present. Its [sic] right hard to get the hang of it in the manufacture of it.

When packed for use, its [sic] about ⅓ the weight, and from 3 to 6 times the explosive power of gun powder.

There never was an invention or discovery that some Jon Bull was not the first to make. He has been for the last year trying to prove that Watt [sic] was the first to invent photography, and as for guns, he invented them all. I should take no notice of the complaint. It was an impudent thing to write such a letter. Suppose you write one back to "Vic."

I hope you get the books all safe.

Thanks for delivering the parcel for my family. I send you another and please send it to R. H. Maury's office.

Love to McCorkle, yours truly. [This letter refers to the fact that Blakely tried to grab credit for discovering the air space principle.]

■ **17 August 1864**
   Lt. Robert D. Minor, Flag Ship *Fredericksburg*, James River Squadron, to Brooke, BP

To burst our shells at the right time and at the right spot where the Yankees are digging, I have removed the percussion fuzes and substituted time fuzes with McEvoys igniters, and the result is very satisfactory.

■ **19 August 1864**
   Secretary of the Navy Stephen R. Mallory to Comdr. James D. Bulloch, England, *Official Records, Navy,* 2d series, p. 708

Since writing my observations relative to operations against the whale trade, conversations with Commander Brooke and Lieutenant [Robert R.?] Carter have confirmed my opinion of the importance of the subject. . . .[6] Enclosed herewith I hand you the views of Commander Brooke who spent much time in surveying the North Pacific and the coast of Japan upon the general fishing grounds of the whalemen.

■ **19 August 1864**
   Memo by Brooke alluded to in Secretary of the Navy Stephen R. Mallory's letter to James D. Bulloch, *Official Records, Navy,* 2d series, p. 708-9

A fast vessel with auxiliary steam power leaving the meridian of the Capt of Good Hope on the 1st January would reach Sydney in Australia in forty days, adding twenty days for incidental interruptions, and leaving the coast of Australia on the 1st of March, passing through the whaling ground between New Zealand and New Holland and the Caroline group, landing at Ascension [Ascension or Assumption I] and allowing thirty days for incidental interruptions, would reach the Ladrone Islands [Marianas] by the 1st of June. She would then, visiting the Bonin Islands, Sea of Japan, Okhotsk, and North Pacific, be in position about the 15th of September, north of the island of Oahu [in the Hawaiian Islands], distant from 60 to 100 miles, to intercept the North Pacific whaling fleet bound to Oahu with the products of the summer cruise.

■ **10 September 1864**

Secretary of the Navy Stephen R. Mallory to Catesby ap R. Jones, chief of Ordnance Works, Selma, Alabama, Jones Family Papers, LC

Your letter of the 5th Inst. has been received. The services which you are rendering at Selma are regarded by this Department as more important to the country than any which you could otherwise perform in the Navy, and not less valuable to its best interests than those which are being rendered by any other Naval Officers.

You can be placed in the Provisional Navy at any time, and you were not so placed, under the Presidents views of its organization, only because your services in your present sphere of duty were regarded by me as indispensable; and were you now withdrawn from it I would find it extremely difficult to supply your place.

I trust that the efficient discharge of the important duties devolved upon you, and which necessarily precluded you from sea service, will not be found to decrease your right to, and your chances of, advancement in a profession in which you are regarded as, in all respects, a most efficient officer.

■ **11 September 1864**

Maj. Francis W. Smith, Commanding Battery Dantzler, Howlett's Farm, to Brooke, BP

In accordance with your request, I beg leave to submit the following report of the double banded VII inch Brooke rifle, No. 2010, in position at this battery.

This gun has been opened 8 or 9 times upon the enemy's fleet & batteries. The results in 3 of these cases are given.

I On the 22nd June, this battery engaged the enemy's fleet of four ironclad monitors, a very high wind prevailed, the vessels lying about 2400 yards from the battery. We commenced with cast iron bolts, and when we had attained the range, made use of the wrought iron projectiles. The accuracy of the gun with this latter bolt was remarked by all, & deserters report that one of the turrets was struck. . . . an indentation several inches deep was made & the turret was cracked some three feet above & below the indentation. They add that a board of survey condemned the vessel & that she was ordered to the Gosport Navy Yard for repairs, & this report was confirmed by parties coming in at different times. Certain it is that on the 23rd the monitor upon which we concentrated, left the fleet and that since the 22nd no monitor has fired a gun at this battery, tho' previous to that time the shelling was very frequent.

II On the day, on which the Confederate fleet engaged the enemy at Signal Hill, orders were received [at] this battery to engage a battery of the enemy distant 3100 yards, & elevated 125 feet above the water, so as to draw its fire from our fleet. Seven percussion shell were fired by this gun at the battery. Two shots only were necessary for the range, the remaining five bursting with unerring precision upon the superior slope of the enemy's parapet.

In conclusion I would remark that the gun is the best heavy piece of ordnance that I have ever seen used. It is worked more rapidly than a 10 inch Columbiad, army carriage, with only 12 men.

■ **22 September 1864**

Brooke, Office of Ordnance and Hydrography, to Lieutenant Commanding James Henry Rochelle, *Palmetto State*, James H. Rochelle Papers, Duke University

Charges for XI inch treble banded Brooke gun Smooth Bore

With shell . . . 15 pounds

With grape . . . 15 pounds

With cast shot, ordinary firing 15 to 20 pounds

With cast shot against Iron Clads—40 to 45 pounds

With wrought shot against Iron Clads—40 to 45 pounds

The high charges of 40 to 45 pounds are only to be employed in <u>close action</u> against <u>Iron Clads</u>.

■ **22 September 1864**

Gen. Robert E. Lee, Headquarters, Petersburg, Virginia, to Brooke, BP

I have received your dispatch of the 21st. I think the 10 inch Columbiads, now mounted at Bishops Battery, are as good for the distance as those you propose. The 7 inch rifle will be mounted to night, & that Battery will be complete. The double banded ten inch & the two 7 inch rifles which you kindly offer, I propose placing in the battery under construction behind Proctors Creek. These guns will be more elevated than those at Bishops, have a broad sweep & will require to be of longer range. I think therefore they will be more suitable for the latter position. The other two 7 inch rifles I propose placing on the north side of the river at Signal Hill, Proctors Creek, Bishops & the bluff to the right of Bishops, that the enemy's boats after passing the Canal, with the aid of our navy, ought to be repulsed. If agreeable to the navy I should like the battery at Proctors Creek to be manned by them.

Will you be so kind as to inform me whether the double banded 10 inch, and the rifles are now aboard the Gunboats, or whether you only propose to make use of the Gunboats to Convoy them to their destination. If aboard the boats it may be better to land those for the south side of the river at the Wharf at Drurys [Drewry's Bluff]. If in Richmond I believe by taking them by rail to Chester [you] may save trouble.

■ **24 September 1864**

Brooke to Commodore Duncan N. Ingraham, Commanding Naval Station, Charleston, South Carolina (copy), BP

I have to request you to obtain information from the proper authorities at Charleston of the time required to load the 600 pdr. Blakely gun, with a view to ascertain its adaptability for vessels and to make a report of the same to this office.

Thru channels to Maj. Blanding, Capt. Parker, & Lt. [Theodore] Bary on Sullivan's Island. Ormsby Blanding, Comdg. Hd. Qrs. 1st Sub. Div. Sullivans [*sic*] Island, Oct. 1, 1864: My experience in firing the Blakely Gun with the Harding shell upon its present carriage, is, that it can be fired once in 15 minutes, but I have no doubt it can be put upon a carriage where it can be fired oftener.

C. W. Parker, Capt. 1st S.C. Arty. 1st Sub. Div. Sullv's Isld., Oct. 1, 1864. I have never loaded the Gun, but conclude from the drill and from raising the projectile by the elevator, that the time required will vary, from fifteen to twenty minutes.

Thos G. Bary, Lt. Oct. 2d—15 minutes on present carriage.

■ **28 September 1864**

Matthew F. Maury, Bowdon, Manchester, to Capt. M. H. Jansen, Matthew F. Maury Papers, LC

We had an interesting discussion upon gun cotton. Baron Lenk has an establishment—Prentice & Co. Strawmarket, Suffolk—for the manufacture of it.

It is now used entirely for blasting in some of the mines. Here is what the committee report in substance:

Guns fired with it, shoot as hard, but recoil less, heat less & foul less, than they do with gun powder.

Shells loaded with gun cotton, burst in the gun & injure it.

Genl. Hay R[oyal] A[rtillery] has been practicing and experimenting with it for small arms. At the distance of 500 yards, and off hand, he lodged 12 shots one after the other, in a space 12x18 in. He made his cartridges of a layer of slow and then quick burning cotton—for it can be made to burn at any speed from 1 to 1000 feet a second. With the gentle layer, he put the ball in motion, leaving time & space for the quickly acting to expand all its force ere the ball left the barrel. He attributes the greater accuracy to the fact that there was no kick to the gun as with powder. In blasting rock they find, that, pound for pound, gun cotton does from 30 to 39 times the work of gun powder. . . .

The British Government has appointed a Board to investigate, experiment & report upon Gun Cotton in all its war-like aspects, and they are also moving upon the question of submarine mining & torpedoes.

These are <u>obliged to make the defence superior to the attack</u>, whenever the contest is between ships & forts. Please my good patient Dutch friend, put that into your pipe & smoke it . . .

No good experiments have been made to determine the relation between depth & torpedo. . . .

The self acting torpedoes are set off in various ways, sometimes by acids so arranged that when a vessel strikes and the phial will break and so set fire to the powder; but more generally they are armed with levers, trigger fashion, so that let a vessel strike one of these things as she may, she will set off a trigger that explodes a percussion fuse.

I prefer gun cotton near the surface, for this reason. Bulk for bulk, gun cotton is $\frac{1}{3}$ the weight of gun powder—and gun powder is heavier you know—a little—than water—consequently you can make magazines of gun cotton to float—but you cant do that with gun powder without extra fittings.

■ **29 September 1864**
   Lt. Col. Joseph A. Yates, Fort Johnson, to Brig. Gen. R[oswell] S. Ripley, BP

I have the honor to acknowledge the receipt of your communication in reference to the time employed in firing the 600 pr Blakely Gun. We in experimenting did not use the apparatus furnished by the Inventor for loading. We had constructed a platform under the muzzle of the Gun, and the shot placed on it before commencing practice. With the Blakely projectile we fired six times in a half hour, but the flanges had been filed off so as to ease them. With the Blakely projectile she can be fired more rapidly, we experienced inconvenience from the groves [sic] becoming fouled, this difficulty was overcome to a great extent by lubricating freely. I would respectfully suggest, that by all means some arrangement be made by which the projectiles can be placed near the muzzle of the gun, convenient for entering, as the delay of lifting the shot is not only very great, but very tiresome to the detachment serving the gun, without such arrangement in my opinion she will not be efficient—I would also call the attention of the Authorities to the difficulty of elevating and the great time consumed in so doing. I would suggest to overcome the difficulty that a Hydraulic Screw be arranged for the purpose.

■ **29 September 1864**

Comdr. James D. Bulloch to Secretary of the Navy Stephen R. Mallory, *Official Records, Navy*, 2d series, p. 729

I had obtained from Captain Maury a set of whale charts published in connection with his Physical Geography of the Sea, but the memorandum enclosed in your dispatch of the 19th ultimo, containing the practical experience and observations of Commander Brooke and Lieutenant Carter upon the periodical localities of the whaling fleet, has reached me at an opportune time and shall be handed to the commander of our cruiser for his guidance.[7]

■ **30 September 1864**

John R. Hamilton, Confederate States Navy, Halifax, Nova Scotia, to Brooke, BP

[Hamilton was unavoidably detained in Halifax.] I was much pleased to hear of the arrival of the "Hope," with the Armstrong Shunt Rifles, 150 pounders. These guns were ordered by Mers. Train, Trenholm Co. by my suggestion, and I furnished those gentlemen with a full description of the guns, in their construction and use, besides interior & exterior drawing, so that I hope in whatever hands they fall, that they will be perfectly informed of the ordnance they have to use. In the experiments which were concluded on the 3d of August at Shoeburyness against iron-plates, it was demonstrated, that no iron clad in the English or any other Navy was invulnerable to this 150 pounder gun when fired with 30 to 35 pounds of powder and <u>steel</u> shot. A target representing the sides of the "Gloire" was riddled and the sides of the ship driven in board in great splinters.[8] The Bellrophon with her 6 inch solid plates of such beautiful manufacture that though penetrated they do not crack, can not resist the steel shell and shot at 1500 yds fired from exactly the same guns the "Hope" took in, and with them are steel shell and spherical steel shot. . . . the 150 pounder, which only weighs 16,000 lbs. can be worked [ea]sily onboard of any vessel. I would call your attention particularly to the fuzes sent with 150 pounders. In all of the experiments at Shoeburyness their success has been complete.

I do not know that you ever received my letter thanking you for kindly offering me the position of Ordnance Officer in England. Had I been disengaged at the time & had Murdaugh not already have taken the duty I would have been much pleased to have the opportunity which the place offers to serve usefully the Government.

■ **5 October 1864**

Diary of Matthew F. Maury, 2 September 1864–13 August 1865, Matthew F. Maury Papers, LC

Instructed Murdaugh how to pack up his 1000 lbs G. cotton for transportation to Brook[e].

■ **6 October 1864**

Lt. Gen. Dabney H. Maury, Headquarters, District of the Gulf, Mobile, Alabama, to Brooke, BP

We have here several 10 and 8 in. Double banded Brooke Guns (smooth bore) recd from the Naval Works at Selma. Their effectiveness would be very materially increased by the use of the <u>wrought</u> iron spherical shot.

I am extremely desirous of obtaining some of these projectiles, even if only a few, and will ask of you the favor to furnish them, if in your power. . . .

■ **6 October 1864**

Brooke, Office of Ordnance and Hydrography, to Flag Officer William W. Hunter, Commanding Squadron at Savannah, Georgia, William W. Hunter Papers, Flowers Collection, Duke University.

Your letter of the 1st instant, reporting the breaking off of 18 inches of muzzle of rifled and banded 32 pdr. on board the C. S. Steamer "Georgia" in Target practice on the 27th ulto, and that it had been replaced by a IX inch shell gun, has been received.

This gun, Register number 1356, was one of a number of 32 pdr. smooth bore guns cast at the Tredegar early in the war.

You will please reserve the broken gun to be employed in testing 6.4 inch shells at Savannah, and direct the Ordnance Officer of the station to report what shells were used, where made, etc. There must be a very considerable number of defective shells at Savannah. It is probable that they were made at Charlotte, if so, the remainder of those received from the Ordnance Works at that place should be condemned.

Commander Jones will be directed to supply, if possible, shells from Selma.

It is desirable that the muzzle of the gun should be cut to a smooth face.

■ **17 October 1864**

Brooke to officers commanding batteries, BP

<u>Charges of VII inch Brooke rifles, double banded</u> with shell, shrapnel, grape, or canister—From 8 to 10 pounds.

With wrought iron bolts—10 to 12 pounds

With wrought iron bolts, only to be used in close action with Monitors—13 to 14 pounds

In all cases the smallest effective charge is to be used. The high charges strain the guns, and their employment is only justified by such emergencies as arise in contact with iron clads.

Charges of 6.4 inch Brooke rifles, double banded
> With shell, shrapnel, grape or conister—From 7 to 8 pounds.
>
> With cast iron bolts. . . . 8 to 10 pounds
>
> With wrought and cast iron bolts in close action with Monitors —12 pounds.
>
> The same rule as regards high charges of VII inch rifle applies to the 6.4 inch rifle.

■ **17 October 1864**

Capt. J. W. Whiting, First Alabama Battery Artillery, Richmond, Virginia, to Brooke, BP

Judging from my observation during the action of the 5th & the siege, I am decidedly of the opinion that the wrought iron bolt is the only effective missile which can be successfully used against iron clads. I saw cast iron shot strike the sides of the Tennessee & break in fragments—when she came up to fight the Fort a few days after her surrender.

■ **20 October 1864**

Brooke to Capt. Sidney S. Lee, in charge of Office of Orders and Detail, Richmond, BP

I have to request that the circumstances attending the bursting (cracking) of VII rifle No. 1867 on board the "Fredericksburg" in action on the 29th ultimo be investigated

It is desirable that the officers appointed to make the investigation should include in their report so far as may be obtained, information upon the following points.

> The total number of fires with this gun while on board the "Fredericksburg."
>
> The charges of powder, and kinds of projectiles used.
>
> The degree of elevation.
>
> Was the cartridge rammed or pushed home?
>
> Were the projectiles lubricated?
>
> Was the gun at any time heated by rapid firing?
>
> Were any shells or bolts observed to break in the gun?
>
> Is it certain that the gun was not cracked prior to the last discharge?
>
> What kinds of projectiles were employed in the last two fires, and what kinds of fuzes?
>
> Were the last two projectiles fired seen after leaving the gun?
>
> What range was obtained by this gun during the action of the 29th ultimo?
>
> Was it worked under the immediate superintendence of a Competent Officer, and by a well instructed crew?

■ **25 October 1864**

Comdr. Robert G. Robb, Lt. A[lexander] N. DeBree, and Lt. Robert D. Minor (Board of Officers), CSS *Fredericksburg*, Richmond, to Capt. Sidney S. Lee, Office of Orders and Detail, BP

Burst onboard the C.S.S. <u>Fredericksburg</u> in action on September 29, 1864, a double banded VII inch Brooke gun loaded with 12 pounds of powder and 15 second time shells with McEvoy igniters. The total number of rounds ever fired from the gun was 113. The gun was cast at Tredegar in 1863. Rifled and banded there, too. On occasion the gun has been fired with 14 lbs. of powder. The elevation was from 4 to 5 degrees on the day the gun burst.

The gun was worked under the immediate superintendence of an officer who has not had much experience in his profession, but the gun's crew had been well instructed in their duties.

[In an endorsement Brooke states:] The 18 pound charges alluded to in this report were furnished with a distinct understanding on the part of Flag Officer Mitchell that they were not to be fired, except in case of extreme emergency. [They were never used.] A communication on this subject was addressed to Flag Officer Mitchell May 27, 1864.

From the allusion in the report to the 4–18 pound charges it might be supposed that 14 lbs. was not considered a high charge. [Apparently the gun was defective.]

■ **4 November 1864**

Brooke to Secretary of the Navy Stephen R. Mallory, *Official Records, Navy*, 2d series, p. 755–58

Early in June, in consequence of the threatening attitude of the enemy before Atlanta, and in accordance with the suggestions of the military authorities, Lieutenant D. P. McCorkle, in charge of the ordnance works at that place, commenced moving stores and machinery to Augusta, and succeeded in transferring safely all the machinery, engines, boilers, and the greater portion of the stores, prior to the evacuation of the city.

Immediate steps were taken by him to commence, with the force at his command, the manufacture of ordnance stores at Augusta. Various causes incidental to the disturbed condition of that portion of the country, have combined to retard the progress of the work. . . . The interruption caused by the removal of the ordnance works from Atlanta to Augusta has been productive of inconvenience, as upon that establishment we were largely dependent for ordnance equipments of vessels at Charleston, Savannah and Mobile. Until the works at Augusta are put in operation, the supplies for those points will be drawn from Charlotte, Selma and Richmond.

Great credit is due Lieutenant McCorkle, for the successful removal of this machinery, etc., from Atlanta to Augusta, and for the energy he now exhibits in re-establishing the works.

As stated in my former report, the force at the Selma works, under the superintendence of Commander Catesby Ap R. Jones, inadequate to carry on the various branches of that establishment, has been employed chiefly in the manufacture of guns, specially adapted for service against iron-clads.

Forty-seven guns of this character have been supplied for the defence of Mobile. . . . In addition to these, twelve guns of the same kind have been sent to other points, including Charleston and Wilmington, chiefly for land batteries, and there are now several on hand, which will be put in service in a few days.

It is to be regretted that the comparatively small number of mechanics required to render the machinery and facilities afforded by this important establishment fully available could not be obtained. Repeated applications for details of mechanics from the army have been made; but as the services of the men were generally considered more important in the field than in the workshop, and the details were therefore disapproved by commanding generals, very few have been granted. In consequence of the want of force, no projectiles have been cast for several months at the Selma establishment, and this is now severely felt, as, owing to the constant interruption of ordnance work in Richmond, the employees have been in the field the greater part of the summer, the suspension of work at Atlanta, and the difficulty of procuring iron of proper quality at Charlotte, the supply of projectiles on hand is inadequate to fully meet the wants of the service, particularly as the ammunition for naval rifles in battery on shore, has been chiefly supplied by this office. Efforts have been made to obtain foreign mechanics; but difficulties incidental to entering the Confederacy from abroad, have hitherto prevented the accomplishment of this desirable object. Commander Jones has made every effort to insure the efficiency of the works, and, although in consequence of the want of assistants, his labors have been unusually arduous and trying, he has rendered service of which the importance can hardly be overestimated.

The naval ordnance works at Charlotte, under the superintendence of Chief Engineer [Henry A.] Ramsay, have been in active operation with excellent results. This establishment is the only one in the Confederacy at which heavy forging can be done. Shafting for steamers and wrought iron projectiles are forged and finished. Gun-carriages, blocks, and ordnance equipments of nearly every description, including the production of an ordnance laboratory, are supplied to the service. Less interruption from the movement of the enemy has been experienced at Charlotte than at any other of the naval establishments. Its position is favorable in this respect, and, being central, its lines of communication with other important points are convenient. The iron produced from the furnaces from which it is supplied, is gradually being improved in quality. . . .

The growing importance of this establishment renders it expedient to add by lease or otherwise to the ground originally purchased and now occupied by the works, which are much cramped for want of room, several lots adjoining.

Urgent applications have been received from Generals commanding at Mobile and Wilmington for wrought iron projectiles, and it is to be regretted that we have not, at other establishments, machinery adapted to their manufacture.

It has long been considered important that the manufacture of steel projectiles, which are undoubtedly superior to those of wrought iron, should be carried on in the Confederacy, or that at least some of the processes employed abroad in the production of material better suited than simple cast or wrought iron for shot and shell to be employed against iron-clads, should be adapted, but, with the limited amount of skilled labor, insufficient to supply the current demands for the ordinary munitions of war, it has not been possible to do so.

At the naval ordnance works at Richmond, under the charge of Lieutenant R. D. Minor, and, during his temporary absence in the James river squadron, under the superintendence of Mr. R. B. Wright, much important work has been executed. Nearly all the equipments of the vessels in James river and at Wilmington have been supplied from these works, and, in addition, the equipments including carriages and ammunition for several heavy navy guns in battery on shore.

The employees of this establishment enrolled in the naval battalion, have, with the exception of a few skillful mechanics whose services were indispensable to prepare ammunition for immediate use, been in the field during the greater part of the summer.

The naval powder mills at Columbia, under the superintendence of Mr. P. M. [T. Baudery] Gareschi, have supplied the wants of the service. The powder there manufactured is of excellent quality, and the operations of the works are conducted in the most satisfactory manner.

The system of instruction and discipline adopted in the naval school, under the superintendence of Lieutenant Wm. H. Parker, has proved of great benefit to the service.

It is recommended that, after the December examination, the second and third classes (now the third and fourth) be ordered on active duty, retaining on board the school ship the Patrick Henry the first (now the second) and fourth classes. . . . this would give about sixty midshipmen to the school, leaving about twenty-four on active duty.[9]

- **5 November 1864**
  Report of Secretary of the Navy Stephen R. Mallory, BP

[In the Battle of Mobile Bay, 5 August 1864,] the enemy's ships, among the finest afloat, were armed with nine, ten, eleven and twenty-inch guns, whose projectiles varied in weight from eighty-four to four hundred and twenty-eight pounds. Their broadsides, the heaviest known, were discharged upon the "Tennessee," at distances ranging from three to thirty yards, and three of their heaviest ships, fitted as rams, ran into her repeatedly at full speed. The massive strength of the frame and the sloping armor of the ship resisted these assaults, and but one shot reached or made any impression upon the woodwork of the shield, and this did not go through it.

The resistance offered by inclined iron armor to the heaviest ordnance ever used upon the sea, was here fully tested at short ranges, and the result so far as known, shows the superiority of this arrangement over similar armor upon vertical planes.[10]

- **20 November 1864**
  Diary of General Josiah Gorgas

The Navy is decidedly out of luck. Mr. Mallory lacks earnestness and devotion to his duty. He is too good company and too generally informed to be worth much at any one thing, tho' a man of undoubted ability. He beats the Secretary of War in every discussion that arises—is in fact too smart for Mr. [James A.] Seddon. p. 151.[11]

- **25 November 1864**
  Matthew F. Maury Diary, 2 September 1864–13 August 1865, Matthew F. Maury Papers, LC

Wrote Brooke about gun cotton and my improvement suggested for Torpedo Boats. . . . Gave Brooke full account of Torpedo Boat.

- **2 December 1864**
  Matthew F. Maury Diary, Matthew F. Maury Papers, LC

[Wrote to] Murdaugh about packing the gun cotton for Brooke.

- **12 December 1864**
  William Garnett to Anna M. Brooke, BP

The winter I spent in Washington, with your mother, she expected to die very soon, as you no doubt remember, as she often talked about it. In this state of mind, she made you a present of a Bible, in which she made a memorandum, alluding to your reading it, after her death. . . . You now have a Mother and three little sisters in Heaven—one who was born before you were. . . .[12]

7

Hard Work to the End

1865

■ **2 January 1865**
Brooke journal, BP

Today the first week day of the New Year I commence recording such incidents as may hereafter possess a certain interest. For the past six months I have led a life at variance with my natural inclinations in the belief and hope that I would thus avoid certain reflections and moods of unhappiness that unchecked would be insupportable. I believe that the necessity of it existed, is now past, and I may direct my thoughts and actions with the divine aid which I now implore to the accomplishment of noble ends.[1] Today engaged in writing brief report on the means upon which we depend for the supply of munitions of war.

Recd. several letters from Comd. C[atesby] ap R. Jones at Selma. He is ready to commence pattern of a new gun. Desires authority to make exchanges of cotton for Naval supplies through Texas. Made New Years call on Mrs. [Stephen R.] Mallory, none other. Genl Anderson & Co. propose selling their machinery etc. to the Government. Shall consult Genl. [Josiah] Gorgas in relation to it. The enemy fleet burst 7–100 pdr. Parrott guns in their attack on Fort Fisher at Wilmington. We burst several. Have not yet received detailed report.

■ **3 January 1865**
Brooke journal, BP

At work today on brief report for information of Congress. Spent the evening at Dr. Gibson's in conversation with him. Remained until 12:30. Snow.

■ **4 January 1865**
Brooke journal, BP

A bright sunshiny day. Authorised Jones to purchase supplies with cotton through Texas. Finished report to Congress and added a brief synopsis.

■ **5 January 1865**
Brooke journal, BP

Fine day, consulted with Messrs Anderson & Col. Gorgas in regard to lease of the Tredegar Works. Did much work at my office. Spent the evening with Miss Mollie Green. Met Major Carrington there. Called at Dr. [Yelverton?] Garnett's. All going out to spend the evening.[2]

■ **5 January 1865**
Secretary of the Navy Stephen R. Mallory to President Jefferson Davis, Jefferson Davis Papers, Flowers Collection, Duke University

I have the honor to submit the following data in response to so much of the Senate's recent Resolution of inquiry addressed to you upon the subject of the general condition of the country as was submitted to me—: the means at the command of this Department for supplying munitions of war.

The Selma, Ala. Foundry. The capacity of this establishment is large; and would enable it to supply per week seven heavy guns of calibres varying from 6.4 to 11 inches, ranging in weight from 11000 to 24000 pounds each, and five field pieces, with all the projectiles for the same, and projectiles also for the general service of the Navy.

It is now delivering two heavy guns and one field piece per week, but no projectiles, the discrepancy between its capacity and its product being due to the want of skilled labor.

The Naval Ordnance Works Charlotte N.C. This establishment manufactures shells, and wrought iron and cast iron shot. Worked to its full capacity it could supply the Navy and Shore batteries in charge of the Navy. The heaviest forgings in the Confederacy are also done here and much machinery manufactured. It is now worked to about one half of its capacity only for the want of mechanics.

Naval Ordnance Works Richmond Va. Ordnance equipments of every description are manufactured and heavy guns are banded here. Its capacity is sufficient for all naval wants in the waters of Virginia, and to meet a large demand from the Army, but for want of skilled labor only one half of its capacity is developed.

Naval Ordnance Works, at Atlanta Geo. The machinery of this establishment was moved to Augusta Geo upon the fall of Atlanta, and from Augusta upon the approach of the enemy to Fayetteville N.C. It will soon be in operation with a capacity to employ one hundred mechanics in the production of all ordnance equipments and projectiles.

Naval Powder Works Columbia S.C. This establishment is worked to its full capacity and makes 20,000 pounds of powder per month with ten experts. In the course of a few weeks its capacity will be doubled by the addition of new machinery and four experts.

The supply of crude material, iron nitre etc. consumed in these works, is shown by the returns of the nitre & mining Bureau.

Means of supplying transportation. Of the three kinds of transportation employed in the public service viz, rail road, field and water transportation the means of this Department enable it to supply but little. We have repaired locomotives and built cars as far as our limited force of experts permitted. With additional mechanics our shops could render very important service in this respect, and we might construct transport vessels when required.

Means of supplying subsistence. We have ample means of supplying all the subsistence required by the Navy; and of accumulating supplies for occasional aid to the Army. We rely upon purchases and upon importations. We have a packing establishment for beef and pork, and grist and flour mills and baking in successful operation at Albany Geo.

I respectfully invite attention to the accompanying paper from Commander Brooke upon ordnance and ordnance supplies.[3]

■ **6 January 1865**
Brooke journal, BP

Writing to Lt [William H.] Murdaugh aboard in relation to importations. Consulted Secretary in relation to Tredegar works etc. Also Col. [Isaac] St John, Chf. Of Nitre & Mining Bureau. Anna sick during the night. Saw Dr. Garnett and breakfasted with him. Lt. [Robert] Minor is shifting his quarters to 4th & Franklin. Did good work at office. Saw Capt. [Sidney Smith] Lee in regard to importance of relieving ord. officer of batteries on the South Side from watch etc.

■ **10 January 1865**
Brooke to Lt. (blank) Bradford (rough draft), BP

I desire to call your attention to an important fact in connexion with the management of rifle cannon which should receive due consideration from Artillerists. It is well known that guns when rapidly fired are heated and that this heat increases the expansive force of the powder gases as indicated by the increased recoil of heated guns and proved by experiment. The increase of force in any given case depends chiefly upon the degree of heat of the gun the length of time to which the cartridge is subjected to it in the bore and the weight of the projectile.

To avoid the danger of parting breechings and bursting guns arising from this increase of strength and to render as nearly uniform as possible the velocities of projectiles was the original and principal cause of the introduction into naval artillery service of three classes of charges for each calibre, viz service charge and first and second reduced charges. But as it has been considered advantageous to use the 1st reduced charge for close action even when the guns are not heated to increase the splintering effect by diminishing the velocity of the projectile they are known as ordinary and neat firing charges and thus Artillerists have been lead [*sic*] to attach more importance to their application in accordance with the distance of the object than with the state—temperature—of the gun, an error which leads in the case of rifles to the worst consequences. For, important as these considerations may be as applied to smooth bores they are still more important when applied to rifles.

Experiment has shown that the pressure of powder gases in guns is directly as the weight of the projectile, in other words the strain upon the walls of the bore of a VII-inch rifle when charged with 10 lbs of powder and a 120 lb bolt is about three times as great as that which is extended when a round 42 pds shot is used with the same charge of powder. Thus with 10 lbs of powder and a 42 pd. shot we suppose the pressure to be 40,000 lbs per square inch, with 10 lbs of powder and a 120 lb bolt the pressure will be 114,285 lbs. per square inch.

If then we further suppose both charges to be equally heated to such a degree as to increase their force by one quarter the pressure with the round 42 pd shot will be 40,000 + 10,000 = 50,000 with the 120 pd bolt will be 114,285 + 28,571 = 142,856. But the greater resistance of the bolt to the development of the expanding gases also causes the evolution of far more heat in the rifle than is evolved by the lesser resistance of the 42 pd. shot. The rifle is therefore sooner heated and to a higher degree than the smooth bore with its appropriate charge. And in addition to this greater heat which materially increases the wide difference of effect shown by the preceding comparison we must consider the further influence of suppression of windage by the expanding sabot, the resistance opposed to the passage of the bolt along the bore by the special grooves, the heat thus generated by friction etc. All of which tend to increase the strain upon rifles.

■ 24 February 1865
T. Baudery Garesché, Charlotte, North Carolina, to Brooke, BP

My telegram, and official letter of this date, will have informed you of the fate of the Columbia powder works, they are a total loss, except so far as they may have escaped the efforts of the enemy to destroy them.

■ 4 April 1865
Diary of John M. Brooke, BP

Left at 8 am for Cumberland C.H. Many stragglers from the army. At 1.20 pm stopped at Dr. Robertsons barn to feed and water, about 2½ miles from the Appomattox. Passed Mrs. Genl. William Mahone in an ambulance.

Reports of movements of our troops very much confused. Say what remains of our cavalry is skirmishing with the enemy near deep creek. The fruit trees are very numerous and covered with blossoms. Gov. ["Extra Billy"] Smith relates an amusing adventure. He got into the canal and was near being [drowned] injured the horse very much. "As you observe" said he "I got him by the tail". . . . We hear an occasional gun in the distance.[4]

■ **5 April 1865**
  Diary of John M. Brooke, BP

Slept at Dr. Crump's last night (Mrs. Isbells). Saw Maltie Goode Mrs. Isbell & Mrs. Crump. Left a note for Anna. turned off from Farmville road and passing through Ca Ina [*sic*] stopped at Mr Donovans for the night.

■ **7 April 1865**
  Diary of John M. Brooke, BP

Left Paces and reached Mrs. Jones' place she entertained us very hospitably. We spent the night there. Before reaching Mrs. Jones we stopped at Mr. Elliots Mill and had a very nice lunch.[5]

■ **8 April 1865**
  Diary of John M. Brooke, BP

Left Mrs. Jones about 7 am. and reached Panill Bridge on Staunton river about half past twelve, Discovered that one of the horses had lost a shoe. Stopped to feed and replace the shoe. Delightful weather. Have a bad cold and consequently do not feel very well. We hear conflicting accounts of the movements of the enemy. Stopped at Mr. Pringles for the night.

■ **9 April 1865**
  Diary of John M. Brooke, BP

Left Pringle, one of the horses was sick last night, bled him he appears well this morning Stopped at Riceville to water. Saw Mr. Anderson and got some tobacco from him.[6]

■ **10 April 1865**
  Diary of John M. Brooke, BP

Slept last night at a widows [house] came on the spring garden road to Danville.[7]

■ **11 April 1865**
  Diary of J. M. Brooke, BP

In the cars for Charlotte N.C. Stopped at Greensboro.[8]

Epilogue

L ike most of his Confederate friends, John Brooke after the war found himself penniless and without a job. Some friends and colleagues were hired for their technical knowledge by foreign governments, and they urged Brooke to do likewise, but he declined such offers. He was constrained by two factors: first, the desire to fulfill Lizzie's wish that he bring up Anna with loving care; and second, that he should, like General Lee, put the war behind him and seek to rebuild the country.

Commander Brooke, a United States Naval Academy graduate, did not qualify for amnesty under President Andrew Johnson's proclamation of May 1865 for several reasons. Therefore, he had to apply directly to the president for pardon. This he did, and with the help of such old friends as Admirals John Rodgers and Samuel Phillips Lee, who had won distinction in the Union navy, he obtained a pardon in August 1866.

In the meantime Brooke, in late 1865, was offered a job to teach astronomy and kindred subjects at the Virginia Military Institute in Lexington. Brooke was familiar with VMI because Lizzie's sister Louisa had married Thomas Williamson, professor of engineering there; Lizzie and her parents had often visited Lexington beginning in the 1850s, and Brooke had joined them when on leave. The pay at VMI was low, and the job was not as exciting as much of his past life had been, but it was a firm anchor. Thinking of what was best for Anna, he apparently planned only to remain a few years. But as things transpired, Brooke continued on the faculty until his retirement as professor emeritus in 1899. While there, Brooke organized the physics department.

During the long period from 1865 to 1899 John Brooke renewed many of his previous friendships, in the North and the South, and carried on a heavy correspondence. For a time he hoped to augment his income through a company he developed with his close Civil War ordnance friends Catesby Jones and Robert D. Minor. The purpose was to supply ordnance and other naval materiel, some of which was unique to the Confederacy, to foreign governments. Though hopes were high at first, the project failed because there was no central office, all three men had other jobs, and they were separated geographically at a time when transportation and communication were slow. Nonetheless, for many years Brooke on the side studied ordnance, conducted scientific experiments, wrote technical articles, and corresponded with ordnance officers in the U.S. Navy and experts abroad. One indication that Brooke was not forgotten was that he was appointed to the Board of Visitors of the United States Naval Academy in 1879 through the efforts of his Annapolis classmates. He was pleased with the appointment and performed his duties conscientiously.

Despite his devotion to Lizzie, Brooke found after a few years that without a wife his life was not fulfilling. Moreover, he realized that a wife could be a tremendous help in rearing Anna. The family records show that after the war he courted several popular daughters of prominent Virginia families. Finally, he won the heart of Kate Corbin Pendleton, the widow of Alexander Swift "Sandy" Pendleton, adjutant general of "Stonewall" Jackson and his successors, who was killed at the Battle of Fisher's Hill in 1864. Sandy was the son of West Point graduate and Episcopal minister William Nelson Pendleton, rector of Grace Episcopal Church in Lexington before and after the Civil War, who during the war served as Lee's chief of artillery in the Army of Northern Virginia.

After Sandy's death Kate lived for a time with the Pendletons, but following the death of her infant son, she accepted a position as governess for the family of William Preston Johnston, a professor at what was then Washington College (now Washington and Lee University). Johnston was the son of Gen. Albert Sidney Johnston, who had been killed at Shiloh and was an old friend of John Brooke's father. John Brooke and Kate Corbin Pendleton were married in 1871. They had a happy marriage and had three children, two of whom lived to maturity. Anna lived with them. She never married and died in 1885 at the age of tewnty-eight. John Brooke died in Lexington in 1906, outliving most of his Civil War friends. Kate died in 1919 in Staten Island, New York, where she was living with her daughter Rosa, Mrs. Henry Parker Willis. Tales of Brooke's adventures in Japan in the 1850s must have inspired his son, George Mercer Brooke, Col. U.S.A., to enlist in the army and apply for service in Japan, where he learned the Japanese language.

Notes

Introduction: *Brooke's Actions on the Eve of War*

1. See George M. Brooke, Jr., *John M. Brooke's Pacific Cruise and Japanese Adventure* (Honolulu: University of Hawaii Press, 1986).
2. Charles Wolcott Brooks, San Francisco, to John Brooke, 19 May 1860, BP.
3. John Brooke, Lexington, Virginia, to Isaac Toucey, 5 May 1860, Officers' Letters to the Secretary of the Navy, RG 45, NA.
4. Toucey to Brooke, 3 May 1860.BP
5. Brooke journal, 3 June 1860, BP.
6. Brooke, Lexington, Virginia, to Matthew Maury, Letters received 4 May 1860, RG 78, NA.
7. Brooke to Toucey, 11 May 1860, Officers' Letters to the Secretary of the Navy, RG 45, NA.
8. Duncan N. Ingraham to Brooke, Washington, D.C., 18 May 1860, Letters to Officers, RG 37, NA.
9. Brooke to Lizzie Brooke, 22 May 1860. John and Lizzie were first cousins, so Lizzie's "pa," William Garnett, was not only John's father-in-law but also his uncle. The relationship was close. During the many years Brooke was at sea, his wife stayed with her parents, first in Norfolk and later in Lexington. William Garnett always manifested a keen interest in his nephew's career. After Brooke's marriage in 1849 he spent a great deal of time at sea. Though the couple wrote frequently, communication was slow and undependable, and Brooke, introverted by nature, found separation exceedingly difficult.
10. John Rodgers to Brooke, 4 June 1860, BP.
11. Brooke to William Gwin, 4 June 1860 (copy), BP.
12. Rodgers to Brooke, 4 June 1860, BP.
13. Toucey to Brooke, 12 June 1860, BP. Isaac Toucey, a Connecticut Yankee, had had wide experience in the field of politics, having served as both representative and senator from his native state in Congress, as governor of Connecticut, and as U.S. attorney general before beginning his four-year term as secretary of the navy. He seems to have borne no animus against Southern officers and was "suspected, possibly without reason, of arranging U.S. naval forces in 1860 so as to aid the South in its secession" (*Webster's Biographical Dictionary,* 1st ed. [Springfield, Mass.: S. & C. Merriam Co., Publishers, 1943], 1480).

14. Brooke to Cyrus Field, 25 June 1860 (copy), BP.
15. Toucey to Brooke, 28 June 1860, Letters to Officers by the Secretary of the Navy, RG 45, NA.
16. The information was obtained from a letter of Nelson M. Blake, Chief Naval Section, War Records Branch, National Archives, to G. M. Brooke, Jr., 4 Feb. 1952, BP. Blake found the information in RG 125, Records of the Office of the Judge Advocate General (U.S. Navy), NA.
17. Brooke, Boston, to Lizzie, 1 July 1860, BP. The "Yankee relatives" derived from Brooke's mother, Lucy Thomas, who was born in Duxbury. In 1860 a number of her cousins still lived there. There is no evidence that national issues were discussed during Brooke's visit or any ill feeling developed. After the war Brooke's Thomas relatives expressed a warm regard for him. William, who worked in New York, was the only one of John Brooke's seven siblings to survive infancy. He had a club foot and was five years younger than John, whom he seems to have admired.
18. Brooke to Toucey, 28 June 1860 (copy), BP.
19. Toucey to Brooke, 30 June 1860, Letters to Officers by the Secretary of the Navy, RG 45, NA; 7 July 1860, Appointments, Orders, and Resignations, RG 24, NA.
20. 18 July 1860, Brooke Diary, BP.
21. Brooke to Capt. J. B. Frisbie, Vallejo, 18 July 1860 (copy); Brooke to Toucey, 24 Sept. 1860 (copy), BP.
22. Duncan N. Ingraham, chief of the Bureau of Ordnance and Hydrography, to Brooke, 8 Aug. 1860, BP.
23. John Van McCollum to Brooke, 16 Sept. 1860, BP.
24. Toucey to Brooke, 29 Sept. 1860, Letters to Officers by the Secretary of the Navy, RG 45, NA; Brooke to Toucey, 3 Oct. 1860, Officers' Letters to the Secretary of the Navy, RG 45, NA.
25. Lizzie to Brooke, 30 Oct. 1860, BP.
26. Robert C. Wyllie, minister of foreign affairs, to Brooke, 15 Nov. 1860, BP.
27. Annual Report of Secretary Isaac Toucey, 1 Dec. 1860, p. 3–9, Senate documents, 2d Sess., 36th Cong., NR, 1861.
28. William N. Brooke to Brooke, 5 Dec. 1860, BP.
29. Robert Wilden Neeser, *Statistical and Chronological History of the United States Navy, 1775–1907*, vol. 2 (New York: The MacMillan Company, 1909), 9.
30. Brooke to Garnett, January 11, 1861 (copy), BP.
31. Neeser, *Statistical and Chronological History*, 9.
32. Diary of John M. Brooke, 25 Jan. 1861, BP. Baron F. von Gerolt was Prussian minister to the United States. Professor Christian Gottfried Ehrenberg (1790–1876) was an eminent German naturalist and a leading German authority on infusoria. For his work in this field Brooke was awarded the Prussian Gold Medal of Science.
33. Brooke Diary, 25 Jan. 1861, BP.
34. Matthew Maury to Brooke, 31 Jan. 1861, Letters sent, RG 78, NA.
35. Alexander Bache to Brooke, Feb. 1861, BP.

36. Joseph Henry to Brooke, 11 Feb. 1861, BP.
37. Brooke Diary, 3 Feb. 1861, BP.
38. Brooke to Robert C. Wyllie, 14 Feb. 1861 (copy), BP.
39. Brooke to Toucey, 14 Feb. 1861, Officers' Letters to the Secretary of the Navy, RG 45, NA.
40. McCollum to Brooke, 18 Feb. 1860, BP.
41. John R. Thomson to Brooke, 27 Feb. 1861, BP; *Congressional Globe*, 2d Sess., 36th Cong., 11 Feb. 1861.
42. William Brooke, New York City, to Brooke, 1 Mar. 1861, BP.
43. Alexander Tunstall, Norfolk, to Brooke, 8 Mar. 1861, BP. Tunstall apparently was in the investment business, as he wrote: "Stocks and the premium on New York funds are constantly fluctuating, and we can't give reliable quotations, two days ahead."
44. Neeser, *Statistical and Chronological History*, 9.
45. Ibid., 10.

Chapter 1: *Brooke's Resignation from the United States Navy and Appointment to Confederate Service*

1. This day saw the partial destruction and abandonment of the Norfolk Navy Yard, Va., by the U.S. naval forces. The following vessels were burnt and scuttled: *Pennsylvania*, 120; *Columbus*, 74; *Delaware*, 74; *Raritan*, 44; *Columbia*, 44; *Merrimac*, 40; *Germantown*, 20; *Plymouth*, 20; and *Dolphin*, 10 (Neeser, *Statistical and Chronological History*.) In the Brooke Papers is a note by Brooke: "On the call of the Governor of Virginia tendered my resignation and went to Lexington with my family and thence to Richmond."
2. Brooke had sent Ehrenberg samples from the bottom of the ocean that he had obtained with his deep sea lead during his recent cruise in the Pacific.
3. John Rodgers had been John Brooke's commanding officer on the North Pacific Exploring and Surveying Expedition and in Washington when they were preparing the report and charts of the expedition. The warm feeling was mutual. Rodgers was an old-timer; listed as a citizen of Maryland he had entered the navy in 1828, and at the time he wrote the letter he was a commander. During the Civil War, Rodgers had a distinguished career in the Union navy. For a good biography see Robert Ervin Johnson, *Rear Admiral John Rodgers, 1812–1882* (Annapolis, Md.: U.S. Naval Institute Press, 1967).
4. On the same day Brooke made this notation, his friend Comdr. John Rodgers was "ordered to report to Maj.-Gen. G. B. McClellan, U.S.A., for the establishment of a naval armament on the Western Waters" (Neeser, *Statistical and Chronological History*, 11).
5. The Annual Report of the Secretary of the Navy, 2 Dec. 1861, Senate Executive Documents, 2d Sess., 37th Cong., vol. 3, no. 1. shows that forty-six lieutenants resigned between 2 April 1861 and 7 November 1861. Five lieutenants including Brooke resigned on 20 April. Among Brooke's good friends who had entered the navy with him in 1841 and resigned about the same time were the following

Virginians: William H. Parker (20 April); William H. Murdaugh (21 April); Robert D. Minor (22 April); Hunter Davidson (23 April). The resignations posed a problem for the new secretary of the navy, Gideon Welles. He wrote: "When I took charge of the Navy Department, I found great demoralization and defection among the naval officers. It was difficult to ascertain who among those who lingered about Washington could and who were not to be trusted. Some belonging to the Barron clique had already sent in their resignations. Others, it was well understood, were prepared to do so as soon as a blow was struck. Some were hesitating, undecided what step to take. Samuel Barron, Franklin Buchanan, Matthew Maury, John Porter, and John Magruder were in Washington, and each and all were, during the unhappy winter, courted and caressed by the Secessionists, who desired to win them to their cause. I was by my friends put on my guard as respected each of them. Buchanan, Maury, and Magruder were each holding prominent places and on duty. Barron was familiar with civil and naval matters, was prepared for any service, ready to be called to discharge such duties as are constantly arising in the Department, requiring the talents of an intelligent officer" (Howard K. Beale, ed., *The Diary of Gideon Welles*, [New York: 1960], 1:20). Barron and Magruder were listed in the 1861 *Register of the Commissioned and Warrant Officers of the Navy of the United States including Officers of the Marine Corps and Others for the Year 1861* as citizens of Virginia, Buchanan of Pennsylvania, and Maury of Tennessee. Barron entered Confederate service on 10 June 1861, Buchanan on 15 September, and Maury on 10 June.

6. Henry Alexander Wise, a Virginia lawyer, was a member of the U.S. House of Representatives (1833–44) and governor of Virginia (1856–60). When Virginia seceded he was appointed a brigadier general in the Confederate army. He was succeeded as governor by John Letcher from Lexington.

7. Brigadier General Robert Selden Garnett, a West Point graduate, was a cousin of Lizzie. He was killed in this campaign, the first Confederate general killed in the war.

8. The Executive Council was established in the early days of the war before the Confederate government moved to Richmond. Davis was certainly Jefferson Davis who had established the Confederate government in Montgomery, Alabama.

9. Robert was probably Robert Mercer Taliaferro Hunter, Brooke's cousin and at that time secretary of state in the Confederacy. He had been a U.S. senator from Virginia at the outbreak of the war.

10. Thomas Hoomes Williamson, who had married Lizzie's sister Olympia, was professor of engineering at Virginia Military Institute in Lexington, and it is with the Williamsons that Lizzie apparently stayed when she was in Lexington.

11. Lizzie had tuberculosis, called consumption then, and had suffered from it for a long time. It was a constant worry to her husband.

Chapter 2: *Conversion of the Merrimac to the Virginia and Experiments in Ordnance*

1. William P. Williamson entered the U.S. Navy from North Carolina in 1842 and held the rank of chief engineer from 1845. He entered Confederate service as

an engineer on 11 June 1861, only twelve days before the meeting, and was appointed engineer-in-chief in Richmond, the new Confederate capital. Though he was experienced, it has been said that "several of his subordinates seem to have been more efficient and capable than he was" (Raimondo Luraghi, *A History of the Confederate Navy* [Annapolis, Md.: Naval Institute Press, 1996], 48). John Luke Porter, born in Virginia, was commissioned a naval constructor in the U.S. Navy on 1 October 1859 and then assigned to the navy yard in Pensacola. A newcomer, he ranked eighth among nine naval constructors (*Register of the Commissioned and Warrant Officers of the Navy 1861*). Porter resigned his commission in the U.S. Navy on 1 May 1861 and, offering his services to the Confederacy, was sent to Norfolk by Secretary Mallory when that city was evacuated by the Federals. Not until late 1862 was Porter officially appointed chief naval constructor. Luraghi has written: "Many historians have been harsh with John Luke Porter, yet he performed his duties commendably. . . . On balance one is amazed by how much one man, amid dreadful adversity, was able to accomplish" (*History of the Confederate Navy*, 36). Prior to the war Stephen Russell Mallory was a U.S. senator from Florida and for seven years chairman of the Senate Committee on Naval Affairs, a position he took seriously (Joseph T. Durkin, *Stephen R. Mallory, Confederate Navy Chief* [Chapel Hill: University of North Carolina Press, 1954]). Often ignored when people discuss the heroes of the Civil War, Mallory gets his due from the latest historian of the Confederate navy, who wrote: "Yet if this navy arose, went to battle, fought so as to gain an immortal place in history, this was mainly because of the work of the quiet, unassuming, apparently colorless Secretary Mallory" (Luraghi, *History of the Confederate Navy*, 10). Luraghi in his excellent history writes that from 1851 onward Brooke "served in the Navy Observatory" (Ibid., 40). But, as has been pointed out, Brooke's life was much more dramatic than that. He served at the Navy Observatory from October 1851 to February 1853, a little more than a year.

2. Brooke misjudged Porter. As will be seen, Porter, in building the ship that evolved from this conference, often disregarded Brooke's plan. The Tredegar Iron Works, founded in 1839, had grown into "one of the better metallurgical firms in America, even though it was far from being a giant like those in Pennsylvania and New York," but it "employed as many as a thousand workers" (Luraghi, *History of the Confederate Navy*, 111). Tredegar would become the mainstay of the Confederate states for the production of armor plate and heavy ordnance. Initially Tredegar was the only facility in the Confederacy capable of producing heavy ordnance. For more information consult Kathleen Bruce, *Virginia Iron Manufacture in the Slave Era* (New York: The Century Company, 1931) and Charles B. Dew, *Ironmaker to the Confederacy, Joseph R. Anderson and the Tredegar Iron Works* (New Haven and London: Yale University Press, 1966).

3. This must have been deemed secret because the Confederate navy did not want the North to know that it was building an ironclad, when it had no ironclads.

4. The matter of submerged ends was important. When the idea was adapted to the *Virginia*, Secretary Mallory reported to the House of Representatives: "The novel plan of submerging the ends of the ship and the eaves of the casemate,

however, is the peculiar and distinctive feature of the *Virginia*. It was never before adopted" (George M. Brooke, Jr., *John M. Brooke, Naval Scientist and Educator* [Charlottesville: University Press of Virginia, 1980], 233–34). The submerged ends was the only feature of his design Brooke claimed to be original. The significance of this point is that later Porter would claim credit for the design of the *Virginia*.

5. These activities when Brooke served in the Virginia navy as naval aide to Gen. Robert E. Lee are described in Brooke, *John M. Brooke*, p. 224–32.

6. Gen. Robert E. Lee had resigned from Federal service on the same day as Brooke and, like Brooke, offered to serve Virginia. He was given command of the Virginia forces as the Old Dominion had not yet been integrated into the Confederate states, whose capital was still in Montgomery, Alabama. From the beginning Brooke had enormous admiration and respect for General Lee.

7. The Parrott Cannon was designed by Robert Parker Parrott, a West Point graduate who was for thirty years the superintendent of the West Point Foundry, a leading producer of ordnance for both the army and the navy (Warren Ripley, *Artillery and Ammunition of the Civil War* [New York: Promontory Press, 1970], 109).

8. Brooke soon developed an aversion to the newspapers's "right to know."

9. Col. Andrew Talcott was of the State Engineer Service. The change meant moving the guns at Powhatan six miles down the river on the left bank. One of the first duties facing the Virginia navy was to protect the rivers from Union attack. This meant establishing forts on the river and manning them. The James, of course, as it flowed past Richmond was of supreme importance. Fort Powhatan was on the south side of the James about halfway between Jamestown Island and Richmond. It is reported that at about that time Brooke and Catesby ap R. Jones, "using the enforced labor of hundreds of impressed slaves and free blacks. . . . constructed a strong fortification on historic Jamestown Island" (John M. Coski, *Capital Navy: The Men, Ships, and Operations of the James River Squadron* [Campbell, Calif.: Savas Woodbury Publishers, 1996], 9–10). Wilson's at Kennon's was six miles down the James from Fort Powhatan on the left bank.

10. Burwell's Bay is in Isle of Wight County. The railroad was the Norfolk and Petersburg.

11. These activities were in the southeastern part of the state. Zuni is on the Blackwater River, which separates Isle of Wight County from Southampton County. The Blackwater flows south joining the Nottoway River near the North Carolina line to form the Chowan River. Gen. Benjamin Huger graduated from the United States Military Academy in 1824. A companion of General Lee in the Mexican War, the latter described him as "an officer of great merit" (Douglas Southall Freeman, *Robert E. Lee*, 4 vols. [New York: Charles Scribner's Sons, 1934], 1:508).

12. Mary Ann Wilson Garnett was the widow of William Henry Garnett and the sister-in-law of Brooke's wife Lizzie. William, the twin brother of Richard Brooke Garnett, was a doctor and died in the yellow fever epidemic in Norfolk in 1855. The Wilson family came from Surrey County on the James.

13. Aquia Creek is in Stafford County in northeastern Virginia and flows into the Potomac. Gen. Theophilus H. Holmes was a classmate of Lee at West Point. Just prior to the Battle of First Manassas he commanded troops at Fredericksburg.

14. The Rip Raps, an old fortification, was near Old Point Comfort in the Hampton Roads area.

15. The governor's Advisory Council gave opinions which Gov. John Letcher usually followed, although he was not bound to do so. Initially the council included Col. Francis H. Smith, superintendent of the Virginia Military Institute; Comdr. Matthew Fontaine Maury, the world-famous oceanographer; and John J. Allen, chief justice of the Court of Appeals. Later Lt. Gov. Robert L. Montague was added.

16. Until the Confederate States Navy Department (see: Tom H. Wells, *The Confederate Navy: A Study in Organization* [Tuscaloosa: University of Alabama Press, 1991], 3-5) was established in Richmond, Brooke remained on General Lee's staff as naval adviser. Secretary Mallory arrived in Richmond to assume his duties there on 3 June 1861 (Luraghi, *History of the Confederate Navy*, p. 16). *The Register of the Commissioned and Warrant Officers of the Navy of the Confederate States to January 1, 1861* shows that Brooke entered Confederate service on 2 May 1861. At the beginning of 1861 Brooke had stood 180 out of 321 lieutenants. In the U.S. Navy promotion had been based on seniority derived from date of entry into the naval service. When transferring to the Confederate navy officers were given the same relative rank they had held in the U.S. Navy.

17. Shells were useful in both the army and the navy; they were defined as "hollow spheres filled with powder. . . . [that] could be fired by most forms of ordnance to achieve long range destruction of men and equipment mainly through blast." Robert Parrott, who produced the Parrott Gun, also produced shells. (See Ripley, *Artillery and Ammunition*, p. 258.)

18. Gen. P. G. T. Beauregard, who had commanded the Confederate forces in the bombardment of Fort Sumter, was now in command of Confederate forces at Manassas Junction, southwest of Washington. This was the prelude to the Battle of First Manassas.

19. The Battle of First Manassas was fought on 21 July 1861.

20. Before the Civil War when Brooke was stranded in Japan, Commodore Josiah Tattnall was in command of the East India Squadron. Shortly thereafter Tattnall took the first Japanese mission to America in the *Powhatan* while Brooke crossed the Pacific in the *Kanrin Maru*.

21. Brooke would remain with the Office of Naval Ordnance for the rest of the war, eventually becoming its chief in March 1863. He succeeded Comdr. George Minor, a Virginian some fourteen years his senior. Minor was more attached to traditional methods and less innovative than his younger colleague.

22. When the Federals evacuated Norfolk on 20 April 1861, they abandoned a number of ships, including the screw steamer *Merrimac*, which they burned to the waterline. The hulk would be raised and converted into the ironclad *Virginia*.

23. In 1851 when assigned to the Naval Observatory in Washington, Brooke and his wife lived at Mrs. Herbert Bryant's boardinghouse at the corner of New York Avenue and Fifteenth Street. I assume that Herbert Bryant was Mrs. Bryant's son. William Williamson was the son of Louisa Williamson, John Brooke's sister-in-law, and the wife of Thomas Hoomes Williamson, professor of engineering at Virginia Military Institute.

24. Sampson & Pae was a Richmond machine shop that finished weapons cast by William James Hubard (Ripley, *Artillery and Ammunition*, p. 364). According to Ripley, Hubard made only the rough casting, and his weapons were finished in the Richmond machine shops of Thomas Sampson and James Pae (Ibid., p. 363). The Sampson and Pae Foundry was at Byrd and Fifth Streets (Coski, *Capital Navy*, p. 76). John A. Dahlgren (1809–70), a career naval officer, was an ordnance expert. From 1847 until his death, with a few short interruptions, he worked on naval ordnance at the Washington Navy Yard. His aim was to produce "a system of boat armament that would remedy the faults brought so glaringly to light under wartime conditions" (Ripley, *Artillery and Ammunition*, p. 87). Dahlgren "invented many of the Navy's weapons. They consisted of varied rifles and smoothbores ranging in caliber from 12-pounder to 20-inch and in weight from 300 to 100,000 pounds"; his achievements are said to have been acknowledged "throughout the world" as "second to none in his field" (Ibid.). From July 1862 to June 1863 he was the U.S. Navy's chief of ordnance (Ibid.). Dahlgren was a favorite of President Lincoln, who wanted to promote him to captain and give him a field command even though he "had not been to sea since the Mexican War"; he has been described as "perhaps the most ambitious officer in the Navy" (John Niven, *Gideon Welles, Lincoln's Secretary of the Navy* [Baton Rouge: Louisiana State University Press, 1978], 383–84).

25. Mary Elizabeth Selden Garnett (Lizzie) was Brooke's wife and a first cousin whom he had married in 1849. At the outbreak of the war they had only one child, Anna, others having died in infancy. Lizzie had tuberculosis, and her health was not good. As before the war, Lizzie frequently visited members of her family in Lexington.

26. This was the Battle of First Manassas. Gen. Joseph E. Johnston and Beauregard commanded the Confederate troops that defeated Gen. Irvin McDowell.

27. In the Office of Ordnance and Hydrography, Brooke spent much of his time designing cannons and ammunition.

28. Hubard, who cast weapons for Sampson and Pae, has been described as an "artist, silhouettist, sculptor, and scientist" (Ripley, *Artillery and Ammunition*, 362).

29. For many years Matthew Fontaine Maury had been superintendent of the Naval Observatory and had done work in hydrography and astronomy, particularly the former. He had a worldwide reputation for his books, *A New Theoretical and Practical Treatise on Navigation* and *The Physical Geography of the Sea*. Brooke, who was twenty years Maury's junior, while working for him at the observatory from 1851 to 1853 invented a deep-sea sounding lead that bears his name; this lead made it possible for the first time to measure accurately the

depth of the deep sea. Brooke at that point had not worked in the field of ordnance. Early in the war Maury experimented extensively with torpedoes (mines)
and became the South's leading authority until he was ordered to England in
June 1862. One authority attributes this in part to "the lack of facilities which
imposed limitations upon serious scientific research." (Milton E. Perry, *Infernal Machines: The Story of Confederate Submarine and Mine Warfare* [Baton
Rouge: Louisiana State University Press, 1965], 16) He would spend the rest of
his naval career in Europe and was succeeded in his experimental work in mines
by Hunter Davidson. Maury is the subject of a number of biographies (see Perry,
Infernal Machines, 1965, 4–16). Maury's removal from the scene and transfer
to England might have stemmed from his deep resentment toward Secretary
Mallory. This resentment was possibly a result of the fact that Mallory, when a
senator, had pushed the formation of a Naval Retiring Board, which removed
from the active list those officers physically unfit for sea service; although Maury
was among the officers removed, he was restored later to the active list after
much effort. (See Luraghi, *History of the Confederate Navy*, p. 68; and Coski,
Capital Navy, p. 26.)

30. Capt. Duncan N. Ingraham, who had entered the U.S. Navy from South Carolina in 1812, had been chief of the Bureau of Ordnance and Hydrography from
1856 until his resignation shortly after South Carolina's secession. Offering his
services to the Confederacy, Ingraham was one of the four officers designated
captain by Jefferson Davis on 16 March 1861. He was appointed the first chief
of the Office of Ordnance and Hydrography and filled that position effectively
until November 1861, when he was assigned to the command of the Charleston
Squadron. He had done an outstanding job obtaining the naval material needed
to fight the war. He was followed as chief of ordnance by George Minor. (See
Luraghi, *Confederate Navy*, p. 15, 40; and *Register of the Commissioned and
Warrant Officers of the Navy 1861*) Capt. George Hollins of Maryland, a senior
captain, had entered the U.S. Navy two years after Ingraham. His last command had been as captain of the steam sloop *Susquehanna*. He had built "a
reputation for recklessness, aggressiveness, and steadfastness." Pearce must have
been acting naval constructor Joseph Pierce, who had been a master carpenter
and was one of Constructor Porter's deputy constructors who has been described
as "able" (Coski, *Capital Navy*, 8; Luraghi, *History of the Confederate Navy*,
121). According to Luraghi, the purpose of the meeting was to meet the threat
in the West by building "a team of ironclads capable of operating not only
along the rivers but on the high seas as well" (*History of the Confederate Navy*,
104). Brooke "strongly supported Mallory's ideas and sketched an organiza-
tional-operational plan for the ironclads" (Ibid.).

31. Lucy was the baby previously mentioned. She must have been named for Brooke's
mother, Lucy Thomas of Duxbury, Massachusetts.

32. U.S. Military Academy Old Trophy Number 183 is an unconventional weapon
long surrounded by mystery. Its slotted bore with rounded ends measures
roughly 6.75 inches long by 1.25 inches high. It is catalogued without identifi-
cation as captured in Richmond on 3 April 1865. Stephen Carr Lyford escorted

it to the Philadelphia International Exhibition of 1876. He identified it as a "disc firing gun," the erratic projectile flight of which is easy to imagine. Leroy H. Corbin finds superior documentation. The *Calendar of Virginia State Papers*, Vol. 11, 206–7, presents the report of Charles Dimmock, Confederate Colonel of Ordnance, stating in part: "The purpose of the Gun is to fire canister shot so that those shot shall be delivered with a vertical spread of the height of a man only, while the horizontal spread shall be the length of a company of Infantry, thus to sweep a whole company." Against a target 100 feet long by 8 feet high, unsatisfactory results were achieved at ranges of 300 and 200 yards. At 100 yard range, ". . . with half pound powder and 48 lead balls (ounce), 26 hit, horizontal spread 15 ft., vertical spread 7 ½ ft. (Aim bad.) . . . Another fire, all things remaining, the hits were 43, horizontal spread 67 ft., vertical 7 ½ ft." Dimmock continued, ". . . a company in line would be destroyed in two or three discharges, and no troops could be brought within the range of such a dreadful weapon."

33. This is usually spelled Drewry; it was named for Maj. Augustus H. Drewry, who owned the bluff (David P. Werlich, *Admiral of the Amazon: John Randolph Tucker, His Confederate Colleagues, and Peru* [Charlottesville: University Press of Virginia, 1990], 37).

34. William G. Cheeney in the fall of 1861 designed a submarine and "supervised its construction" at the Tredegar (Dew, *Ironmaker to the Confederacy*, 123). According to Dew, "it was to be used in conjunction with Maury's torpedoes to destroy enemy ships in Virginia waters"; also, Cheeney "was in charge of torpedoes (mines) strung in the James River below Richmond in June 1862" (Ibid.). It is stated that Cheeney, "a New York–born former United States Navy officer subsequently commissioned in the Confederate navy, worked . . . on what was described as a submarine boat" (Coski, *Capital Navy*, 117). In November 1861 J. R. Anderson at Tredegar sent Cheeney "a detailed estimate about the building of an iron submarine, specifying that the cost of construction approached $6,000, with another $200 for erecting a shed over her so that workers would be protected from prying eyes" (Luraghi, *History of the Confederate Navy*, 252). William was John Brooke's only sibling to survive infancy. He was five years Brooke's junior and was handicapped by a club foot. He held a variety of clerical jobs and never married.

35. Lizzie was deeply religious, and for years when Brooke was at sea she chided him to read the Bible daily.

36. This was probably the Reverend William Nelson Pendleton, who had been rector of Grace Episcopal Church in Lexington. A West Point graduate, he resigned as rector and offered his services to the Confederacy. In time he became chief of artillery of Gen. Robert E. Lee's Army of Northern Virginia.

37. It is clear that John Brooke's separation from his wife, aggravated by such wrangling and the constant worry about Lizzie's and Lucy's health, placed a heavy burden on him. This was at a time of mounting responsibilities in Richmond. John Brooke had married his cousin in Norfolk in 1849 when twenty-two. From then until the Civil War the couple was separated much of the time, John

Brooke on cruises to remote parts of the world where communication was slow and irregular, and Lizzie with her family in Norfolk. As Lizzie was the youngest of the five Garnett children and the only one at home during those years, it is natural that she should have been close to her father, collector of customs in Norfolk for a time and a respected citizen.

38. An act making additional appropriations for the navy of the Confederate states, for the year ending 18 February 1862 (*Laws for the Army and Navy of the Confederate States*).

39. Lt. Robert D. Minor, a close friend of Brooke, had entered the U.S. Navy the same year as Brooke and the Confederate navy one month later. He was a younger brother of Comdr. George Minor, at that time chief of naval ordnance. He would later serve aboard the *Virginia* and then as chief of the Richmond Naval Ordnance Works. Shirley was one of the great plantation houses on the James River; it was owned by the Carter family. The *Patrick Henry*, originally the *Yorktown*, was a wooden side-wheel steamship 250 long and 34 feet wide that was used before the war as a packet and passenger boat between New York and Virginia; converted into a warship in Richmond, she became a part of the James River Squadron (Coski, *Capital Navy*, 8). City Point is today known as Hopewell, Virginia. It is twelve miles below Bermuda at the place where the Appomattox River flows into the James. John Randolph Tucker, a veteran of thirty-five years' service in the U.S. Navy, had entered Confederate service on the same day as Matthew Fontaine Maury. Tucker superintended the conversion of the *Yorktown* to the *Patrick Henry* and was her first commander; he became the commander of the James River Squadron (see Werlich, *Admiral of the Amazon*). Joseph Pierce was a master carpenter and assistant naval constructor who helped convert the *Yorktown*. Lt. Catesby ap R. Jones, an expert in ordnance, conducted gun experiments and later served as the executive officer on the *Virginia*. Nelson Tift and his brother Asa from Key West, Florida, were close friends of Secretary Stephen Mallory. About this time the Tift brothers informed Mallory "that they would gladly assume the task of building an iron-clad warship according to new, almost revolutionary, principles" (Luraghi, *History of the Confederate Navy*, 108).

40. Brooke did make the sketch. During his long cruises in the navy Brooke had often made sketches and painted.

41. Capt. Samuel Barron was a senior officer, a Virginian who had entered the U.S. Navy in 1812. At the time Barron was commander of coastal forces in North Carolina and Virginia. It is reported that the attack on "Hatteras Inlet, which leads into Pamlico Sound" was directed by Commodore Silas H. Stringham. Barron was made a prisoner, and the South was "dismayed" at the disaster. (See Luraghi, *History of the Confederate Navy*, p. 183.)

42. There were two McCorkle brothers in the Confederate navy. Joseph P. was chief clerk of the Office of Ordnance and Hydrography and had served in a similar capacity in the U.S. Navy. Lt. David P. McCorkle, his brother, later would be in charge of the Atlanta Naval Ordnance Works. He had entered the U.S. Navy the same year as Brooke. Lt. James Rochelle, another of Brooke's contemporaries,

was the first commander of the *Teaser,* "the only warship put into commission by the Virginia State Navy" (Coski, *Capital Navy,* 8). Dr. Yelverton Garnett was a cousin of Brooke.

43. An authority has said, "The testing was a disaster. An eight inch ball fired from three hundred yards pierced the three sheets of iron as though they were cardboard and penetrated five inches into the solid oak planking" (Luraghi, *History of the Confederate Navy,* 97).

44. She was the daughter of Col. William Byrd of Westover. By the middle of the twentieth century her tombstone had "entirely disappeared" (John McGill, comp., *The Beverley Family of Virginia: Descendants of Major Robert Beverley (1641–1687) and Other Families* [Columbia, S. C.: The R. L. Bryan Company, 1956], 534–35).

45. Richard Brooke Garnett was one of Lizzie's brothers. A West Point graduate, he was for a number of years aide to Gen. George Mercer Brooke, John Brooke's father. Serving in the West at the outbreak of the war, he resigned his commission and offered his services to the Confederacy. In time he was given command of the Stonewall Brigade in Gen. Thomas J. Jackson's Valley Campaign until the Battle of Kernstown. His relationship with John Brooke was close.

46. French Forrest's naval service went back to 1811; he had been put in charge of the rehabilitation of the Norfolk Navy Yard after the Federal evacuation, had done an excellent job, and was in command when Brooke was sent there (Luraghi, *History of the Confederate Navy,* 96).

47. Col. John T. L. Preston, a graduate of Washington College in Lexington, Virginia, was a founder of Virginia Military Institute and one of its first professors.

48. Lt. Benjamin Gallaher, a paymaster, was a Virginian who did not "go South." He was stationed in Washington in 1861.

49. In designing cannons Brooke, of course, did not start from scratch. The United States Navy in 1859 had adopted a smooth bore cannon designed by John A. Dahlgren. Also, during the war Brooke made every effort to keep abreast of ordnance experiments abroad and studied the material collected for him by Confederate agents in England and on the Continent. From the first, however, Brooke recognized the superior penetrating power of solid shot fired from rifled cannons against armored vessels. On the other hand, smooth bores firing shells and canisters were effective against wooden vessels and personnel. The Confederacy had to develop range tables for its new guns in a hurry, and this responsibility devolved on Brooke. While in Confederate service Brooke designed three calibers of rifled cannons: 6.4-inch (thirty-two pounder), 7-inch, and 8-inch; and to permit larger charges he put one, two, or three iron bands on his guns. He also designed 10- and 11-inch smooth bores. There is a description of Brooke's 6.4-inch and 7-inch rifled cannons with illustrations in Ripley, *Artillery and Ammunition,* p. 127–36.

50. According to Charles B. Dew, Dr. Robert Archer was Joseph R. Anderson's father-in-law. Archer "had retired from the army and moved to Richmond" and with his son Robert, Jr., had constructed the Armory rolling mill. The company called R. Archer and Company in the 1850s had specialized in the production

of bar iron. In 1859 Archer joined forces with Anderson and Company and became active in the production of cannons. Dew states that Dr. Archer "was an inventor of some distinction having designed rifle shot for Tredegar cannons and a safety device to prevent premature explosions of cannon shell." See Dew, *Ironmaker to the Confederacy*, p.16–17, 96–97.

51. Comdr. Archibald B. Fairfax, a Virginian, was a navy inspector of ordnance. Many years Brooke's senior, he had entered the U.S. Navy in 1823, eighteen years before Brooke. Ripley states that Fairfax "rifled and banded a number of 32-pounders captured at Norfolk Navy Yard" (*Artillery and Ammunition*, 362). According to Luraghi, Fairfax, "Ordnance Chief at Norfolk, was a resourceful and energetic man. He went to work without delay to convert as many of the 32 pounder smoothbores as he could by rifling them and reinforcing their breeches with a strong iron band, greatly improving their efficiency" (Luraghi, *History of the Confederate Navy*, 43).

52. Luraghi writes that Secretary Mallory noted, "Rifled cannon are unknown to naval warfare; but those guns have attained a range and accuracy beyond any other form of ordnance, both with shot and shell, I propose to introduce them into the Navy" (*History of the Confederate Navy*, 66).

53. Brooke had married in Norfolk at the bride's home in 1849. Brooke's father-in-law, William Garnett, was his uncle. At the time Brooke was attached to the Coast Survey in Washington.

54. Joseph Reid Anderson was a graduate of West Point. Resigning from the army, in 1848 he became owner of the Tredegar Iron Works in Richmond. The Tredegar before the war was a "supplier of cannon for the federal government, furnishing a reported 1,200 during the years prior to the war" (Ripley, *Artillery and Ammunition*, 127). At this time Brooke "began to assemble data when any gun burst, so that the source could be analyzed and proper safeguards be enforced" (Brooke, *John M. Brooke*, 244). David Graham of Wythe County had produced gun iron of high quality in the late 1850s, but early in the war Graham iron "proved to be completely unreliable" (Dew, *Ironmaker to the Confederacy*, 78, 135).

55. Lt. John N. Maffit, a North Carolinian born in Ireland, had entered the U.S. Navy in 1832 and the Confederate navy in May 1861. During the Civil War he won fame as the skipper of the public cruiser *Florida*.

56. The *Register of the Commissioned and Warrant Officers of the Navy 1861* of the Confederate navy listed F. Volck, a native of Germany, as a draftsman in the Office of Ordnance and Hydrography.

57. Port Royal is a town on one of the South Carolina sea islands in Beaufort County. The Union navy established a base at this port on 7 November 1861. Mallory's biographer called its fall "the crowning disaster of the year" (Durkin, *Stephen R. Mallory*, 164).

58. According to Warren Ripley, gunpowder during the Civil War "was a combination of charcoal saltpeter (Potassium nitrate, or niter) and sulphur in the proportions 75-15-19 or 74-14-10 by weight" (*Artillery and Ammunition*, 241). The niter was produced by the Bureau of Nitre and Mining. As quoted by Joseph

Durkin, it aimed to "work to the last our material deposits (as distinct from artificial nitrates), at times even within the enemy's lines" and to examine carefully for new deposits in every possible locality (*Stephen R. Mallory,* 324-25). Gen. Josiah Gorgas was chief of army ordnance during the Civil War and did an effective job.

59. Gen. Gideon Pillow served under Gen. John B. Floyd during the Fort Donelson campaign.

60. An authority writes that Maury thought reliance on the conversion of the *Merrimac* into the *Virginia* was not enough for the defense of Southern rivers and harbors. He pushed hard for what he called "big guns and little ships"; what he envisioned was "a large fleet of small steam-powered wooden gunboats, each armed with two guns," and the Confederate congress authorized the building of 100 of them (Coski, *Capital Navy,* 26-27). Though Secretary Mallory approved, Brooke must have been aware of the great division between Maury and Mallory going back to the 1850s. With the simultaneous building of an ironclad, a rivalry of sorts developed. Adding to the general excitement at this time was the *Trent* Affair precipitated by the seizure of the Confederate commissioners James M. Mason and John Slidell.

61. Jones had been conducting gun experiments at Jamestown. Catesby ap R. Jones, a Virginian, had entered the U.S. Navy as a midshipman in 1836. In 1853 "he was ordered to ordnance duty at the Washington Navy Yard. Here Jones assisted Dahlgren in perfection of that inventor's shell gun and later went to sea as ordnance officer aboard the *Merrimac* and other vessels on which the new Dahlgrens were installed" (Ripley, *Artillery and Ammunition,* 128). With Virginia's secession Jones was appointed captain in the Virginia navy. When he transferred to the Confederate navy, Jones was commissioned as a lieutenant. It is interesting that he served on the *Merrimac* when it was a wooden vessel and later when it was an ironclad (Ibid.). Jones is said to have had "such gifts of character as 'energy, steadiness, carefulness, and courage'" (Luraghi, *History of the Confederate Navy,* 44).

62. This must have been the *Galena,* which was launched at Mystic, Connecticut, on 14 February 1862. Although the British and the French had built armored vessels in the 1850s, the U.S. Navy had lagged. With the outbreak of the Civil War the Confederacy quickly saw armored ships as a way to break the Union blockade and began the conversion of the wooden frigate *Merrimac,* scuttled by the Federals in Norfolk, into the ironclad *Virginia.* In late September 1861 a navy board in the North with a number of plans to choose from recommended the construction of the *Monitor,* the *Galena,* and the *Ironsides.*

63. To keep abreast of ordnance developments abroad, Brooke read avidly the papers that were sent to him by Confederate agents abroad, such as James D. Bulloch and Samuel Barron. Initially Sir William Armstrong founded Elswick Ordnance Company in 1859 at Newcastle-on-Tyne to manufacture "rifled cannon solely for the government." In 1862 the British government withdrew its support and Elswick merged with other interests to form Sir W. S. Armstrong and Company (Ripley, *Artillery and Ammunition,* 364).

64. Brooke and Maury had worked closely together over a span of many years. For two years, 1851–53, Brooke had worked for Maury at the Naval Observatory where the latter was superintendent. While there Brooke had invented his deep-sea sounding device for measuring accurately ocean depths greater than two thousand fathoms. Later while in charge of hydrography on the North Pacific Exploring Expedition, Brooke corresponded with Maury. At the outbreak of the Civil War the two officers resigned their commissions in the U.S. Navy on the same day.

65. Joseph W. Barney, a Maryland native, had entered the U.S. Navy in 1835, and following his resignation at the beginning of the Civil War he entered Confederate service on 2 July 1861. In 1863 Barney commanded the *Harriet Lane*, which vessel was the cause of controversy between the army and the navy when "the navy had apparently transferred the *Harriet Lane* to the War Department." The problem arose when Barney was ordered by the army to make alterations in the vessel, which he did not feel authorized to do "without sanction from the Secretary of the Navy." (See Durkin, *Stephen R. Mallory*, p. 291.)

66. John Tyler died less than two months later on 18 January 1862.

67. In what is known as the *Trent* Affair, Confederate commissioners John Slidell and James M. Mason, while en route to England on the British steamer *Trent*, had been seized by Capt. Charles Wilkes of the U.S. Navy in the *San Jacinto* and removed. This causing a crisis in U.S.-British relations, Secretary of State William H. Seward ordered their release.

68. Fort Pickens, held by the Federals during the Civil War, lay at the entrance to Pensacola harbor.

69. 1st Lt. Henry K. Stevens was involved in the naval defense of St. Marks, Florida. Brooke had served with him on the North Pacific Expedition in 1853–56, when Stevens commanded the *Fenimore Cooper* and then the *John Hancock*. William Sharp, a first lieutenant, was with the James River Squadron. He had entered the U.S. Navy in 1841, the same year as Brooke. Fort Lafayette was a Federal prison in New York harbor.

70. The *Niagara* was a steam frigate of twelve guns built in Brooklyn in 1853. It had recently returned from taking the Japanese embassy staff back to Japan. Bragg was Gen. Braxton Bragg. First Lt. David P. McCorkle had entered the U.S. Navy in 1841. He and Brooke had been shipmates on the *Vincennes* during the North Pacific Expedition in the 1850s. In 1862–64 McCorkle was in command of the Atlanta Ordnance Works. When Sherman threatened Atlanta, McCorkle began moving his plant to Augusta and "was successful in saving the machinery, engines, boilers, and most of the stores before the Federals moved into Atlanta" (Brooke, *John M. Brooke*, 281). The Evansport Battery had been designed to block the channel of the Potomac. "As cannon intended for the defenses of Richmond had been sent to advanced positions and could not be replaced, the President was most solicitous that those at Evansport, as well as those at Manassas, should be saved" (Douglas Southall Freeman, *Lee's Lieutenants* [New York: Charles Scribner's Sons, 1944], 1:135).

71. John Newland Maffit has been described as a man of "daring, boldness, initiative, and stern sense of duty." It is reported that for a number of years he

served in the African Squadron and "distinguished himself in chasing slavers." After minor assignments in the Confederacy he was given command of the blockade runner *Nassau.* Later he was selected to command the *Florida,* "the first warship 'built under contract' for the Confederate Navy." The vessel was constructed in England. (See Luraghi, *History of the Confederate Navy,* p. 220.)

72. The commodore was French Forrest, who commanded the Norfolk Navy Yard. Webb was probably Lt. William A. Webb, who had entered the U.S. Navy in 1838, three years before Brooke, and commanded the small gunboat *Teaser* during the Battle of Hampton Roads. Henry Ashton Ramsey, noted as a first assistant engineer in the U.S. Navy, had been engineer of the *Merrimac* when she was a wooden ship before the war. He helped Williamson with the conversion and became chief engineer of the *Virginia.* Ramsey has been described by Luraghi as "a very able officer"; he had entered the U.S. Navy in 1853. Forrest had protected Craney Island at the mouth of the Elizabeth River by "laying obstructions, building earthworks, and placing coast pieces." Luraghi describes the difficulty of recruiting: "Even though the South succeeded in gathering a suitable number of officers [for the *Virginia*] the same was not true for sailors. One reason was that the army, also urgently in need of personnel, had already enrolled in its ranks even those who had maritime experience." (See Luraghi, *History of the Confederate Navy,* p. 96, 114.)

73. A description and illustrations of shot and shell designed by Brooke can be found in Ripley, *Artillery and Ammunition,* p. 318–20. Ripley states, "Confederate rifle ammunition is a particularly difficult subject since few records have survived and identifications must be based partially on supposition, much of it open to argument" (Ibid., 304).

74. This is evidence of the growing friction between Brooke, a naval officer then serving at the Tredegar Works in Richmond, who had designed the transformation of the wooden vessel *Merrimac* into an ironclad, and John L. Porter, the constructor on the scene in Norfolk, who was inclined to do things his own way.

75. This must have been 1st Lt. Charles C. Simms of Georgia, who had ranked Brooke by forty-three files in the U.S. Navy before the war.

76. George T. Sinclair, a Virginian, was a very senior first lieutenant who had joined the U.S. Navy ten years before Brooke.

77. Luraghi commends Fairfax for his work as ordnance chief at Norfolk. "He went to work," says Luraghi, "without delay to convert as many of the 32–pounder smoothbores as he could by rifling them and reinforcing their breeches with a strong iron band, greatly improving their efficiency." He describes Fairfax as "a resourceful and energetic man." (See Luraghi, *History of the Confederate Navy,* 43.)

78. Comdr. Richard L. Page was one of the few navy officers selected for army duty when President Davis in December 1861 "was authorized to assign temporary military rank and command to navy officers serving with troops." This was because of the shortage of experienced officers in the army and the large surplus of senior officers in the navy. John Taylor Wood is another well-known

example. (See Tom H. Wells, *The Confederate Navy, a Study in Organization* [University: University of Alabama Press, 1971], 21.)

79. Capt. Franklin Buchanan, the senior officer in the Confederate navy, would command the *Virginia* when it was launched.

80. Anna Maria Brooke, Brooke's first child, was born in 1856.

81. Mary Selden was one of Brooke's many Garnett cousins.

82. William Garnett was Brooke's uncle and father-in-law, who often stayed in Lexington with his daughter Louisa Garnett Williamson. Before the war he had been collector of customs in Norfolk.

83. England took a hard line, and as a result Secretary of State William H. Seward released Mason and Slidell on the grounds that Wilkes, who had seized them, had erred in not bringing the British ship, rather than just the Confederate agents, to court.

84. When Brooke's surveying vessel, the *Fenimore Cooper*, was wrecked on the coast of Japan in 1859, he lost almost his entire private library. He was an avid collector of books in his field, and when he went to Richmond at the time he joined the Virginia navy he left most of his remaining books in Lexington, where his brother-in-law Thomas Hoomes Williams, a VMI professor, lived.

85. It is reported that during the war the Tredegar Iron Works, under Anderson's ownership, "became the major supplier of ammunition for the Confederacy and from 1861–1863 was almost the sole source of heavy weapons, including the Brooke" (Ripley, *Artillery and Ammunition*, 128). It was at the Tredegar that Brooke produced his cannons and ammunition and the iron plates for the *Merrimac*.

86. This refers to the *Trent* Affair.

87. Warren Ripley writes: "Four rifles tested at Fort Monroe in 1859 are listed as the design of 'Dr. Reed.' This appears to be Dr. John Brahan Read (1816–1899), Tuscaloosa, Alabama physician and inventor of the celebrated Read projectile which also is often misspelled 'Reed'" (*Artillery and Ammunition*, 176).

Chapter 3: *The* Virginia *in Hampton Roads*

1. Capt. Franklin Buchanan had been appointed to command the *Virginia*.

2. Jones, an expert in naval ordnance, in 1853 had been ordered to the Washington navy yard to assist John Dahlgren "in perfection of the inventor's shell gun" (Luraghi, *History of the Confederate Navy*, 128). Dahlgren was perhaps the navy's most experienced ordnance officer before the war and for a time served as chief of the Bureau of Ordnance in the Federal navy.

3. With Brooke's familiarity with the problem and easy access to Secretary Mallory he might well have pushed for such legislation.

4. John Letcher of Lexington, a Democrat, was elected governor of Virginia in 1859 and was a strong supporter of the Confederacy. He had opposed secession until Lincoln called for troops to invade the South. Robert L. Montague of Middlesex County, Virginia, served as lieutenant governor while Letcher was governor.

5. Maury was still a commander. Brooke apparently called him captain out of respect.

6. Early in the war the Confederacy suffered from the small production at the few small mills. But Josiah Gorgas, army chief of ordnance, turned to Maj. George Washington Rains, who found that the necessary machinery for a large powder mill could be obtained only at the Tredegar.

7. Catesby Jones, recognized as a man "of outstanding skill in artillery matters," was appointed executive officer of the *Virginia,* then being constructed, and on 11 November 1861 was ordered "to proceed immediately to Norfolk and there personally survey the testing and placing of the guns with the utmost speed" (Luraghi, *History of the Confederate Navy,* 99). Jones fired in the Hamptons Roads area at such places as Craney Island and the hospital, but because of limited time and the range limits imposed by the area, firing was difficult (Ibid.). The Blakely guns manufactured in England were "12 pounder rifles, muzzle-loading, and fired well with English ammunition (built-up shells with leaden bases) but with the Confederate substitute they experienced the same difficulties which attended this ammunition in all guns" (Ripley, *Artillery and Ammunition,* 138). Lacking the resources of the North, the Confederacy imported all the guns it could. The Blakely was one of three English guns greatly admired, the others being the Armstrong and the Whitworth.

8. The older Williamson, Thomas Hoomes, was Brooke's brother-in-law and one of the first professors at Virginia Military Institute, where he taught engineering.

9. Hunter Davidson, a Virginian, had entered the U.S. Navy the same year as Brooke did. Early in the war he worked with Maury on torpedoes, and when the latter went to England, Davidson continued this work. He is described by Luraghi at the time the *Merrimac* was being sheeted in iron as "the future genius of submarine weapons" (*History of the Confederate Navy,* 114).

10. In planning the armament for the *Virginia,* Mallory decided that the forward and stern guns should be "the most modern rifled guns, of a new design, capable of firing either shells or armor-piercing bolts" (Luraghi, *History of the Confederate Navy,* 98). The Tredegar was making ready to produce rifled cannons, and Brooke was given the job of designing the new gun. The result was "a piece of ordnance of the most modern conception, one that soon proved superior to any enemy cannon and to almost any cast in Europe, to rank among the most powerful muzzle-loading cannon ever built" (Ibid.). Mallory described the 6.4-inch and 7-inch Brooke cannons as "superior in strength, precision, and range to any available in America" (Ibid.). For details on the Brooke Gun, see Ripley, *Artillery and Ammunition,* p. 127–36.

11. "Fingal" probably refers to the iron-hulled ship of that name that was made in England as a blockade runner. On its first voyage the *Fingal* arrived in Savannah, Georgia, on 12 November 1861 with a cargo including four rifled naval guns and eight hundred projectiles (Luraghi, *Confederate Navy,* 200).

12. Jones seems to have been aware that the North was building ironclads, which put pressure on him to complete the conversion of the *Merrimac* quickly. A week earlier, on 30 January, the *Monitor* was launched at the shipyard of Thomas Rowland at Greenpoint, Long Island. (See Neeser, *Statistical and Chronological History,* 13.)

13. Captain Buchanan was not formally appointed to command the *Virginia* until 24 February, but Luraghi states that the appointment of Buchanan had been in the wind "for at least five months, and Jones knew it." Jones had hoped for the command himself, but Mallory could not pick him over so many senior officers. While Jones was in Norfolk, Buchanan was in Richmond as chief of the Office of Orders and Detail, and in that capacity "he carefully surveyed all the work to outfit the *Virginia,* and it was to his credit that he detailed some first-rate officers to her." Despite his own impatience to challenge the Union fleet, Jones had a high opinion of Buchanan, a veteran of forty-five years' service in the U.S. Navy. (See Luraghi, *History of the Confederate Navy,* 117.)

14. James Dunwoody Bulloch, according to the Confederate states' navy Register of the Navy of the Confederate States, to January 1, 1863, was promoted on 17 January 1862 from lieutenant to commander for the war. This was in recognition of his service in obtaining for the Confederacy fast vessels to serve as public cruisers, which the South because of its limited means could not build itself.

15. No commander was ordered to the *Virginia.* It must have been that since Jones had been with the *Virginia* from the beginning and Captain Buchanan had not yet arrived, Jones must have felt that another person would be a fifth wheel.

16. Mercer was the daughter of Lizzie's sister, Mrs. Thomas Hoomes Williamson.

17. This was a problem that worried Brooke until the vessel put to sea, because it left a strip of the hull above the water exposed to gunfire.

18. It is reported that "the lead mines near Wytheville, Virginia, were the only lead mines in the Confederacy" (Bruce, *Virginia Iron Manufacture,* 346n. 83).

19. The historic Roanoke Island near the entrance to Albemarle Sound, North Carolina, was captured by a Federal army under Gen. Ambrose Burnside on 8 February 1862.

20. William J. Hubard had a bronze foundry near Richmond where, Ripley says, he produced brass cannons "and by fall 1861, was furnishing weapons to state and Confederate governments," but he "apparently made only the rough casting and his weapons were completed in the Richmond machine shop of Thomas Sampson and James Pae" (Ripley, *Artillery and Ammunition,* 362–63). Ripley writes that Hubard's powder experiments "resulted in his death . . . from accidental explosion of a shell" (Ibid., 363). The government detailed men to various manufacturers, including Hubard's foundry (Bruce, *Virginia Iron Manufacture,* 346 n 80).

21. Capt. William F. Lynch, a veteran of over forty years of naval service who was charged with the coastal defense of North Carolina, in January 1862 complained to Secretary Mallory about the "serious deficiencies of the army's preparations at Roanoke Island and Hatteras Inlet" (Durkin, *Stephen R. Mallory,* 190).

22. Capt. French Forrest was in charge of the Office of Orders and Detail. According to Durkin, Forrest, an old-timer who had entered the U.S. Navy in 1811, was one of Mallory's two principal aides (*Stephen R. Mallory,* 136). Sewell's Point was near Norfolk. There was a battery there that fought Federal gunboats in June 1861 (Freeman, *Robert E. Lee,* 1:500).

23. This was a smooth bore cannon.

24. Coski writes that Powhatan was "25 miles below Richmond" in Prince George County and, "weak and short-lived though it was[,] . . . the naval defense point closest to Richmond" (*Capital Navy,* 10, 39).

25. After capturing Fort Henry in February 1862, General Grant threatened Fort Donelson, which lay twenty miles west on the Cumberland River. Grant attacked on 13 February without success, and the following day the Confederates counterattacked but made little headway. Seemingly trapped, the Confederates asked Grant for his best terms. His famous reply was: "No terms except unconditional and immediate surrender can be accepted." On the night of the 15th Fort Donelson and fourteen thousand Confederates were surrendered. (See Wayne Andrews, *Concise Dictionary of American History* [New York: Charles Scribner's Sons, 1962], 296.)

26. In referring to the *Virginia* and other Confederate ironclads in the pictures in *Iron Afloat,* William Still uses the term "CSS" (William N. Still, Jr., *Iron Afloat: The Story of the Confederate Ironclads* [Nashville, Tenn.: Vanderbilt University Press, 1971]).

27. Muscoe Russell Hunter Garnett (1821–64), a lawyer, was Brooke's cousin. A strict constructionist and defender of slavery, he served in the U.S. House of Representatives from 1856 to1861 and, following secession, in the Confederate Congress. (See Joseph Hopkins, ed., *Concise Dictionary,* 329.)

28. William Porcher Miles, an eloquent supporter of slavery and secession, was a member of the Confederate Congress representing the Charleston, South Carolina, district.

29. This was probably George T. Sinclair, a Virginian.

30. Rifled cannons were far more effective against ironclads than were smoothbores.

31. Buchanan had by no means been idle; on 2 March 1862 he wrote from the *Virginia* to General Magruder, commanding at Yorktown:

> On my arrival here on Tuesday last, the 25th inst. I found the ship by no means ready for service, she required eighteen thousand two hundred pounds of powder, for her battery. Howitzers were not fitted and mounted on the upper deck to repel boats & boarders & none of the port shutters are fitted on the ship. Much of the powder has now arrived, and the other matters shall not detain me. You may therefore look out for me at the time named [early on Friday morning next]. My plan is to destroy the Frigates first, if possible, and then turn my attention to the battery on shore. I sincerely hope that acting together we may be successful in destroying many of the enemy.

Along the same line, he wrote on 3 March 1862 from the *Virginia* to Comdr. John R. Tucker, CSS *Patrick Henry:*

> I am informed by the Hon. Secretary of the Navy that the Patrick Henry under your command, the "Jamestown," Lieut. Comdg. Barney & the Teazer Lt. Comdg. Webb are placed under my command as

composing part of my squadron. It is my intention, if no accident occurs to this ship to prevent it, to appear before the enemy off Newport News at daylight on Friday morning next. You will, with the "Jamestown" & "Teazer" be prepared to join me. My object is first to destroy the Frigates Congress & Cumberland, if possible and then turn my attention to the destruction of the battery on shore, and the Gun boats. You will, in the absence of signals use your best exertions to injure or destroy the enemy, much is expected of this ship & those who cooperate with her, by our countrymen, and I expect and hope that our acts will prove our desire to do our duty, to reflect credit upon the country and the Navy.

You will communicate this communication to Lieuts. Commdg. Barney & Webb.

No. 1 signal hoisted under my pennant indicates "sink before your surrender."

On 4 March on the *Virginia*, Buchanan wrote to Secretary Mallory:

I have the honor to acknowledge the receipt of your order and instructions (received yesterday) appointing me Flag Officer for the command of the Naval defences of the James River. Today I assumed command and hoisted my flag on board this ship. . . .

On Thursday night the 6th inst. I contemplate leaving here to appear before the enemy's ships at Newport News, should no accident occur to this ship, when I feel confident the acts of the Virginia will give proof of her officers & crew to meet the views of the Department as far as practicable, From the best and most reliable information I can obtain from experienced pilots it will be impossible to ascend the Potomac in the Virginia with the present draft of water, nearly 22 feet.

None of the port shutters are fitted on the Virginia, nor are the Howitzers placed on the upper deck, the latter may be ready by Thursday. The shutters for the two bow & quarter ports, I will have temporarily placed there to keep out shot or shells. The last of our powder shells will be received on board on Wednesday.

All three letters are from Admiral Franklin Buchanan Letter Book 1862–63, Southern Historical Collection, University of North Carolina at Chapel Hill.

32. The North must have known that the *Virginia* was about ready. On 7 March 1862 U.S. Secretary of the Navy Gideon Welles sent the following telegram to Capt. John Marston, senior naval officer at Hampton Roads: "Send the St. Lawrence Congress and Cumberland immediately into the Potomac river. Let the disposition of the remainder of vessels at Hampton Roads be made according to your best judgement after consultation with Genl. Wool. Use steam to tow them up. I will also try and send a couple of steamers from Baltimore to assist. Let there be no delay. 9:50 PM" (John A. Dahlgren Papers, LC [copy]).

33. Robert Dabney Minor was a younger brother of George Minor, chief of the Office of Ordnance at the time. Robert Minor had entered the U.S. Navy the same year as Brooke and spent much of the Civil War on ordnance duty.

William H. Parker, who had stood first in Brooke's class at Annapolis, became head of the Confederacy's naval academy, which was established on the *Patrick Henry*. Robert Minor was the flag lieutenant of the James River Squadron of which the *Virginia* was flagship and Franklin Buchanan the commander. Fairfax was ordnance chief in Norfolk, and he did not succeed George Minor as Confederate chief of ordnance in Richmond; Brooke did.

34. Much has been written on this battle, but it is interesting to get some con temporary observations. James B. Jones, a Southerner, wrote to his sister, Mrs. Bettie Hayes, on 8 March from Camp Arrington, near Norfolk: "The iron plated steamer, Merrimack has been finished some time—and was expected down last night to attack New Port News. The Merrimack is thought to be impregnable by any guns mode in Yankeedom, some even think [she] could pass Old Point with impunity." On 10 March he wrote:

> You will see I commenced to write the 8th but was disturbed by the report that the Merrimack had passed down the river. I went immediately to the beach, about one o'clock, the Merrimack in company with the gun boats, Raleigh and Beauford [*sic*] had passed Sewels [*sic*] Point and turned up the Channel in the direction of New Port News and the blockaders of James River, they passed the blockade round to the mouth of the river, without firing or being fired on, at the mouth of the river they were met by two gun boats from Richmond and then the fight commenced, the Merrimack proceeded first to shell New Port News which she did handsomely silencing every gun which presumed to fire on her; burning every tent and house in sight.
>
> While she was engaged with the fort two of the largest frigates in the U.S.N. and several gun boats started up from Old Point and, in passing opened fire on Sewell's Point broadside and broadside without an effect, Sewels [*sic*] Point returning the fire with rifled guns and disableing [*sic*] one of the ships so much that she could not reach the scene of action but had to draw off and wait for night to screen her retreat and it is not known whether she made good her retreat or went down after night, in the mean time our fleet above was hotly engaged, the fire was incessant and such excitement I never saw before, the beach for a mile was covered with men. The Merrimack after satisfying herself with the battery turned her attention to the Yankee fleet which she managed as follows: she first attacked an iron plated gun boat, her sides proving too hard for balls, the commander gave the order to advance and sink her at all hazards, which was done, sinking the Yankee and all on board instantly, next sinking a smaller gun boat and then turning her attention to blockaders running in forty yards of the Cumberland (the ship that burnt the navy yard) and sinking it with the first fire. (You never saw such cheers as rent the air when it went to the bottom) the next was the Congress, which was disabled and silenced and raised a white flag, our boats ceased firing and sent an open boat to it which was fired on, the commander of the Merrimack then gave

the command to sink it, but took fire instead of sinking, it now being night our boats drew off and anchored near Sewels [*sic*] Point, thus ended the first day's work with the exception of the burning which I saw the whole of as I was on guard on the beach, it was a beautiful sight, it burned steadily untill [*sic*] about one o'clock when the magazine took fire and such an explosion I never saw before, an immense column of fire ascended, apparently a mile high, with the most terriffic [*sic*] report I ever heard.

Our fleet attacked them again on yesterday morning which lasted three or four hours but at long range, striking and injuring one of the enemy's largest ships, which is thought to be a complete ruin.

Our fleet drew off yesterday and returned to Norfolk, our loss is thought to be 25 killed and 100 wounded, that of the Yankees is not known but it is thought to be at least 1000. I hope the Militia will breathe more freely as the attack on this place is indefinitely deferred.

The previous letters are in the Mrs. J. Boyd Massenburg Collection 1862–70 to 1932, Southern Historical Collection, University of North Carolina at Chapel Hill.

A memorandum in the John A. Dahlgren Papers, LC, dated 8 March 1862 offers another description.

The *defence* has been gradually making slow way against Ordnance —But the events of this day will definitely shape the future in such matters.

Our squadron had been quietly occupying Hampton Roads since the Insurrection without dispute or the prospect of it. Meanwhile rumor from day to day reported that the frigate Merrimac, which it was supposed we had destroyed in retiring from Norfolk Navy Yard, was being cut down & plated with Iron. Notwithstanding it had been recently said also that the project had failed because the plates applied were too heavy, still the work was believed to be in progress. We had also been preparing some Iron plated batteries and the readiness of one of them probably precipitated the catastrophe.

About one PM of this day the Merrimac was seen coming down from Norfolk and was signalled by the Congress & Cumberland lying at Newport News. The Minnesota was near Fort Monroe & also the Roanoke. Transports and a fleet of small craft were about. Two light steamers Jamestown & Yorktown coming down the James River joined the Merrimac & the three steamed straight for the two ships at Newport News. . . . [The battle with the *Cumberland* and *Congress* is then described.] The continuous fire of the vessels was of no avail, the shot & shells poured from their guns & fell harmlessly on her. [The Merrimac returned to Norfolk at the close of day.]

It was about this time that Mr. [Gustavus Vasa] Fox, Ansn Sec of Navy who had come to examine in person if there was any reason to expect the M. had full evidence of the fact. . . . [The writer then describes the arrival of the *Monitor* and then the battle.] The iron casing of the Monitor was scarred, but no more and the Comd. was nearly blinded by the explosion of a shell at the slit just as he was looking through it—no other personal damage was done to any one in the Monitor.

Several thought that the Merrimac was pierced in three places by the XI shot of the Monitor, but others thought not.

If the Merrimac could have succeeded, she could have scathed every one of our Naval^in positions and had access to all our ports where the draft of water was sufficient. On the outside of this memo is written: The contest of the *Merrimac & the Monitor* the first *battle test* of the Xi^in gun—The two XI in guns then saved all our ports.

35. This was probably Maj. Isaac M. St. John, whom Dew describes as "another one of the superbly efficient officers Gorgas attracted to the [army] ordnance service. This is an example of the close co-operation in ordnance matters between the army and the navy, particularly in river defense (*Ironmaker to the Confederacy*, 145–46). In time St. John became chief of the Bureau of Nitre and Mining. He worked closely with the navy.

The emergence of the *Virginia* caused considerable activity by the Federals. John Dahlgren, chief of naval ordnance, sent a series of messages on 9 March. He advised President Lincoln at 3 P.M.

that upon consultation with such Pilots as I have in the yard, I find them to be of opinion that a vessel drawing 22 feet water can pass up the Potomac within a hundred yards of the arsenal. . . . The actual blocking of the River is only to be resorted to when the exigency arises. . . . I would advise that some heavy Ordnance be got ready for placing at the Arsenal, at Giesberry Point and at Buzzard Point. Fort Washington should also have suitable cannon. . . . It happens unfortunately that the only two good Steamers belonging to the Yard are at Fortress Monroe. [To Secretary of the Navy Gideon Welles, Dahlgren wrote at 3:30 P.M.:] Two of the large yard steamers are at Fort Monroe. One of them is not yet repaired, so that I have but one little tug. . . . I would suggest authority to charter or hire one or two of the best Steamers on the River, if necessary without consent of the owner. [Ten minutes later he notified General McClellan:] I am making arrangements to place an Eleven inch Gun and some Ten inch Mortars on Giesberry Point, which will command at short Range the nearest Point that a vessel drawing 22 feet can approach the Capital; the channel passes within 50 yards of this position. [At 4:20 P.M. Dahlgren wrote Welles:] I have but one Eleven Inch Gun here and not one nine inch gun on the yard—it is highly desirable to have some pieces if only for precaution or use down the River.

At 6:00 P.M. the telegraph operator at the Navy Yard was notified by Headquarters, Army of the Potomac that "Secretary Stanton is in the Navy Yard, find him immediately and say the Military Telegraph is in circuit with Fortress

Monroe that the 'Merrimac' did not go to sea but has put back to Norfolk. The message reads as if she has had an encounter with the 'Erricson' [*sic*]." At 7:25 the army chief of engineers asked Dahlgren, "How many guns of large calibre could be spared for fort Washington? state kind and calibre also what kind of carriages." Forty minutes later Dahlgren notified General Barnard, chief of engineers, "I have but two guns in the yard of proper caliber, which with a few mortars, I am preparing to place on Giesberry Point." At 9 P.M. Dahlgren informed the president and the secretary of the navy: "The proposed measures for guarding the Potomac are in progress. I am informed from the Quarter Master's Department that eight Canal Boats loaded with stone were about to leave and eight more would leave during the night. I have sent instructions to the Comd't of Flotilla as to their disposition and use at the three places where the Channel has least depth of water." Fifteen minutes later Dahlgren was informed by Brigadier General Hooker, "Captain Wyman is of the opinion that the Merrimac cannot ascend the Potomac." (See John A. Dahlgren Papers, LC.) Most readers are aware that Secretary of War Stanton was fearful that the *Virginia* would attack Washington. These messages indicate that he was not the only leader so concerned. No one was aware that the Confederate navy did not feel that the *Virginia* was seaworthy. Perhaps she could have operated in the Potomac, but how would she get there?

In his diary Secretary of the Navy Gideon Welles gives a somewhat different account of what transpired:

When intelligence reached Washington on Sunday morning, the 9th of March, that the Merrimac had come down from Norfolk and attacked and destroyed the Cumberland and Congress, I called at once on the President, who had sent for me. Several members of the Cabinet soon gathered. Stanton was already there, and there was general excitement and alarm. Although my Department and the branch of the Government entrusted to me were most interested and most responsible, the President ever after gave me the credit of being on that occasion, the most calm and self-possessed of any member of the Government. The President himself was so excited that he could not deliberate or be satisfied with the opinions of non-professional men, but ordered his carriage and drove to the navy yard to see and consult with Admiral Dahlgren and other naval officers, who might be there. Dahlgren, always attentive and much of a courtier, had, to a great extent, the President's regard and confidence, but in this instance Dahlgren, who knew not of the preparation or what had been the purposes of the Department, could give the President no advice or opinion, but referred him to me. The inability of Dahlgren to advise seemed to increase the panic. . . . But the most frightened man on that gloomy day, the most as I think of any during the Rebellion, was the Secretary of War. He was at times almost frantic, and as he walked the room with his eyes fixed on me, I saw well the estimation in which he held me with my unmoved and unexcited manner and conversation.

The Merrimac, he said, would destroy every vessel in the service, could lay every city on the coast under contribution, could take Fortress Monroe; McClellan's mistaken purpose to advance by the Peninsula must be abandoned, and Burnside would eventually be captured. Likely the first movement of the Merrimac would be to come up the Potomac and disperse Congress, destroy the Capital and public buildings, or she might go to New York and Boston and destroy those cities. (Beale, *Diary of Gideon Welles*, 61–64)

On 15 March 1862 Matthew Fontaine Maury in Richmond was prompted by the battle to write a twenty-seven-page letter to Captain De la Marcha at the Depot De la Marine, Paris, France, in the hope of getting French naval aid for the Confederacy. He wrote:

Our "Virginia" by her performances in Hampton Roads has, at a single dash, overturned the "wooden walls" of Old England and rendered effete the navies of the world. She has reduced at one blow many a strong fortification on the land, Happily for us and the causes of truth, officers of your navy were witnesses to that sea-fight, and Europe I trust, will at least for once, have something like a correct account of *one* of our engagements with the enemy.

But when we come to the "Virginia" and other iron clad men-of-war, they can pass forts with impunity, and bring such cities as New York and London into terms under their guns. The forts of the Thames below London can not now prevent a shot-proof vessel from passing up to London. Such a vessel would be invulnerable to the wooden navy of England, and as the case now stands mighty lay that ancient city in ashes, or bring it under contribution, according to her pleasure.

It may be said therefore that we, whom the powers of Europe refuse to recognize as worthy of a place in the family of nations, have, at a single dash wiped out their wooden navies, rendered impotent their coast defenses, and exposed their seaport towns to the first enemy that chances to appear before them in the shot proof armour of a steel clad man-of-war. (Matthew T. Maury Papers, LC)

Maury ignores the fact that with the building of the *Gloire* in 1858 the French were pioneers in ironclad construction, and that both the French and British had turned increasingly to armored ships to supplant their wooden vessels. According to James Phinney Baxter: "When France stopped building wooden ships of the line, produced the *Gloire*, and announced a program of sixteen seagoing and seventeen coast-defence ironclads, built or building, the death knell of the wooden walls had sounded. . . . The battle of Hampton Roads demonstrated and emphasized the foresight of the French" (James Phinney Baxter, *The Introduction of the Ironclad Warship* [Cambridge, Mass.: Harvard University Press, 1933], 4). Baxter states that there were "five great naval revolutions of the nineteenth century—steam, shell guns, the screw propeller, rifled ordnances, and armor." (p. 3). He notes that when the *Virginia* sank the

Cumberland, the Confederate ironclad "embodied all five of those revolutionary features" (p. 3). In his letter Maury also ignores the fact that "in the three years preceding the Battle of Hampton Roads, the [British] Admiralty ordered sixteen seagoing ironclads, including the *Prince Albert*" (p. 316).

36. The battle of the *Virginia* and the *Monitor* must have eased tensions in Washington, for at 1:00 A.M., 10 march 1862, Gideon Welles, from Army of the Potomac headquarters, sent Captain Dahlgren a military telegraph ordering him to "suspend operations for the present for sinking boats or placing obstructions in the Potomac" (John A. Dahlgren Papers, LC).

37. Lt. John Taylor Wood (see Still, *Iron Afloat,* p. 33). As previously mentioned, Wood was one of the naval officers selected for army duty.

38. The *Monitor* that fought the *Virginia* was sometimes called by the name of its inventor, John Ericsson, a Swede.

39. George T. Sinclair, one of seven Sinclairs who served in the Confederate navy, had been ten years senior to Brooke in the U.S. Navy and was near the top of the list of lieutenants in the Confederate navy; later he would be sent to Great Britain by Secretary Mallory to procure an armor-plated commerce raider (Luraghi, *History of the Confederate Navy,* 206). Sinclair's letter must have shaken Brooke out of any euphoria he was enjoying from reports of the battle. Although well aware of the *Virginia*'s limitations, Brooke must have been surprised, if not startled, at the strength of the Northern ironclad. Sinclair was very perceptive. With its enormous facilities and the apparent success of the *Monitor,* the Union began turning out such vessels in large numbers. Also the war proved that the seven-inch Brooke rifle with wrought iron bolts could penetrate the armor of ships like the *Monitor.* The day before Sinclair wrote, Brooke had wrought iron bolts made for the seven-inch rifle.

40. In Ripley (*Artillery and Ammunition,* 283–340) there is considerable information on the smoothbore and rifled ammunition Brooke designed. Hunter is probably Robert M. T. Hunter, Brooke's cousin, who was Confederate secretary of state from 1861 to 1862. John T. and William E. Tanner were Tredegar partners. The Union was thinking along the same lines as the Confederacy. On the same day that Brooke wrote of his experiments in his journal, Gustavus Fox, assistant secretary of the navy, wrote to Dahlgren: "Don't you think you can allow the wrought iron shot to be used in the eleven inch Guns. It is the only thing that will settle the Merrimac. If you think so she ought to have more, we must have more of these Boats with fifteen inch Guns and you must go check with your furnaces at once to make them to stand solid shot. The monitor is anxious for another Brush. Buchanan commanded the first day and was wounded. Catesby Jones the second day" (by telegraph: S. V. Fox, Fort Monroe, to Capt. Dahlgren, Comdg. Navy Yard, John A. Dahlgren Papers, LC).

41. Sampson and Pae is described by Ripley as a "Richmond machine shop which finished weapons cast by William James Hubard" (*Artillery and Ammunition,* 364). Charles A. McEvoy is listed by Ripley among manufacturers and inspectors in the Confederate Navy Office of Ordnance and Hydrography (*Artillery*

and Ammunition, 363). McEvoy is listed in the Confederate navy Register of the Navy of the Confederate States to January 1, 1863 as a "master not in line of promotion." After the war he lived in England, continued to experiment in ordnance, and corresponded with Brooke.

42. The most thorough study of balls and shells used in the Confederate navy is Ripley's *Artillery and Ammunition*. He states that much Confederate ammunition "was manufactured by relatively small shops that made little attempt to meet specific standards other than caliber" (p. 289). According to Ripley, "the name 'Tennessee Sabot' or 'Tennessee Shell' also crops up on occasion in either Mullane or Brooke projectiles, but unfortunately it is difficult to determine which" (p. 321). "Mullane had a copper cup bolted to the base of the projectile" (p. 313). Brooke went beyond Mullane in that shallow indentations or ratchets were placed on the copper base (p. 317).

43. Secretary Mallory put Comdr. Charles McIntosh in command of the *Louisiana* on 2 March 1862, and on the latter's arrival he "immediately started working to overcome the great obstacles that still hindered her completion" (Luraghi, *History of the Confederate Navy*, 128). With the loss of such key forts in the West as Forts Henry and Donelson and Island No. 10, Mallory endeavored to strengthen the Confederate position on the Mississippi. Part of his plan involved the building of ironclads at Memphis and New Orleans. According to Still, "With the exception of Gosport Navy Yard at Norfolk, New Orleans was the most important shipbuilding center of the Confederacy" (*Iron Afloat*, 43). The Confederacy laid the keels for two ironclads in New Orleans in October 1861, the *Louisiana* and the *Mississippi*, the former in the yard of E. C. Murray, just north of the city. The Tift brothers, Asa and Nelson, built the *Mississippi* (Ibid., 43–44). At this time veteran commander John K. Mitchell was in command in New Orleans. He had entered the U.S. Navy in 1825. In facing the delays at New Orleans, Mallory decreed that the *Louisiana* "should have not two but four bow and stern guns and that they would be powerful 7-inch Brookes weighing six tons each" (Luraghi, *History of the Confederate Navy*, 129).

44. This was probably Charles E. Thorburn, the only commissioned officer to serve with Brooke on the surveying schooner *Fenimore Cooper* in 1858–60. Thorburn resigned from the U.S. Navy in July 1860. He was a native of Ohio and six years Brooke's junior.

45. The new shipyard in Richmond was to be built across the James River from Rocketts. William A. Graves was a naval constructor. Lt. Robert D. Minor, a Virginian, had entered the U.S. Navy in 1841, the same year as Brooke. He had been wounded while serving as flag lieutenant of the *Virginia* and later took command of the Naval Ordnance Works in Richmond.

46. Hunter Davidson, a contemporary of Brooke, was one of the first officers assigned to the *Merrimac*. He would later win fame for his work with torpedoes and has been called "the future genius of submarine warfare" (Luraghi, *History of the Confederate Navy*, 114). The *Fingal*, referred to earlier, was an iron-hulled merchant ship made in England for the Confederacy and run through the blockade to Savannah. The Tift brothers with Mallory's consent converted

her into the ironclad *Atlanta*. Still writes that her "machinery was relatively new, English built, and included probably the best propulsion unit in any Confederate ironclad" (*Iron Afloat*, 129).

47. Lt. William H. Murdaugh of Virginia had entered the U.S. and Confederate navies the same years as Brooke.

48. As cited earlier, Lt. Robert D. Minor, flag lieutenant, had warned Brooke of this possibility. This was the beginning of a heated altercation of the time and for many years thereafter. The first blow was struck by Porter through a letter published in the *Charleston Mercury* on 19 March 1862. It was Brooke's belief, or so he wrote to a friend many years later, that "Porter 'first wrote a friend making a most extravagant claim in regard to what he had done' in designing the *Virginia* and the friend had had the letter published" (Brooke, *John M. Brooke*, 253). The following day a number of newspapers joined in giving Porter credit. On 29 March the report of Secretary of the Navy Mallory to the House of Representatives giving full credit to Brooke was published in the *Richmond Examiner* (Ibid., 233–34). But this did not stop Porter, whose response was the letter referred to in Brooke's journal. To settle the matter Brooke applied for "a patent on his design for ironclad warships based upon the unique feature of his plan that had been applied to the *Virginia:* the submerged ends, extending beyond the forward and after ends of the shield" (Ibid.). Brooke was granted Patent 100 by the Confederate Patent Office on 29 July 1862. This should have settled the matter, but it was renewed many years later by a book published in 1886 by J. Thomas Scharf titled *The History of the Confederate Navy from Its Organization to the Surrender of Its Last Vessel* (New York: Rogers and Sherwood; see p. 145–53). Scharf had been a midshipman at the Confederate Naval Academy. After extensive quotations from various people on the subject Scharf concludes that "it appears at this time that there was some similarity of plan between that offered by Lieut. Brooke and the model exhibited by Constructor Porter; but that the model, rather than the 'rough drawings,' received the approval of the Board and adoption by the department. That to Constructor Porter is due the honor of the plan—the only original thought or idea about the ship" (Scharf, *History of the Confederate Navy*, 151). In response Brooke published a pamphlet, *The Merrimac or Virginia: Her Real Projector*. James Phinney Baxter, in *Introduction of the Ironclad Warship* (p. 225–26), briefly discusses the controversy but makes no judgment. William N. Still, Jr., in a careful examination of the facts, notes that "the really significant and unique difference" between Brooke's plan and Porter's "was Brooke's plan for submerging the ends (bow and stern) of the vessel"; he also notes that Brooke obtained a Confederate patent on this and that "Porter never contested it" (Still, *Iron Afloat*, 14). But, Still notes, "Although Porter's claim that he designed the *Virginia* is apparently not valid, he did provide the plans and drawings for most of the other armored vessels" (Ibid., 15). John M. Coski states that "Mallory assigned Brooke the task of drafting a preliminary design for an ironclad ship, then summoned Porter and Williamson to discuss Brooke's ideas. Porter brought to the meeting the model of an ironclad ram apparently based on Brooke's proposal. The four men

inspected the model and approved Porter's design for a casemate shaped armor shield. They also approved Brooke's modification to submerge both ends of the deck" (Coski, *Capital Navy*, 24). Luraghi stresses that Porter's model was like that of the French floating batteries used in the Crimean War "intended mainly for harbor defense"; Brooke's plan calling for extended and submerged ends was for "a true warship not only capable of steaming by herself but of fighting any enemy ship," while Porter's plan called "for a hull ended (like that of the French floating batteries) abruptly at both ends of the casemate"; he concludes that "a scrutiny of the original draft, in the archives of the Confederate Museum at Richmond, shows that the early Porter plans would *not* include the elongation of the bow and stern of the hull which would have resulted in a 'ship,' and that Porter instead had stuck stubbornly to the idea of a floating battery, as he continued to call his" (Luraghi, *History of the Confederate Navy*, 93–94).

49. On 19 March 1862 Buchanan gave Mallory his views on an "attack on New York by the 'Virginia'":

> On her passage she would no doubt be followed by the heavy steam ships of the enemy and the "Monitor," and having the speed of the "Virginia" would annoy her exceedingly with their guns.
>
> When off New York I consider it would be impossible to obtain Pilots who would venture to run the ship over the shoals and through the channels with such an exposure of life as they would be subjected to: Under the present state of things no confidence can be placed in any New York or Jersey pilot.
>
> Ships drawing 22 feet water are frequently obliged to remain outside of New York Bar a week or more before they are able to enter.
>
> I have passed the bar in a Frigate drawing 21 feet water and stuck. I have also with an experienced pilot stirred up the mud in a Sloop of War coming out.
>
> The fortifications in the harbour of New York near which the ship is obliged to pass are armed with the heaviest of guns. . . .
>
> One of the most vulnerable points of the "Virginia" is her projecting stern with her propeller and rudder, and had the "Monitor" succeeded in running against it as she attempted, the result would have been disastrous to this ship. (Admiral Franklin Buchanan Letter Book, 1862–63, Southern Historical Collection, University of North Carolina at Chapel Hill)

On 27 March 1862 Buchanan gave a full report of the *Virginia*'s actions on March 8–9 to the secretary of the navy. On the same day he wrote: "While in the act of closing this report, I received the communication of the Department dated 22nd Inst. relieving me temporarily of the command of the squadron for the Naval defences of James River. I feel honored in being relieved by that gallant Flag Officer Tatnall" [Tattnall]. (Admiral Franklin Buchanan Letter Book, 1862–63, Southern Historical Collection, University of North Carolina at Chapel Hill)

50. Gen. Albert Sidney Johnston was killed at the Battle of Shiloh. One of the South's most promising senior officers, he had served with Brooke's father in the old army.

51. Brooke's estimate seems to have been general. Henry Stuart Foote, though born in Fauquier County, Virginia, in 1804, became a Democratic politician in Mississippi and a personal and political enemy of Jefferson Davis. He was governor of Mississippi from 1852 to 1854 but opposed secession.

52. This was Maj. Gen. George Brinton McClellan's Peninsula Campaign.

53. On that date McClellan began the siege of Yorktown, which was not occupied until a month later. John Magruder was the Confederate general.

54. This was on the eve of the Battle of Shiloh. The Confederates surrendered Island No. 10 in the Mississippi. Beauregard and Gen. Leonidas Palk joined forces with Gen. Albert S. Johnston to attack Grant at Pittsburg Landing across the Tennessee border from Corinth.

55. This is probably C. P. Leavett, a mechanic, with whom Brooke worked after the war in perfecting a pneumatic and hydraulic pump.

56. See footnote 48 for a discussion of this topic.

57. This is in connection with McClellan's advance up the peninsula between the York and James Rivers.

58. The *Register of the Navy of the Confederate States to January 1863* includes a statement approved 21 April 1862 that amends "An act to provide for the organization of the navy, approved March 16, 1861." In section 2 the order stipulates: "All the admirals, four of the captains, five of the commanders, twenty-two of the first lieutenants, and five of the second lieutenants, shall be appointed solely for gallant or meritorious conduct during the war. The appointments shall be made from the grade immediately below the one to be filled and without reference to the rank of the officer in such grade and the service for which the appointment shall be conferred shall be specified in the commission."

59. After naval bombardment by Admiral Farragut on 24–25 April, New Orleans surrendered on 29 April. It was occupied by Gen. Benjamin Butler.

60. The rifled thirty-two pounders were Brooke's 6.4-inch guns. The banding strengthened the guns, thus permitting heavier charges.

Chapter 4: *James River Defense, Inventions, Personal Woes, and Promotion*

1. The *Warrior* was Great Britain's first seagoing ironclad with armor of four and a half inches, constructed as an answer to the French ironclads (Baxter, *Introduction of the Ironclad Warship*, 131). The British were aware that France "had laid down no wooden line-of-battle ships since 1855, and that they had four ironclads under construction" (p. 130). So Brooke was an avid student of what was being built abroad.

2. Cheeney's thinking extended beyond his submarine. In a separate communication to Brooke on the same day he gave a full description of the enemy forces in Hampton Roads and stated that the *Monitor* and the *Galena* were apparently the only ironclads. He wrote:

Without venturing to advise, I would, simply as an individual citizen of the Confederacy, who has her best interests at heart, state to you my own views as to what the "Virginia" might and ought to do. First— should she remain on the *defensive* simply to protect Norfolk and James River, in a short time the enemy will have multiplied his *iron clad vessels* and *rams* to such an extent that the "Virginia" will be powerless then either for offensive or defensive operations. I believe that she could now, with her improved shot, and other facilities which she has provided herself with, destroy or capture the Monitor in a very short time. The Galena has upright sides, and I do not believe she could stand the shot of the Virginia's big guns one-half hour. In my opinion the only guns she [*Virginia*] has to fear are the large ones in front of Old Point. By passing near the Rip Raps in the night the probabilities are that she would escape their shot uninjured. She could then attack and destroy the shipping below the forts, and blockade McClellan's army on the Peninsula. Could she succeed in this, McClellan's Army and Fortress Monroe would soon yield from want of supplies, or at least, Johson [Joseph E. Johnston], by a decisive victory would capture all. Is not this a stake worth the greatest risk? *Now* the "Virginia," if successful, may do a great and glorious work. In a short time, the enemy, with their superior facilities, will have added so many iron-clad auxiliaries that the Virginia will then be unable to accomplish anything. Had she not better run the risk of getting sunk now, rather than wait inactive until she will be an easy prey for the enemy?

In describing Southern submarine efforts, Coski writes, "William S. Cheeney, a New York–born former United States Navy officer, subsequently commissioned in the Confederate navy, worked in the Southern capital from the late summer of 1861 through the late spring of 1862, on what was described as a 'submarine boat.' Records reveal that Tredegar Iron Works provided him with boiler plate, castings, bolts, cloth, timber, an air pump and articles for 'diving bells'"; he adds, "Whether Cheeney's man-powered submarine was actually used against the Federal fleet is unclear because of discrepancies in dates" (Coski, *Capital Navy*, 117–19).

3. Neeser, in *Statistical and Chronological History*, states that on 11 May the *Virginia* was destroyed off Craney Island, which is at the mouth of the Elizabeth River. Though many blamed the captain, Flag Officer Josiah Tattnall, for a grievous error, Brooke, who knew Tattnall well, did not. The ship was scuttled to prevent capture by the enemy. In his diary Secretary Mallory wrote: "The destruction of the Virginia was premature" (Diary of Stephen R. Mallory, 15 May 1862, Southern Historical Collection, University of North Carolina at Chapel Hill).

4. Chaffin's Bluff was across the James River from Drewry's Bluff (see Coski, *Capital Navy*, p. 41–52).

5. Brooke is referring to Drewry's Bluff, eight miles from Richmond, which rises fifty feet above the James River. Robert Minor had seen the bluff's importance

for the defense of Richmond, and at his suggestion engineers began to construct a fort there. When the *Virginia* was abandoned, her crew under the leadership of Catesby Jones "hurried to Drewry's Bluff . . . and began to mount some heavy guns that had been sent there in great haste" (Luraghi, *History of the Confederate Navy*, 166). According to Luraghi, "Tattnall had correctly considered them the most important part of the ironclad to save for the Confederacy, rather than foolishly throwing them against the enemy in a ship that would be doomed to destruction" (p. 167).

6. Alarmed at the advance of enemy wooden vessels and ironclads up the James River, Mallory wrote to his wife on 15 May: "The enemy will do his best to get here, and we will do our best to keep him away; & we will not leave Richmond without a determined contest to hold it. If the boats ascend the river I hope we shall have manhood enough left to fight him at the wharves & at the street corners, if necessary to repel him" (Stephen R. Mallory Letters and Papers, 1846–72, Southern Historical Collection, University of North Carolina at Chapel Hill). On the same day Mallory confided to his diary his innermost thoughts about the dangers emanating from the loss of Norfolk and the Federal ascent of the James River:

> now Richmond is assailed, and saved from the presence of the enemy's vessels only by the poor & temporary obstructions at Drury's [Drewry's] Bluff, which the first freshet may destroy. . . .
>
> This day was set apart as one of humiliation & prayer & it was generally thus observed, all places of business being closed. I did not attend church, but I went to Rocketts & hurried off guns, men and materials to meet the enemy at Drury's [Drewry's] Bluff." (Diary of Stephen A. Mallory, Southern Historical Collection, University of North Carolina at Chapel Hill)

7. The Naval Ordnance Works in New Orleans was moved to Atlanta under the direction of Lt. David McCorkle. In Atlanta gun carriages, shells, and armor-piercing projectiles were produced (Luraghi, *History of the Confederate Navy*, 46). The victory on the James River was the Battle of Drewry's Bluff on 15 May.

8. The *Galena* was an ironclad. Rifled cannons firing iron bolts had much greater penetrating capability than smoothbores firing shells, and Brooke was convinced that had he been able to get some of the bolts for his rifled cannons on the *Virginia*, they would have penetrated the armor of the *Monitor*. It was ironic for Brooke that John Rodgers, his old commander in the northern Pacific, commanded the *Galena*.

9. Comdr. Ebenezer Farrand was an old-timer who had entered the U.S. Navy in 1823 and the Confederate navy in 1861. Secretary Mallory had ordered Farrand at Drewry's Bluff "to make the best arrangement in your power to resist the enemy. Three of the enemy's gunboats and one of their ironclads, are in the James River, and they may be at Drewry's Bluff tomorrow morning. . . . The enemy must not be permitted to pass" (Mallory to Farrand, 8 May 1862, quoted in Durkin, *Stephen R. Mallory*, p. 212). Sidney Smith Lee, an older brother of

Gen. R. E. Lee, had been senior to Farrand in the U.S. Navy but was listed as a "captain for the war" in the Confederate navy *Register of the Navy of the Confederate States to January 1863* with date of entry into Confederate service of June 1861. On 15 May, Lee was ordered: "Proceed to Drewry's Bluff and take command of the naval defenses of the James river, relieving Commander Farrand, who will remain there second in command" (Mallory to Lee, 15 May 1862, quoted in Durkin, *Stephen R. Mallory*, p. 215). Lee had been a reluctant rebel, but according to one authority he had "an unrewarding but praiseworthy Confederate career as commandant of the Norfolk Navy Yard, of the James River Squadron, and of the naval batteries at Drewry's Bluff" (Wells, *Confederate Navy*, 17). The Battle of Drewry's Bluff, May 15, 1862, is ably described by John Coski in *Capital Navy*, p. 41–52.

10. Brooke overlooked the fact that this was an army responsibility. Fearing the fall of Richmond, Gen. Robert E. Lee "pressed Mallory for more naval guns at Drewry's Bluff and for more obstructions in the river" (Durkin, *Stephen R. Mallory*, 212). When Capt. S. S. Lee was ordered to relieve Farrand at Drewry's Bluff, he was told: "General [William] Mahone has been assigned to the Chief command, but the naval force is expected to fight all the batteries, complete the obstructions, and mount additional guns where you may deem them necessary. . . . Consult freely with General Mahone and defend the river to the last extremity" (as quoted by Durkin in *Stephen R. Mallory*, p. 122 n, 215).

11. The time was critical, as Lt. John Taylor Wood at Drewry's Bluff, writing to his wife in Greensboro on 24 May, explained: "What to do in case we have to evacuate this place is something I have thought about a good deal recently; the Navy for the time has been destroyed & we must seek other ways of rendering ourselves useful; most of the officers will join the Army in some capacity. I have no place yet and want to see you before I do anything. . . . The Pilots are out in a letter denying the statements in Com. Tattnall's report. . . . There is one thing which is undeniable & that is they said they could take the ship up James River until the time came & then they declined to do so, & after lightening the ship we were more helpless & vulnerable than an ordinary wooden vessel" (John Taylor Wood Papers, Southern Historical Collection, University of North Carolina at Chapel Hill).

Wood, who had trained the crew of the *Virginia*, and Jones were the last to leave the ship when it was scuttled, "spreading flammable material everywhere and setting the fuses" (Luraghi, *History of the Confederate Navy*, 166). Three days later, on 27 May 1862, Secretary Mallory thought the situation had eased when he wrote to his wife: "I have worked night & day upon the defenses of the river, and have now got them so strong that I am afraid the enemy will not make a second attempt to pass them. I want him to try them once more. You will see in the papers the results of their last attempt; and on that occasion we had but four heavy guns in battery, whereas we now have fourteen, & many of superior calibre" (Letters and Papers, 1846–72, Southern Historical Collection, University of North Carolina at Chapel Hill).

12. Col. Josiah Gorgas, the Confederate army's chief of ordnance.

13. I do not know the date of Lucy's death, but this event probably precipitated Lizzie's move to Lexington, where she could be with the Williamsons. No railroad had been built to Lexington at that time. In this letter Brooke wrote much about the Confederate victory on the Peninsula that led to the withdrawal of Federal troops. He complained that news was slow in coming from the front. Thomas Williamson, Brooke's brother-in-law, on 25 June had forwarded to him for consideration the plan for a new projectile suggested by a Major Elisha Paxton. Paxton's idea was that a round case for shot was inefficient because of uniform dispersion when used against personnel. He believed that an elongated projectile with a time fuse would serve better.

14. Brooke, as indicated earlier, was too optimistic about an early settlement of the controversy with Porter. The baby apparently was a new one, and its birth perhaps precipitated Lizzie's move to Lexington. A daughter was born on 23 June 1863.

15. Yelverton Garnett, a cousin of John Brooke and Lizzie, had served for a time in the U.S. Navy with John Brooke and later set up a medical practice in Richmond. He offered his services to the Confederacy and was the physician for President Jefferson Davis. Barry commanded the railroad gun that Brooke had built at the request of General Lee. George Minor remained as chief of the Office of Ordnance and Hydrography until March 1863, when he was succeeded by Brooke, who was some fifteen years his junior.

16. The court martial was for sinking the *Virginia* in the James River because of her excessive draft.

17. The *Richmond* was the first ironclad completed at the Rocketts navy yard in Richmond (Coski, *Capital Navy,* 78). She was commissioned in late November 1862 and was "the only ironclad in operation on the James River for 16 months" (p. 91).

18. Louisa Garnett Williamson, Thomas Williamson's wife, had died in 1858. Louisa, Lizzie, and Richard Garnett, children of William Garnett (Uncle William), were siblings and first cousins of John Brooke. Apparently Thomas Williamson wanted Lizzie and her father to move out, since Louisa had died.

19. At this time Richard Garnett was a brigadier general in the Confederate army. He had been in command of the Stonewall Brigade at the Battle of Kernstown in March 1862. When Garnett ordered the withdrawal of the Stonewall Brigade, Jackson relieved him of his command. At the time Garnett and Brooke were rooming together, Garnett was awaiting trial by Jackson on 6 August. Charlotte Derby, who lived in South Carolina, was Richard Garnett's sister, and Mary Ann Wilson was the widow of his twin brother, Dr. William Garnett, who had died in the yellow fever epidemic in Norfolk in 1855.

20. Robert B. Pegram, a Virginian, who would be promoted to commander for the war on 13 September 1862, with Catesby Jones had commanded the naval detachment that took over the powder magazine at Norfolk in April 1861. The *Arkansas,* an ironclad constructed near Memphis, distinguished herself in combat along the Mississippi River during May–August 1862. (See Still, *Iron Afloat,* p. 62–78.)

21. The *Richmond,* commanded by Lt. Robert Pegram, was commissioned in November 1862; launched in Norfolk in May 1862, she had been hauled up the James for completion in Richmond (Coski, *Capital Navy,* 78).

22. Charles M. Conrad was chairman of the Committee of Naval Affairs in the House of Representatives. The South's desperate efforts to hold New Orleans in April 1862 is discussed in Luraghi, *History of the Confederate Navy,* p. 155–63; and in Durkin, *Stephen R. Mallory,* p. 203–10.

23. Conrad was "a wealthy planter and lawyer from New Orleans"; this matter is discussed by Luraghi, who says that Conrad "was envious of Mallory" (*History of the Confederate Navy,* 3, 181–82).

24. As demonstrated earlier, Brooke had complained bitterly in the past about the lack of promotion in the Confederate navy. The navy *Register of the Navy of the Confederate States to January 1863* of 1 January 1863 shows only four promotions to commander for the war up until that time.

25. The Whitworth was a muzzle-loading rifled gun. Brooke had complete instructions on how it should be loaded and cleaned, the weight of the powder charge, etc. Also, apparently, a sample flannel powder bag and a wooden sabot were sent to him and, the latter to be used as an edge when the gun was depressed below zero elevation. According to Ripley, Sir Joseph Whitworth was asked by the British government "to design machines for making rifled muskets." He developed "a form of rifling which instead of grooves utilized a polygon shape with gently rounded edges and similarly shaped projectiles." He used the same technique in his cannons. Though not adopted by the British government, the Whitworth cannons were used by both the North and the South, and the latter was "quite fond of them." Though Whitworth made both breech and muzzle loaders, the former "proved a failure for larger calibers." (See Ripley, *Artillery and Ammunition,* 142.)

26. Benjamin Huger was Confederate inspector of ordnance from 1862 to 1865 (Ibid., 357).

27. Lt. George W. Harrison had entered the U.S. Navy nine years before Brooke and was near the top of the list of lieutenants in both the U.S. and Confederate navies. It is reported that he "was the lieutenant commanding the *Jamestown* and the *Hampton* during the squadron's assent up the James River in May 1862" (Coski, *Capital Navy,* 272).

28. The view of Gideon Welles, the Northern secretary of the navy, on this subject is interesting. On 9 October 1862 he wrote in his diary:

> Dahlgren is grieved with my action in his case. He desires, beyond almost any one, the high honors of his profession, and has his appetite stimulated by the partiality of the President, who does not hesitate to say to him and to me, that he will give him the highest grade if I will send him a letter to that effect, or a letter of appointment. Title irregularly obtained cannot add to Dahlgren's reputation, yet he cannot be reasoned with. He has yet rendered no service afloat during the war,—has not been under fire,—and is not on the direct road for professional advancement. But he is a favorite with the President and knows it. The

army practice of favoritism and political partyism cannot be permitted in the Navy. Its effect will be more demoralizing than that of the military, where it is bad enough. I am compelled, therefore, to stand between the President and Dahlgrens promotion, in order to maintain the service in proper condition. Dahlgren has the sagacity and professional intelligence to know I am right, and to appreciate my action though adverse to him. He therefore now seeks service afloat. Wants an opportunity to acquire rank and distinction, but that opportunity must be a matter of favor. His last request was to be permitted to capture Charleston. This would give him eclat. I told him I would not rob Du Pont of that honor. . . .

It . . . would be wrong to the service, and a great wrong for the country, for him to leave the Ordnance Bureau, where he is proficient and can be most useful. His specialty is in that branch of service; he knows his own value there at this time, and for him to leave it now would be detrimental to the object he desires to attain. He is conscious of it, but he has Dahlgren more than the service in view. (Beale, *Diary of Gideon Welles*, 1:164)

Dahlgren had been appointed the federal chief of ordnance on 18 July 1862 following his promotion to captain. In the end Dahlgren got his wish; he was promoted to admiral in February 1863 and five months later left the Bureau of Ordnance "and took command of the South Atlantic Blockading Squadron" (Mark M. Boatner III, *The Civil War Dictionary* [New York: David McKay Company, Inc., 1959], 218).

29. The Battle of Sharpsburg had been fought on 16 and 17 September 1862. It ended Lee's first invasion of the North. Boatner puts Confederate losses at 13,724, of whom 2,700 were killed (Ibid., 21).

30. Raphael Semmes had entered the Confederate navy on 26 March 1861 and was promoted to captain on 15 July 1862. Maffit had entered Confederate service as a first lieutenant on 8 May 1861. Semmes, a native of Alabama, had entered the U.S. Navy in 1826, six years ahead of Maffit, a North Carolinian. Semmes "was commissioned commander, put in charge of the lighthouse bureau, and then fitted out the cruiser *Sumter* in New Orleans. Cutting through the river blockade for a six months' cruise, he took 18 prizes" (Ibid., 731). Certainly Semmes's later exploits on the *Alabama* would justify his promotion. Semmes had ranked John R. Tucker by seventeen files in the U.S. Navy at the beginning of the war and had entered Confederate service three months earlier when the seat of government was in Montgomery, Alabama.

Chapter 5: *Developments in Ordnance*

1. In 1863 the Confederate congress authorized the establishment in the navy of the office of chief constructor. John L. Porter was appointed to that position. Two acting constructors were appointed, of whom William A. Graves was one. Coski says that Graves was initially a Norfolk shipbuilder and became "the primary naval architect for the yard opposite Rocketts" (*Capital Navy*, 67).

2. Chaffin's (sometimes spelled Chafins or Chapins) Bluff is on the north side of the James River, a short distance downriver from Drewry's Bluff. Its importance in preventing a gunboat attack on Richmond is given in Still, *Iron Afloat*, p. 172–82. At this time Thomas Jefferson Page was a commander. He had a career of long naval service, having entered the U.S. Navy in 1827.

3. Lt. Alexander F. Warley, a South Carolinian, in October 1862 commanded a small force that commandeered the private ironclad *Manassas* (Still, *Iron Afloat*, 46). Later Warley won fame when in command of the *Manassas* he attacked Admiral David Farragut's fleet off New Orleans (Ibid., 56–58). Warley is described as "determined," "daring," and "bold" (Luraghi, *History of the Confederate Navy*, 105, 159).

4. Dew in his study of the Tredegar writes: "Experiments with various brands of high quality Virginia charcoal pig iron . . . soon revealed what seemed to be an ideal combination for cannon— Cloverdale and Grace iron, produced by two Botetourt County furnaces" (*Ironmaker to the Confederacy*, 11). Dew also noted that "by giving close attention to his casting methods and using only Cloverdale and Grace iron, [Joseph R.] Anderson reestablished and maintained a high reputation for his cannon" (Ibid., 12).

5. Hunter Davidson, a contemporary of Brooke, had entered the U.S. Navy in 1841. During the war he won a reputation working in submarine mines, first under Maury and then when the latter went to England in October 1862, as chief of the unit conducting such experiments. (See Wells, *Confederate Navy*, p. 58, 61; and Perry, *Internal Machines*, p. 16–19.) Luraghi called Davidson "the future genius of submarine warfare" (*History of the Confederate Navy*, 114). In June 1962 Davidson was appointed by Mallory to take charge of devising, placing, and superintending submarine batteries on the James River (as quoted by Coski in *Capital Navy*, p. 122).

6. In 1854 Matthew Delany, "a skilled machinist, bought a part interest in the Tredegar foundry and machine shops" (Dew, *Ironmaker to the Confederacy*, 16). Frederick Chatard, a veteran of thirty-seven years' service in the U.S. Navy, "was considered an expert in heavy artillery"; he commanded the batteries at Drewry's Bluff on the James in 1862–64 (Coski, *Capital Navy*, 104).

7. Rocketts was a suburb of Richmond on the James River (see Still, *Iron Afloat*, p. 90–91). The *Richmond*, whose construction began at Gosport Navy Yard, was with the fall of Norfolk hauled up the James to Rocketts for completion. On the eastern edge of Richmond, Rocketts had become by 1860 "a somewhat dingy working-class neighborhood . . . home to men who worked in Richmond's shipping industry" (Coski, *Capital Navy*, 14). When the Federals took over Norfolk in 1862, "the Rockett's waterfront was given over to the Confederate navy and army"; its wharves were used by both warships and commercial vessels and its warehouses by the James River Squadron, and it became "one of the Confederacy's most prolific and longest-lived shipyards" (Ibid.).

8. Robert Minor remained in command of the Richmond Naval Ordnance Works until 1 October 1863.

9. The *Hampton* was apparently one of the one hundred steam-powered wooden gunboats that Maury proposed and the Confederate congress authorized in late 1861; built in Norfolk, it became part of the James River Squadron and was a sister ship of the *Nansemond* (Coski, *Capital Navy*, 26).

10. According to Ripley, "The Columbiad made its appearance in 1811 as a 50-pounder, the invention of Colonel George Bomford." The Columbiads were produced in a number of calibers and are described as "large-caliber, long pieces capable of firing shot and shell with heavy charges at high angles of elevation." They were said to be "ideally suited for defending narrow channels as well as distant roadsteads." (See Ripley, *Artillery and Ammunition*, p. 71.)

11. This is the first indication we have that Lizzie had returned to Richmond from Lexington.

12. Capt. Samuel Barron, a Virginian, was an old salt who had entered the U.S. Navy in 1812. The vital defense of Richmond from attacks in the South depended on the heavy guns emplaced at various places along the James, the widespread use of submarine mines, and a flotilla of small vessels.

13. Actually, by this time Lincoln had become frustrated by McClellan's dilatory tactics and on 7 November had replaced him with Gen. Ambrose Burnside. This brought on the battle of Fredericksburg in December.

14. Lt. Alexander M. DeBree, a Virginian, had entered the U.S. Navy the same year as Brooke, 1841. At the time of these tests he was detailed at Tredegar as assistant inspector of ordnance. Belle Isle is located in the middle of the James River where it passes through Richmond, and for a time it was used for prisoners of war.

15. Col. Thomas S. Rhett was with the army Ordnance Department and was an inspector of ordnance. Comdr. Robert B. Pegram of Virginia commanded the ironclad *Richmond* of the James River Squadron.

16. Brooke reported to Capt. S. S. Lee on 6 December. Capt. Sidney Smith Lee, brother of Robert E. Lee, was in command at Drewry's Bluff. It is interesting at this point to get the view on the vulnerability of ironclads from Brooke's old colleague John Rodgers, who had led the May attack on Drewry's Bluff in the ironclad *Galena*. On 1 December 1862 Rodgers wrote to ordnance expert John Dahlgren: "I have looked with a great deal of interest at your iron targets—They give a more impressive idea of the force of gun powder than one has, before seeing them—they confirm me still more in the opinion that iron clads are not to fight forts, too close. —Indeed the great point of interest now is, at what distance may the Ironsides, one of a very important class, be considered safe from the effects of modern artillery" (John A. Dahlgren Papers, LC). The lightly armored *Galena*, one of the North's first ironclads and the flagship of the invading fleet, was ably handled by Rodgers but badly peppered by the Confederate guns on Drewery's Bluff and in the James River Squadron. It is ironic that much damage should have been done by Brooke Guns, designed by his old friend of the North Pacific Cruise.

17. Lt. James Waddell, a North Carolinian, would later command the public cruiser *Shenandoah*.

18. This is an example of the close cooperation between the navy and the army in the defense of the James River.

19. Anton Schönborn, an instrument maker, had been appointed assistant astronomer of the North Pacific Expedition (1853–56) on Brooke's recommendation.

20. Capt. Duncan N. Ingraham of South Carolina had been chief of the Bureau of Ordnance and Hydrography in the U.S. Navy at the outbreak of the war. The Confederates withstood two years of siege before evacuating Charleston in February 1865.

21. Lt. William A. Webb.

22. Gen. John Bankhead Magruder. Jones was an ordnance expert, and this appears to be another case of army-navy cooperation in the defense of rivers.

23. This probably refers to Asa and Nelson Tiff, old friends of Secretary Mallory, who had conferred with him as early as August 1861 about the building of ironclads. Nelson Tiff's plan to build an ironclad had been used in the construction of one in New Orleans. (See Still, *Iron Afloat*, p.16.)

24. His prediction was correct. The Federals never took Charleston from the sea.

25. John Luke Porter was appointed.

26. Luraghi gives a comprehensive description of the Selma foundry and its importance to the Confederacy (*History of the Confederate Navy*, 44–45, 191–94). He notes that "upon assuming management of the foundry in June 1863, Jones found it in deplorable condition. Yet during the entire war the Selma Foundry turned out at least 143 guns, of which more than 100 were heavy naval cannons" (Ibid., 45). Luraghi praises Jones's contribution. Stating that Selma was initially a joint army-navy operation, he observes that in time it became exclusively a navy project and that "the new chief of ordnance, John Mercer Brooke, appointed his most valued collaborator, Capt. Catesby ap R. Jones, as commander of the foundry. Brooke's choice could not have been better. Beyond such gifts of character as energy, steadiness, carefulness and courage Jones had an exceptional mind and was a scientist and a mechanical engineer" (Ibid., 44). The Naval Gun Foundry at Selma became the Confederacy's "most efficient" (Ibid.). The Simmes mentioned here by Jones was probably Lt. Charles C. Simms, a Virginian who had served with Jones on the *Virginia* as an ordnance officer. According to testimony quoted by Scharf, Simms fired the first Confederate naval gun in the Battle of Hampton Roads, and when Jones took command of the *Virginia*, Simms followed him as executive officer; Jones praised Simms for his experience, energy, and zeal (Scharf, *History of the Confederate Navy*, 208).

27. Charles Dew describes the fire in *Ironmaker to the Confederacy*, p. 193–95.

28. Samuel Cooper, the highest ranking general in the Confederate army, served as adjutant general and inspector general.

29. The baby would soon die, as did all the other Brooke infants except Anna.

30. Webb was in command of a special gunboat expedition detailed for an attack on Federal monitors in Charleston harbor. See Durkin, *Stephen R. Mallory*, p. 262–63; and Luraghi, *History of the Confederate Navy*, 211–13, who suggests that perhaps Webb was too confident and daring.

31. Brooke was too optimistic. He was, of course, referring to the twin disasters at Gettysburg and Vicksburg but did not have complete information.

32. General Garnett, who was ill, led the center brigade in the famous charge.

33. Elliott Lacey was a civilian inspector of ordnance at Tredegar.

34. George W. Gift from Tennessee had been appointed a lieutenant for the war when he entered Confederate service on 18 March 1862. He had not served in the U.S. Navy.

35. Brooke labeled this principle as "the utility of the air space" and deemed it significant. See Brooke, *John M. Brooke*, p. 265–67.

36. On 26 August 1862 Franklin Buchanan was promoted to admiral and took command of the Mobile Station. The city of Mobile on the northern edge of Mobile Bay was an important center for blockade running and naval construction. The *Tennessee* was commissioned in Mobile in February 1864 and the *Nashville* six months later. Still gives a good description of the building of these two vessels in *Iron Afloat*, p. 194–96. According to Still, "Finding seamen to man the ships was probably the most irksome problem Buchanan encountered" (Ibid, 196). Bragg's victory probably refers to the Battle of Chickamauga, referred to as a tactical but Pyrrhic victory for Bragg (Boatner, *Civil War Dictionary*, 149–53).

37. George Peacock was an English technician who, according to Luraghi, was "gifted with a lively and bright mind." Early in the war "he was superintendent of a foundry at Columbiana, Alabama, but Jones had hired him at the urging of General Rains at twice his own pay. Described as "a scholar, a scientist, and a man of genius of international fame," Peacock became superintendent of the naval foundry in Selma. See Luraghi, *History of the Confederate Navy*, p. 193.

38. I have found no record of any orders for Jones or Simms such as the rumor suggested. Jones continued his good work at Selma.

39. Parker had stood first in the first class of Annapolis.

40. Many of these conclusions, such as the greater penetrating power of flat-headed bolts and the advantage of inclined plates on ironclads in deflecting shot and shell, Brooke had reached earlier on his own.

41. For a comprehensive description of British rifled cannons see Ripley, *Artillery and Ammunition*, chap. 8, "British Rifles," p. 137–60. Ripley writes, "England, which had been experimenting with rifles for several years prior to the American Civil War, was a natural shopping ground for North and South in their frantic search for weapons during the early stages of the conflict. . . . The Confederacy needed every gun it could get and English rifles were imported in a steady stream until perfection of the federal blockade narrowed the flow to a trickle" (p. 137). The information Hamilton supplied must have been a great help to Brooke in his experimentation in a field that was new to him. Lt. John R. Hamilton, a South Carolina veteran of fifteen years' service in the U.S. Navy, had resigned on 15 December 1860, nine days before South Carolina's secession. He was commissioned a lieutenant on 21 March 1861.

Chapter 6: *Personal Sorrow and Continued Activity in Ordnance*

1. The *Tennessee* was placed in commission on 16 February 1864, but Jones's hopes were not to be realized; the command was given to Lt. James D. Johnston, who had taken care of naval affairs in Mobile in the early days of the war when the city was largely ignored by the Confederate navy (Still, *Iron Afloat*, 186–87). In 1862 Johnston had commanded the *Baltic*, a converted tug which had been armored and provided with six guns (Luraghi, *History of the Confederate Navy*, 280). Jones's contribution to the *Tennessee* would be to supply heavy Brooke Guns from Selma for the formidable new vessel.
2. Rep. Colin J. McRae is identified by Luraghi as a "merchant and businessman from Mobile, Alabama, who would later have prominent if indirect ties with the Confederate navy" (*History of the Confederate Navy*, 3). He had much to do with converting the Alabama Manufacturing Company into the Naval Gun Foundry in Selma (p. 44). In time McRae was appointed "financial agent for Europe with the duty of consolidating the administration of Confederate funds abroad" with those of a French loan (p. 267).
3. When Georgia seceded from the Union, James Dunwoody Bulloch, who had served in the U.S. Navy at one time, was appointed a commander in the Confederate navy and sent to Europe as a naval agent.
4. The Confederate navy established a powder works in Petersburg, but it was moved to Columbia in the summer of 1862. T. Baudery Garesché was appointed superintendent and did a splendid job (Luraghi, *History of the Confederate Navy*, 47). It is recorded that he "improved the quality of his powder through experimental firing" (Wells, *Confederate Navy*, 56).
5. The commanding Cooke who had supervised the building of the ironclad *Albemarle* in North Carolina rammed the *Southfield* in the battle of Plymouth and sent her to the bottom. The *Southfield* had six guns (Luraghi, *History of the Confederate Navy*, 292–95). A good description of the *Albemarle*'s engagement is given in Still, *Iron Afloat*, p. 157–63; Still notes that Cooke won recognition in the Confederate navy as "an able and aggressive officer."
6. This must have been Robert R. Carter of the famous Virginia family whose home was Shirley Plantation on the James. Carter had entered the U.S. Navy one year after Brooke and had been in the North Pacific Expedition of 1853–57 commanded first by Cadwalader Ringgold and then by John Rodgers. When Virginia seceded, Carter resigned his commission and was appointed a lieutenant in the Confederate navy on 10 June 1861.
7. Before the Civil War, John Brooke had established his reputation as a surveyor and hydrographer, particularly in the western Pacific along the coast of Asia and in the northern Pacific as far north as Bering Strait. From 1853 to 1857 Brooke surveyed much of this area when in the *Vincennes* with the North Pacific Surveying and Exploring Expedition under Commodore John Rodgers. Later, 1858–60, he continued this work in the surveying schooner *Fenimore Cooper*. There was probably no one in the Confederate navy who knew more about the sailing patterns of the American whalers that left New England and cruised for

several years in the northern Pacific and rendezvoused in Honolulu and Lanai. The memo was for the use of a fast public cruiser, the *Sea King*, built in Glasgow and obtained by Bulloch for the Confederacy. In October 1864 Lt. James Waddell took over the command of the vessel, rechristened the *Shenandoah* in Madeira, where she took on arms and supplies. Heading for the northern Pacific to destroy the whaling fleet, the *Shenandoah* sighted the Kurile Islands north of Japan on 14 April when she arrived five days after Lee's surrender at Appomattox. Not until 2 August 1865 did Waddell learn from a British merchant vessel that the war was over. Meanwhile he had played havoc with the Northern whaling fleet. When he learned the war was over, Waddell hauled down the last Confederate flag and sailed for Liverpool where he turned over his ship to the British authorities (Luraghi, *History of the Confederate Navy*, 341–44). More information can be found in James D. Horan, ed., *C.S.S. Shenandoah: The Memoirs of Lt. Commanding James I. Waddell* (Annapolis: U.S. Naval Institute Press, 1996). The records show that before the *Shenandoah* hauled down its flag it had captured thirty-eight Northern ships and burned thirty-two.

8. According to James Phinney Baxter, an authority on ironclad ships: "When France stopped building wooden ships of the line, produced the *Gloire*, and announced a program of sixteen seagoing and seventeen coast-defence ironclads, built or building, the death knell of the wooden walls had sounded" (*Introduction of the Ironclad Warship*, 4).

9. The report shows that in addition to his work in ordnance, Brooke was responsible for the operation of the naval school. As at the Naval Academy today, the entering midshipmen were in the fourth class. From this status they move upward, graduating from the first class four years later.

10. The strength of sloping armor corroborated Brooke's views when he designed the *Virginia*.

11. This view of Mallory seems to have been general, but according to Luraghi, a thorough historian, it was not correct, or was at least incomplete. Luraghi writes: "Mallory was all and everything: administrator and head of the navy, author and executor of naval strategy, and the man responsible for the conduct of maritime and coastal operations"; and he concludes that Mallory, "through almost five grim years of war, burdened by almost inhuman responsibility . . . did indeed do his duty well (if not without unavoidable blunders) . . . and produced the best naval strategy possible in such a grievous situation" (Luraghi, *History of the Confederate Navy*, 14). Luraghi writes that in Mallory the Confederates states' navy found "a leader of outstanding competence, foresight, and talent" (Ibid., 348). A different view is that Mallory started his career as an unpopular man and received little if any credit for the navy's subsequent achievements" (Wells, *Confederate Navy*, 6). For a balanced view see Durkin, *Stephen R. Mallory*.

12. Garnett was probably living with Charlotte Olympia Garnett, the sister of Lizzie and Richard Garnett. Charlotte had married Derrill Hart Darby of South Carolina, who had died in 1859.

Chapter 7: *Hard Work to the End*

1. Lizzie had died of consumption on 14 June 1864 at the age of thirty-seven. This was the culmination of a long struggle with tuberculosis aggravated by frequent trips to Lexington and the births and deaths of two babies. Brooke was disconsolate, and his wife's death affected him deeply. The responsibilities and pressure of his work during the war had forced him to neglect his home life. Lizzie was a devoted Christian and had always urged Brooke to read the Bible. With her death he apparently tried to make up for his shortcomings.

2. This was probably Dr. Yelverton Peyton Garnett, Brooke's cousin and the personal physician of President Jefferson Davis.

3. From this report made near the end of the war it is obvious that the Confederacy did not collapse from the failure of the Office of Naval Ordnance to set up adequate establishments to meet its needs. But it is also clear that a lack of production can be attributed to a lack of skilled labor and mechanics. The grabbing of all manpower by the army, frequently alluded to in the Brooke journals, definitely hampered production. This report and previous ones made by Brooke show that he was fully in control of ordnance operations. Brooke's reputation has been built on his scientific and inventive talents as demonstrated by the design of the *Virginia* and the Brooke Gun. But his reports and correspondence as chief of the Office of Ordnance and Hydrography show that he was also a careful and efficient administrator and that Mallory relied heavily upon him.

4. General Lee had evacuated Petersburg and Richmond on 2 April, following his unsuccessful assault on Grant at Five Forks the day before. On 4 April, Lee was headed west hoping to effect a junction with Gen. Joseph E. Johnston in North Carolina.

5. Brooke did not record who he was traveling with. John Coski reports that Brooke and Robert Minor left Richmond at 1:00 P.M. on 2 April "in an old ambulance" (*Capital Navy*, 219).

6. This was the day that Lee surrendered to Grant at Appomattox Court House, but apparently Brooke was unaware of this fact and continued his flight.

7. With the fall of Richmond, Jefferson Davis moved the Confederate government to Danville and then to Greensboro, North Carolina. For a good account of Davis's retreat or flight to Greensboro see Burke Davis, *The Long Surrender*, (New York: Vintage Books, 1985), 20–62.

8. At a final cabinet meeting in Charlotte on 24 April, President Davis conceded the end of the war but continued his own flight. Joseph Johnston had surrendered to Sherman six days earlier.

Bibliography

Andrews, Wayne. *Concise Dictionary of American History.* New York: Charles Scribners Sons, 1962.

Baxter, James Phinney. *The Introduction of the Ironclad Warship.* Cambridge, Mass.: Harvard University Press, 1933.

Beale, Howard K., ed., *The Diaries of Gideon Welles,* 3 vols. New York: W. W. Norton, 1960.

Boatner, Mark M. III. *The Civil War Dictionary.* New York: David McKay Company, Inc., 1959.

Brooke, George M., Jr., *John M. Brooke, Naval Scientist and Educator.* Charlottesville: University Press of Virginia, 1980.

———. *John M. Brooke's Pacific Cruise and Japanese Adventure.* Honolulu: University of Hawaii Press, 1986.

Bruce, Kathleen. *Virginia Iron Manufacture in the Slave Era.* New York: The Century Company, 1931.

Coski, John M. *Capital Navy: The Men, Ships, and Operations of the James River Squadron.* Campbell, Calif.: Savas Woodbury Publishers, 1996.

Dew, Charles B. *Ironmaker to the Confederacy, Joseph R. Anderson and the Tredegar Iron Works.* New Haven and London: Yale University Press, 1966.

Durkin, Joseph T. *Stephen R. Mallory, Confederate Navy Chief.* Chapel Hill: University of North Carolina Press, 1954.

Freeman, Douglas Southall. *Lees Lieutenants.* 3 vols. New York: Charles Scribner's Sons, 1944.

———. *Robert E. Lee.* 4 vols. New York: Charles Scribner's Sons, 1934.

Luraghi, Raimondo. *A History of the Confederate Navy.* Annapolis, Md.: Naval Institute Press, 1996.

Neeser, Robert Wilden. *Statistical and Chronological History of the United States Navy, 1775–1907.* 2 vols. New York: The MacMillan Company, 1909.

Niven, John. *Gideon Welles, Lincoln's Secretary of the Navy.* Baton Rouge: Louisiana State University Press, 1978.

Perry, Milton E. *Infernal Machines: The Story of Confederate Submarine and Mine Warfare.* Baton Rouge: Louisiana State University Press, 1965.

Ripley, Warren. *Artillery and Ammunition of the Civil War.* New York: Promontory Press, 1970.

Scharf, J. Thomas. *History of the Confederate Navy from Its Organization to the Surrender of Its Last Vessel.* New York: Rogers and Sherwood, 1886.

Still, William N., Jr. *Iron Afloat: The Story of the Confederate Ironclads.* Nashville, Tenn.: Vanderbilt University Press, 1971.

Vandiver, Frank, ed. The Civil War Diary of General Josiah Gorgas. Tuscaloosa: University of Alabama Press, 1947.

Wells, Tom H. *The Confederate Navy, A Study in Organization.* Tuscaloosa: University of Alabama Press, 1971.

Werlich, David P. *Admiral of the Amazon: John Randolph Tucker, His Confederate Colleagues, and Peru.* Charlottesville: University Press of Virginia, 1990.

Index

Archer, Dr. Robert: percussion fuzes 45; 62, 91

Armstrong, Sir William: smooth bore cannon; report on production of Armstrong Gun, 160-61, 166; report of Lt. Hamilton in Liverpool, 165; shunt rifles, 162

army ordnance: progress in three years, 181

Barron, Capt. Samuel: capture of, 34

Beauregard, Gen. Gustav T., 86, 119, 131; instructions from Brooke on use of naval guns, 140-42

Bessemer Process: use in making guns in England, 161

Blakely Rifle, 145, 146-47; powder for second Blakely, 151; construction of in England, 160, 161, 165, 166-67, 174, 176, 190, 191

blockade of Southern States, 28, 40, 82

blockade runners for Apalachicola, 180

Brooke, Anna Maria, 2, 66, 136, 137, 198

Brooke, Lizzie: criticism of Brooke, 27-28, 32; death, 185; impending death, 136; interest in Merrimac, 38; letter to Jefferson Davis, 38; new baby, 25, 26; rooms in Richmond, 40, 41; 123; premonition of death, 7, 8; sickness, 1, 3, 5, 6, 26, 69; strong religious faith, 8, 31

Brooke, Lucy, 26, 30, 31, 40, 41, 42, 66

Brooke, William (brother): sale of western land, 9; sketch of John Brooke's ordnance accomplishments, 170-73; views on slavery and secession, 123-24

Brooke's Deep Sea Sounding Lead, 11, 13

Brooks, John Wolcott, 1

Bryant, Herbert, 38

Buchanan, Capt. Franklin, 64, 65, 68, 70-71, 129

Bulloch, James D., 162, 181, 185, 187, 192

Charleston, S.C.: assault by Dahlgren, 138, 144, boarding enemy ironclads, 124, 128; excellence of two Brooke VII inch rifles, 173-74; ordnance sent to defend, 129; proper weights of charges and projectiles for heavy artillery used in defense of, 156-60

Charlotte, N.C.: no leather for fuze washers, 156

Cheyney, William G., 47, 54, 66, 78, 89-90

Index